实用商务英语写作教程

(第3版)

主　编　董晓波
副主编　董宇冉　周志伟
参编者　戚珊珊　韩佳音　王　凡

清华大学出版社
北京交通大学出版社
·北京·

内 容 简 介

本书从各种商务写作实践入手,致力于解决学习者在商务英语写作中面临的主要问题,涉及主题范围广,大量写作实例均来源于最新的商务案例,适合读者模仿。同时,本书也把一些基础性的写作知识和语言知识穿插在各个章节之中,给学生的学习和教师的课堂教学留有较大的自主选择空间。

本书是涉外商务人员的必备之书,既可供普通高等教育商务英语专业、国际贸易等外向型专业的学生使用,也可供有志于从事国际商贸工作的人员阅读。

本书封面贴有清华大学出版社防伪标签,无标签者不得销售。
版权所有,侵权必究。侵权举报电话:010-62782989 13501256678 13801310933

图书在版编目(CIP)数据

实用商务英语写作教程/董晓波主编. —3 版. —北京:北京交通大学出版社:清华大学出版社,2023.2 (2025.3 重印)
ISBN 978-7-5121-4842-0

Ⅰ. ①实… Ⅱ. ①董… Ⅲ. ①商务-英语-写作-教材 Ⅳ. ①F7

中国版本图书馆 CIP 数据核字(2022)第 220912 号

实用商务英语写作教程
SHIYONG SHANGWU YINGYU XIEZUO JIAOCHENG

责任编辑:田秀青
出版发行:清华大学出版社 邮编:100084 电话:010-62776969 http://www.tup.com.cn
　　　　　北京交通大学出版社 邮编:100044 电话:010-51686414 http://www.bjtup.com.cn
印　刷　者:北京鑫海金澳胶印有限公司
经　　销:全国新华书店
开　　本:185 mm×260 mm　印张:17.25　字数:442 千字
版 印 次:2008 年 2 月第 1 版　2023 年 2 月第 3 版　2025 年 3 月第 2 次印刷
印　　数:2 001~3 000 册　定价:49.00 元

本书如有质量问题,请向北京交通大学出版社质监组反映。对您的意见和批评,我们表示欢迎和感谢。
投诉电话:010-51686043,51686008;传真:010-62225406;E-mail:press@bjtu.edu.cn

Preface
前言

大力培养复合型外语人才

  我国外语教育始终服务于国家战略方针，不同时代对外语教育有着不同的要求。党的十九大确立了中国特色社会主义发展进入了新时代的历史方位。全球化时代，我国正从"本土型"国家向"国际型"国家转型，构建人类命运共同体、"一带一路"倡议、讲好中国故事、推进国际传播等，为外语人才培养提出了更高的要求。2017年我在《光明日报》载文：明确提出复合型外语人才是国家重要的战略资源，在构建"人类命运共同体"的过程中发挥重要作用。2018年年初，教育部宣布实施《普通高等学校本科专业类教学质量国家标准》（以下简称《国标》，外国语言文学类《国标》要求学生具有"中国情怀""国际视野""人文素养""国别与区域知识""跨文化能力""创新能力"等，彰显了新时代外语教育助推构建人类命运共同体的价值追求。

  目前我国外语人才培养存在的问题：首先，教育理念落后。"外语工具说"思想一直主导我国外语教育，影响外语学科、外语专业的独立性，进而影响外语专业人才培养定位，学生在大学四年期间以接受语言技能培训为主，与其他专业毕业生相比，外语专业学生在知识结构、思想深度、思辨能力、创新能力等方面还有较大差距。其次，课程设置单一，教学方法落后。课程设置与专业人才培养的目标不匹配，语言技能课程居多，教材内容陈旧，知识结构狭窄，无法真正拓宽学生的视野和知识面；教学方法流于"应试教育""填鸭教育"，"互动式""启发式""讨论式""探究式"等多是纸上谈兵，因材施教难以落地，学生学习积极性、主动性不高。再次，复合型专业内容融合度较低。受制于师资力量的困境，外语专业系统的开放性程度较低，对于有行业背景、综合实力较强、办学历史悠久的院校来说，走复合型道路，比如，商务英语、旅游英语、法律英语等能够凸显一定特色，取得较好的成绩，但对于新建本科院校、师范院校、理工科类院校来说，外语和专业融合尚存不少困难。最后，外语教学受到人工智能、机器翻译的冲击。由于科技进步，机器翻译、语言技术服务大有取代人力翻译之势，比如，故宫博物院目前可以提供近30种外语语种的"解说机"，这对于外语人才培养似乎造成很大威胁，但可以肯定，机器翻译终究难以胜任高层次的文化翻译，以及跨学科的专业知识翻译，外语人才培养必须顺应时代发展，亟待优化升级，提高质量。

  总而言之，目前我国外语教育所面临的形势，一方面表现为单一外语人才过剩；另一方面，由于缺少管理、创新等能力，外语专业人才的社会适应性差，职场成就低。可见，传统的以语言技能为主的纯语言型人才培养模式已不能服务于经济全球化，更不能服务于

"一带一路"建设和"构建人类命运共同体"的需要。因此,高校外语专业走复合型人才培养之路是大势所趋,也大有作为。

新时代外语人才培养的原则:第一,强化外语学科、外语专业地位,明确外语人才培养定位。以人为本,关注学生个体发展,培养现代社会的公民精神,向来是本科教育的本质属性。一直以来,由于"工具说"盛行、对"复合型外语人才"的理解片面,外语学科的专业性质逐步弱化,学科属性趋于模糊。经过多年的实践、摸索与深刻反思,近些年来,外语教育"人文性""人文英语教育论""人文价值取向"等逐渐成为学界共识。第二,坚持质量提升、内涵式发展的准绳。不管以语言文化,还是以复合型外语人才为定位,外语专业都面临着新时代对其内涵、质量的诉求。以语言文化为中心的专业,需要纠偏"重工具""轻人文"的倾向,改革课程设置,改变教学方法,着力提升学生的综合能力、人文素养;以复合型外语人才为定位的专业,要打破外语与专业的形式化、机械化"拼盘",实现学科专业之间的内在勾连和深度融合。第三,坚持"学生本位",给学生自由的选择权。党的十九大报告提出,要不断促进人的全面发展。有学者提出外语教育要坚持"全人教育"的思想。须知,这个目标的实现需要学生具备自由、充分的选择权。诺贝尔经济学奖获得者阿马蒂亚·森认为,扩展自由既是发展的首要目的,又是发展的主要手段。没有自由、没有足够的选择权,学生的个性、主体性便无法得到充分发挥。

新时代外语人才培养的优化与升级是个系统工程,外部需要政府制定科学的外语教育政策、给予充沛的资源配置,学校管理部门也要健全灵活的教学管理制度;内部需要外语专业在培养模式、课程设置、师资队伍、评价机制等方面加强建设,形成有机整体。

第一,打破专业壁垒,突出培养方向。外语教育要满足国家战略需要、社会经济发展需要,以及学生个人需要的多元目标,就必须建立配套的、灵活的教学管理制度。一般而言,学生受制于专业限制,知识与视野无法拓展,可以通过设立专业方向,拆掉专业隔阂这堵"墙",避免把学生限制在某一专业之内,同时也可以避免专业定位过于功利化、职业化。比如,设立语言文化方向(语言文化+语言科学),国际社会方向(区域国别+国际传播+文化安全),跨专业方向(外语+某专业)等,不同方向配置不同课程体系,开设丰富多样的课程,形成"课程超市"或"课程模块",彼此互联互通,通过完善选修制度,增加学生跨方向选择权,让每个学生的学习、生活都能增值。

第二,拓宽课程广度与深度,给学生更大的选择面。课程建设是人才培养的核心。外语专业的课程设置一般包括基础课程(通识教育),专业课程(外语教育),相关专业课程(跨专业教育)以及实践环节4大块。学校应该尽己所能,开发、提供多元、合适的课程:(1)通识教育,需要学校教务管理部门统筹全校课程资源,比如,针对《国标》中提到的"中国情怀",可以开设汉语专业相关课程,帮助学生了解中国文化;针对《国标》中提到的"科学素养""自然科学基础知识",可以增设计算机、物理、化学、生物等方面基础课程;(2)外语专业课程,需要加大国际化、人文性的内容与比重,比如,在低年级将技能训练与文化、人文素养、专业知识课程交叉融合,在高年级文学、语言学、翻译学、区域国别研究、国际关系、国际传播等专业课程中强化技能训练,或者在低年级开设面向"一带一路"沿线国家的文化、宗教、地理、历史等研究导论课程,将语言技能单独以项目培训的方式,综合强化学生听说读写译的五种语言能力;(3)跨专业课程,通过建立双学位制度、辅修制度,联合政法学院、商学院、管理学院等的课程资源,在课程难度、学分要求上相对降低标准，激励学生选修的积极性。（专业方向构想见图1，不同学校可根据办学资源、师资条件，动态调整设置。）

	语言文化方向		国际社会方向			跨专业方向		
本科四年级	语言文化	语言科学	区域国别	国际传播	文化安全	法律外语	商务外语	医学外语
本科三年级								
本科二年级	基础课程（通识教育＋技能训练）							
本科一年级								

图1　外语专业方向构想

第三，加强师资队伍建设。师资队伍是人才培养质量提升的关键。提高外语人才的"人文性"，需要教师要具备更宽广的专业知识。教师要在区域国别研究、文化文明研究等人文性较强的领域内有所建树，就需要继续攻读跨专业的学历学位，拓宽专业研究方向，开出有质量、有深度的课程。

第四，变革教学方法，强化能力培养。教师要改变传统"一言堂""满堂灌"的教学方法，注重研讨班、个别或集体辅导性的课程模式，加强学生写作、语言表达等基本功训练，课堂教学由知识传授向能力提升转变。

第五，完善外语人才培养评价机制。科学的评价机制为调整人才培养思路提供参照和依据。评价机制应具有过程性和多元性，过程性是指不仅对学生在校学习的过程进行评价，也包括对其就业过程中的能力和素质表现进行评价，多元性既指囊括课程标准、学业基础和能力标准的多维评价，也指吸纳专家、教师、行业企业、用人单位、学生个人等多元主体的评价体系。

第六，进一步推动外语教育政策与规划。外语教育已然成为国家软实力建设的重要组成部分，外语人才培养离不开科学的政策。一者，政府部门要将外语教育规划作为国家战略的有机组成部分，科学制定外语教育发展的总规划；二者，政府要为中外合作办学、校企合作办学建立桥梁，拓宽人才培养渠道，通过设立基金、资金支持，鼓励更多的外语专业学生到目标国留学、交流，切实培养学生的国际视野，引导行业企业参与人才培养，提高学生实习实践的含金量；三者，考察国外一流高校外语专业的人才培养，小班化教学是优质教育的重要前提，政府要在资源配置上加大投入，保障硬、软件资源充足。

商务英语是对外经济活动中的重要工具，商务英语写作则是各国、各企业之间相互沟通、开展业务、达成交易、友好合作的重要媒介。当今，随着国际商务不断发展和活动范围日益扩大，各行各业需要大量精通商务英语写作的专业人才，准确、全面地掌握商务英语的文体写作已经成为每一个高素质、复合型人才的必备技能。《实用商务英语写作教程》一书致力于解决学习者在商务英语写作中面临的主要问题，即如何学以致用，把课堂学习同就业需要有机结合，把商务背景知识、语言知识和语言技能有机结合；从各种商务写作实践入手，涉及主题范围广，涵盖了学生在商业企业中面临的大多数写作需要；在介绍每种文体时都提供了大量的范例，通过讨论范例熟悉该文体，总结出其核心模式和常用术语及习惯用语，并配有操作性强的技巧训练。范例均附中文译文，习题均附参考答案和必要的引导性评论。

本书共涵盖18种商务文体的写作，分为18个单元。各单元遵循统一体例，分成4

部分。

第 1 部分为概述部分，简要介绍当前单元所涉及商务文体的性质、特点和格式等。

第 2 部分为样例部分。在这部分，编撰者们在广泛搜集商务英语写作真实素材的基础上，精选了一定篇幅的适合教学的例文，并在每篇例文后附上中文译文，供学习者研究学习。此外，每篇例文后均附有新词难词注解及编者的简要分析评论，以帮助学习者更好地理解掌握每一种商务文体的写作技巧和要点。

第 3 部分为句式集锦。这部分归纳总结了每单元商务文体写作中可能用到的一些术语或句式表达，供学习者参照和举一反三。

第 4 部分是练习部分。这部分为学习者提供了自我检查的机会。学习者可以按照自己不同的学习需求，选择适合自己的习题进行实际操练。所有的习题均在书后附有参考答案。

在整个编写过程中，我们力求完美，但是限于水平和时间，偏颇和疏漏在所难免，恳请广大同人和读者不吝指正，以便再版充实与完善。

本书既可供普通高等教育商务英语专业学生，以及国际贸易、国际经济、国际工商管理等外向型专业的学生使用，也可供有志于从事国际商贸工作的人员，同时准备参加 BEC 等各类商务英语考试的考生阅读，亦是涉外商务人员的必备之书。

董晓波

2022 年 1 月于南京河西

Contents

Unit 1　**Résumés** ··· 1
　　　　简历
Unit 2　**Certificates** ·· 16
　　　　证书与证明
Unit 3　**Application Letters** ··· 27
　　　　求职信
Unit 4　**Memorandums** ·· 37
　　　　备忘录
Unit 5　**Notes** ··· 44
　　　　便条
Unit 6　**Notices & Announcements** ··· 52
　　　　通知及公告
Unit 7　**Meeting Minutes** ·· 62
　　　　会议记录
Unit 8　**Itineraries & Agendas** ·· 77
　　　　行程表和议程表
Unit 9　**Business Reports** ··· 88
　　　　商务报告
Unit 10　**Business Letters** ··· 104
　　　　商务书信
Unit 11　**Contracts & Agreements** ·· 144
　　　　合同与协议
Unit 12　**Bidding** ··· 159
　　　　招标
Unit 13　**Advertisements** ·· 169
　　　　广告

I

Unit 14	**Introduction of Company** ………………………………………	182
	公司及产品介绍	
Unit 15	**Brochures, Instructions & Manuals** ……………………………	190
	指南、说明书及手册	
Unit 16	**Invitations** ………………………………………………………	197
	邀请函	
Unit 17	**Social Letters** ……………………………………………………	206
	社交信函	
Unit 18	**Public Speeches** …………………………………………………	214
	致辞与演讲	
Keys	………………………………………………………………………	224
练习答案		
References	……………………………………………………………………	264
参考文献		

Unit 1

Résumés(简历)

- General Introduction
- Sample Reading
- Useful Expressions
- Writing Practice

General Introduction & Sample Reading

What Is a Résumé?

Résumé 又称 Curriculum Vitae（CV），是极为重要的求职材料。在求职时，求职者往往要随求职信一起，向招聘者提供一份履历，可以制成履历表形式。简历是求职者介绍自己、推销自己的有力武器，把求职者的能力、学历、工作经历、成就业绩、奖励、兴趣爱好、特长等展示给用人单位。而对招聘单位来说，简历是决定是否给予求职者面试机会的重要依据。

Functions of a Résumé

简历和求职信是有密切联系的。好的简历可以使应聘者赢得招聘者的好感，加深印象，从而获得面试的机会。反之，如果简历过于简略、夸大其词或者过于自谦，则会适得其反。

Contents of a Résumé

简历的内容通常包括以下几点。
① 本人情况：姓名、性别、出生年月、国籍、婚姻状况、居住地址、电话号码等。
② 学历：就读过的学校（一般只写大学），何年获得何种学位等。
③ 工作经历：何年何月在何处工作，任过何种职务等。
④ 兴趣爱好。
⑤ 其他：有何著述，获得过何种奖学金、资助、奖励，参加过哪些学术团体、委员

会、基金组织等，推荐人或证明人的姓名、地址、职位等。

Principles for Writing a Résumé

英文简历和中文简历有着诸多不同之处，因而，在写英文简历时，应注意如下一些原则。

1. 掌握语言运用技巧

① 尽量少用长句/复杂句，尤其是以 I 或 My 开头的句子，要多用短句和短语；
② 冠词可在不影响意思的情况下省略；
③ 同一部分的表达应当一致。

2. 突出业绩能力

① 可以 Summary 的方式先概括地写出业绩和能力，使招聘人员一目了然；
② 以 Related Work Experience 为抬头，将相关经历提前突出说明，即 Functional Résumé 的形式；
③ 用具有说服力的数据强化说明所取得的业绩；
④ 用字体等格式方面的调整突出要强调的部分，但不宜过度，否则会令人眼花缭乱，适得其反。

3. 使用列举方式

如非填写招聘单位的履历表格，一般自行写作时，不宜用表格的形式书写，而应以列举的方式表达，这既能强调重点，也能使信息整齐醒目，节省招聘人员的时间。

4. 长短适宜

一般而言，招聘人员看一份简历的时间很短，因而过长的简历会令招聘人员失去耐心，而过短的简历会给招聘人员留下能力有限的印象。所以，简历的长度通常在 200～500 字，约一页纸篇幅。

Layout of a Résumé

简历的要素主要包括如下部分。

① 姓名（Name）：应使用全称，不必加称谓等。
② 地址（Address）：应与求职信及信封上的地址一致。
③ 电话号码（Tel）：应与求职信中的一致。
④ 电子邮件（E-mail）：同样应与求职信中的一致。
⑤ 目标（Objective）：希望申请得到的职位。
⑥ 概述（Summary）：对以前的工作经历、业绩等做简要概括，一般经历丰富的申请人会加上这一部分内容。
⑦ 工作经验（Working Experience）：简历的重点，是招聘者最感兴趣的部分，申请人需仔细说明。
⑧ 教育状况（Education Background）：受教育的情况、毕业院校、学位等。

⑨ 资格及职业称谓（Qualifications & Professional Designations）：拥有的职业资格。

⑩ 爱好（Hobbies）：不属于必写部分，但是恰当的描述，能够使招聘者对申请人的状态、看法、思维等方面作出良好的评估。

⑪ 备询人（Reference）：同样不属于必写部分，其作用在于强调所述的真实性，并以备招聘人员查证。

Types of Résumé

英语简历并无固定不变的格式，应聘者可根据自身具体情况确定所应采用的形式。一般来说，按照侧重点的不同，简历可分为3种基本形式，即以学历为主的简历（Basic Résumé）、以经历为主的简历（Chronological Résumé）和以职能为主的简历（Functional Résumé）。

① 以学历为主的简历通常适用于即将毕业的学生，由于一般缺乏工作经历，此种简历的重点在学历上。其内容主要包括：个人资料、应聘职位、学历、特别技能、业余爱好等。

② 以经历为主的简历侧重于工作经历，适合于有工作经验的求职者。其内容包括：个人资料、应聘职位、工作经历、学历、资格及特别技能、成果业绩。相关经历和业绩应按时间顺序由近及远书写。

③ 以职能为主的简历同样侧重于工作经历，与以经历为主的简历的差别在于：后者按时间顺序排列工作经历，而前者以工作职能或性质排列工作经历，不强调时间上的连续性，旨在强调求职者在某些方面的工作经历和能力。

Sample Reading

【Sample 1】

下面是一份个人简历，由于应聘者工作经历相对较少，故将工作经历与教育状况合在一起，按时间顺序排列。最后也注明了备询人的详细信息。但这份简历最大的不足之处在于作者未明确说明其具体的求职目标/意向，而求职目标往往是面对众多应聘者的招聘单位在筛选简历时最先关注的信息，因此这条信息的缺失很有可能会减少应聘者被考虑的机会。

```
PERSONAL DATA
Name：Liu Ping                    Sex：Male
Date of Birth：20 April, 1996     Place of Birth：Beijing
Marital Status：Single            Nationality：Chinese
Home Address：32 Heping Road Zhongguancun
Beijing, 100031
Tel：(010) 6483-9201
```

EDUCATION & EXPERIENCE

Oct. 2018 – Present: Employee at Beijing Huafeng Stock Co., Ltd.
 (Department Manager since Dec. 2019)

Nov. 2018 – Sept. 2020: Part-time student at Beijing Foreign Trade College (diploma in Business Administration, 2020)

Sept. 2014 – June 2018: Undergraduate in the Economics Department of Hebei University (BA in Economics, 2018)

Sept. 2011 – June 2014: Senior high student at Beijing Jingshan Middle School

Sept. 2008 – June 2011: Junior high student at Beijing Jingshan Middle School

AWARDS:

Third prize in University Public Speaking Competition, 2017

Second prize in University English Competition, 2018

SPECIAL INTEREST:

Computer programming

REFERENCES:

Mr. Gao Hong

(General Manager of the Beijing Huafeng Stock Co., Ltd.)

23 Hepingmenwai

Beijing, 100009

Tel: (010) 7463-6352

Ms. Lin Bing

(Dean of the Economics Department of Hebei University)

45 Changjiang Avenue

Baoding

Tel: (0311) 836-2726

个人情况:

姓名:刘平　　　　　　　　性别:男

出生年月:1996年4月20日　　出生地:北京

婚姻状况:未婚　　　　　　　国籍:中国

家庭地址:北京市中关村和平路32号　　邮编:100031

电话:(010) 6483-9201

学历及工作简历:

2008年9月—2011年6月 北京景山中学初中部学生

2011年9月—2014年6月 北京景山中学高中部学生

2014年9月—2018年6月 河北大学经济系本科生
（2018年获经济学学士学位）
2018年11月—2020年9月 北京外贸学院业余进修生
（2020年获企业管理专科毕业证书）
2018年10月迄今 受雇于北京华丰股份有限公司
（2019年12月晋升为部门经理）

奖励情况：
2017年获"河北大学演讲比赛"三等奖
2018年获"河北大学英语竞赛"二等奖

个人爱好：
计算机程序设计

备询人：
高宏先生 北京华丰股份有限公司总经理
地址：北京市和平门外23号　　邮编：100009
电话：(010) 7463-6352
林冰女士 河北大学经济系主任
地址：保定市长江路45号
电话：(0311) 836-2726

【Sample 2】

下面是一名应届毕业生的履历表。包括其受教育背景（其中列举了详细的课程成绩）、工作经历、技能水平等内容。总的来说是一份中规中矩的简历，并不特别出彩，也没有明显的不足。若写作者在用词方面少一些生涩，也许可以使其简历更有吸引力一些。

Qiao Yifeng

135 Binjiang Road

Chengdu, 610001

(028) 74638292

qiaoyf@sina.com.cn

Objective：To obtain a position in corporate finance
Certificate：CPA
Education：Sichuan University, Chengdu, Sichuan, 2019-Present
　　　　　　B.S. in Economics to be obtained in June 2023
　　　　　　Related courses and scores on the 100 marking system：

Macroeconomics	83	Industrial Accounting	89
Microeconomics	91	Cost Accounting	92

	Economic Decision-making	85	Management Accounting	86
	Economic Law	91	Financial Management	91
	Accounting Principles	81	Finance and Tax	90
	Money and Banking	90	Investment	84

Experience: Accountant
Leda Industrial Corporation Leshan, Sichuan, Summer, 2022
Analyzed financial position
Made proposals related to investment
Prepared accounting reports
Bookkeeper
Minjiang Company Chengdu, Summer, 2021
Entered variety of data into books
Tutor 2020-2021
Taught middle school students Maths, Physics and English three hours a week

Computer: Working knowledge of operation and support of hardware
Good at such softwares as Office, Photoshop, AutoCAD
Mastery of Python, MATLAB and C++ programming skills

English: Scored 636 on TOEFL   2021
Scored 91 on College English Test, Band 4   2020
Won Highest Prize in English Speech Contest of Sichuan University   2020

Membership: Member, Society of Regional Economics of Sichuan University

Reference: Chen Zhiyuan, Professor
Department of Economics
Sichuan University
15 Wangjiang Road.
Chengdu 610073

Yuan Can, President
Leda Industrial Corporation
12 Dafo Street.
Leshan, Sichuan 614001

乔义枫
成都市滨江路135号 邮政编码：610001
电话：(028) 74638292
电子邮箱：qiaoyf@sina.com.cn

应聘职位：公司财务
证书：注册会计师

学历：2019年至今，就读于四川大学
　　　2023年6月将取得经济学学士学位
　　　相关课程及按百分比计算的成绩如下：
　　　宏观经济学　　83　　　工业会计　　89
　　　微观经济学　　91　　　成本会计　　92
　　　经济决策　　　85　　　管理会计　　86
　　　经济法　　　　91　　　财务管理　　91
　　　会计学原理　　81　　　财务与税收　90
　　　货币银行学　　90　　　投资学　　　84
工作经历：2022年暑假，在四川乐山乐达实业公司实习
　　　　　任会计，主要职责是：
　　　　　分析财务状况
　　　　　提供投资建议
　　　　　编制财务报表
　　　　　2021年暑假，在成都岷江公司实习
　　　　　任簿记员，主要职责是：
　　　　　把各种数据记入账册
　　　　　2020年至2021年担任家庭教师
　　　　　辅导中学生的数学、物理和英语，每周3小时
计算机能力：掌握了硬件操作和维护知识
　　　　　　擅长Office、Photoshop、AutoCAD等软件操作
　　　　　　掌握了Python、MATLAB和C++语言编程技巧
英语水平：2021年，参加了TOEFL考试，成绩是636分
　　　　　2020年，参加了大学英语4级考试，成绩是91分
　　　　　2020年，荣获四川大学英语演讲比赛一等奖
会员资格：四川大学区域经济学会会员
证明人：邮政编码：610073
　　　　成都市望江路15号
　　　　四川大学经济系教授
　　　　陈志远
　　　　邮政编码：614001
　　　　四川省乐山大佛街12号
　　　　乐达实业公司总裁
　　　　袁灿

【Sample 3】

　　下面这份简历来自一位工作经验相对丰富的求职者。该简历内容丰富又不失简洁。该求职者对自己在相关领域的工作经历做了较为详细的陈述，重点突出，有利于吸引招聘单位的兴趣。并且，该简历在语言表达上也相对流畅，显示了求职者良好的受教育背景，这一点对提高其竞争力也有一定帮助。

501 Chaoyang Street, Beijing 100012　（010）3838-4759

Gong Qing

Objective　Director of Human Resources

Profile
- **Nine years' experience in** human resources administration
- **Comprehensive knowledge of recruitment; screening and interviewing**
- **Demonstrated ability to work effectively with employees at diverse levels**
- **Adept at labor negotiations on behalf of** management
- **Innovator with ability to increase employee morale and improve communications**

Personal Experience

2011-Present　Beijing Bio-Medical Corporation

Personnel Manager
- Responsible for recruitment, screening and interviewing of personnel
- Extensively involved in labor relations such as contract negotiations
- Interpreted and oversaw implementation of all personnel policies; controlled administration of comprehensive employee benefit programs
- Introduced measures to improve employment incentives
- Conducted wage and salary analyses to assure competitive compensation position in industry
- Supervised a six-person department

Other Experiences

2009 – 2011 Jinghua Corporation

　　　　Assistant Sales Manager
- Increased sales from ￥50 million to ￥100 million
- Managed 100 sales representatives in 10 provinces
- Trained new employees

2007 – 2009 Hengda Corporation

　　　　Purchasing Manager
- Supervised 12 staff members
- Lowered unit purchasing price by five percent due to good communication with suppliers

Education

2007 – 2009 Beijing University of Finance and Trade
　　　　　　On-the-job training of management skills

2003 – 2007 Beijing College of Commerce
　　　　　　BA in Marketing

Affiliations　International Association of Personnel
　　　　　　　Beijing Society of Personnel Management

北京市朝阳街501号　　邮政编码：100012　　电话：(010) 3838-4759

宫青

应聘职位：人力资源部经理

概述：
- 具有9年的人力资源管理经验
- 具有广博的筛选、面试等招聘知识
- 能与各种层次的员工进行有效合作
- 擅长代表管理层进行劳资谈判
- 能改善与员工的沟通，提高他们的工作热情

人事经历

2011年至今在北京生物药品公司工作

　　人事经理
- 负责招聘员工，应聘者筛选、面试
- 广泛参与各种劳动关系事务，如：进行劳动合同谈判
- 负责监督劳动政策的执行并对其进行解释，监督各种员工福利方案的执行
- 采用各种措施以提高员工的积极性
- 进行工资待遇分析以确保公司在行业中的竞争地位
- 领导本部门的6位员工

其他经历

2009年至2011年在北京京华公司工作

　　销售部经理助理
- 把年销售额从原来的5 000万元提高到1亿元
- 管理遍及10省的100个销售代表
- 培训新员工

2007年至2009年在北京恒达公司工作

　　采购部经理
- 领导12名职员
- 善于与供应商沟通，使单位的购买价降低了5%

学历

2007年至2009年在北京财经大学学习

　　进行管理技能的在职培训

2003年至2007年在北京商学院学习

　　获营销学学士学位

会员资格：国际人事协会会员
　　　　　北京人事管理协会会员

 Useful Expressions

As mentioned above, résumé writing can cover a wide range of subject matters. However, there are some structures and expressions which can always be used in composing résumés.

Useful Expressions about Education

academic activities	学术活动
bachelor	学士
commissary in charge of entertainment	文娱委员
commissary in charge of organization	组织委员
commissary in charge of physical labor	劳动委员
commissary in charge of publicity	宣传委员
commissary in charge of sports	体育委员
commissary in charge of studies	学习委员
courses completed	所学课程
curriculum included	课程内容
degree	学位
doctor (Ph.D)	博士
excellent League Member	优秀团员
excellent leader	优秀干部
extracurricular activities	课外活动
grades	分数
in-job/off-job training	在职/脱产培训
League branch secretary	团支部书记
major	主修
master	硕士
minor	辅修
monitor	班长
part-time job	业余工作
Party branch secretary	党支部书记
post doctorate	博士后
refresher course	进修课程
reward	奖励
scholarship	奖学金
social activity/practice	社会活动/实践
special training	特别训练
student council	学生会
summer job	暑期工作
Three Goods student	三好学生
vacation job	假期工作

Common Expressions

(1) assist manager in routine affairs
协助经理处理日常事务

(2) assume higher responsibilities than co-workers
比同事承担了更重要的职责

(3) authorized to represent company on numerous occasions
被授权在许多场合代表公司

(4) budget time scientifically
科学安排时间

(5) change previously deficit financial position
改变以前的财务赤字情况

(6) commended for my diligence and efficiency
因刻苦勤奋、效率高而受到称赞

(7) complete assigned task ahead of schedule
提前完成安排的工作

(8) conceive measures to increase sales volume
构思增加销售量的措施

(9) consider solutions to problems in fierce competition
考虑激烈竞争中出现的问题的解决方案

(10) construct ambitious but practical enterprise plans
制订大胆可行的企业计划

(11) contact end users for feedback about products
与终端用户取得联系，征求他们对产品的反馈意见

(12) contribute substantially to the present prosperity of this company
为公司目前的繁荣做出了很大贡献

(13) cooperate well with other staff members
与其他员工合作良好

(14) coordinate functions of company's departments
协调公司各部门的职能

(15) create friendly atmosphere
创造友好氛围

(16) demonstrate ability to exceed quota
表现能超额完成任务的能力

(17) discharge responsibilities of my position faithfully and efficiently
忠诚有效地履行岗位职责

(18) expand business in other countries
扩展在其他国家的业务

(19) expedite development of the company
加快公司的发展

(20) furnish adequate service to customers
为顾客提供充分的服务
(21) handle personnel problems skillfully
熟练处理人事问题
(22) harmonize relations with external organizations
和外部机构协调关系
(23) intensify sense of responsibility
增强责任感
(24) motivate staff to meet goals
激励员工实现目标
(25) prepare weekly, monthly, quarterly, and yearly reports
编制周报表、月报表、季报表和年报表
(26) promoted from an ordinary worker to supervisor and then to director
从一般工人,晋升为主管,再升为经理
(27) provide training, guidance and assistance to newcomers
对新来的员工提供培训、指导和帮助
(28) render perfect after-sale service to customers
为顾客提供完美的售后服务
(29) schedule quality training programs for staff members
为员工安排高质量的培训
(30) systematize working arrangements
使工作安排系统化

Writing Practice

I. Rewrite the following sentences in résumé.

(1) My duties are to write periodical reports, update and distribute company address lists, draft correspondences, make travel arrangements, and complete special projects as assigned.
(2) As a result of my efficient discharge of duties, I was promoted.
(3) I have seven years of business administrative background.
(4) I was ranked second in a class of thirty-two.
(5) I analyzed the opportunity to invest in the operations of a national fast food chain.
(6) Directed as MIS for headquarter
Provision of advice on computer to branches
(7) Career Objective: I want to get a position in Mechanical Design.

II. Fill in the following résumé table with your own information.

HORIZON

Construction Company

Application form

Please complete all sections in your own handwriting.

Section 1. Personal Particulars-Use BLOCK CAPITALS when completing this section

Position wanted _____

Date of application _____

Surname _____

First name _____

Date of birth _____

Place and country of birth _____-_____

Nationality _____

First language _____

Sex: male/female

Marital status: single/married/divorced

Husband's or wife's name _____

No. of children and their ages _____

Present address _____

_____

Section 2. Education

Primary School: Name of School _____

Town _____

Region/State _____

Dates, state month and year: From _____ to _____

Secondary School: 1. Name of School _____

Town _____

Region/State _____

Dates, state month and year: From _____ to _____

2. Name of School _____

Town _____

Region/State _____

Dates, state month and year: From _____ to _____

Name of examinations taken _____

Results _____

Details of subjects and grades _____

_____

Higher or Further Education: Give details of colleges attended, dates, courses followed,

examinations taken and results.
_____
_____

Correspondence or Evening classes: Give details of any Courses you are following at the moment.
_____
_____

Section 3: Languages
Give details of Languages you know apart from your first language. Delete as appropriate:
Name of language
I can speak it a little/fairly well/very well/not at all.
1. _____ I can write it a little/fairly well/not at all.
I can speak it a little/fairly well/very well/not at all.
2. _____ I can write it a little/fairly well/very well/not at all.
I can speak it a little/fairly well/very well/not at all.
3. _____ I can write it a little/fairly well/very well/not at all.
I can speak it a little/fairly well/very well/not at all.

Section 4: Employment
Present employer's name _____
Present employer's business address _____
_____

Date: employment began _____
length of notice required _____
Position _____
Duties _____

Previous employment: List in chronological order the names of your previous employers. State the position you held, your main duties and the beginning and ending dates of each period of employment:
_____
_____
_____

Section 5: Interests: Mention any activities (e.g. sports, hobbies) you engage in during your leisure time. State any positions of responsibility you have held or competitions, prizes, etc., that you have won:

Unit 1   Résumés（简历）   15

_____
_____
_____

Date _____ Signature _____

III. Write résumés according to requirements.

（1）张东，东南大学计算机科学与工程学院应届毕业生；平均成绩 91，学生会副主席，电子协会会员，计算机科学协会理事；每年均获得奖学金；取得微软系统工程师证书，在杂志上发表论文；在数家电子公司担任过职务；精通英语；提供证明人。

（2）高欣，谋求中小型建筑公司办公楼设计师职位；建筑学学士；列举相关课程内容；列举相关技能；暑假工作经历；兴趣。

Unit 2

Certificates (证书与证明)

- General Introduction
- Sample Reading
- Useful Expressions
- Writing Practice

General Introduction & Sample Reading

What Is a Certificate?

证明是一种涉及面非常广的文书,凡是用来表明或证明一个人的身份、经历、学历,或者某件事情真实情况的文书,都可以称为证明。与其他文书信函相比,证明更加简单明了,是单位或有关人士对其管辖范围内或了解范围内的人或事情的真实情况开具的证明信件。

Characteristics of a Certificate

证明通常简明扼要,用词较为正规。证明可以仿照普通英文书信书写,也可以按照英语证明特有的格式和用语书写。但多省掉收信人的姓名、地址和结束用语。称呼多用"To Whom It May Concern",意即"有关负责人",但此项也可省略。

Types of Certificates

证明可分为两大基本类别,一类是证明信,另一类是证书。

证明信是国家机关、社会团体、企事业单位为证明有关人员的身份、经历及其与某事件关系而出具的函件,用真实、可靠的材料表明或断定人或事物的真实性,证实和说明人和事物具体表现或特性的专用文书;有公文式、书信式、便条式3种格式;有的是主动发往对方的,有的是答复对方来函询问的;有时用于差旅事项的证明,有时用于证明事实材料的真实性。

证书是政府机关或有权单位出具的证明有关人员具有某种资格的证明文件,一般均加有单位印章。

根据内容的不同，证明主要包括：毕业证明、学历证明、工作经验证明、身份证明、病情证明、留学生经济担保书、学业成绩证明书、证书，等等。

Styles of a Certificate

1. 证明类

证明类文书通常体现为证明信的格式，与普通英文书信格式一样，同样由信头、日期、信内姓名与地址、称呼、正文、结束问候语、署名或印章等7个部分构成。除了正文的内容不同之外，其他部分的格式与普通英文信函基本一致。

证明信的样式也可以分为齐头型（Blocked Style）、缩进型（Indented Style）和综合型（Modified Style）。齐头型证明信中的每个部分都是顶格书写，段落的开头也不空格，方便编排。缩进型证明信的信头和日期位于右上方，各段开头空5格，结束问候语及署名位于右下方，其他部分顶格书写。综合型证明信的信头和日期位于右上方，结束问候语及署名位于右下方，其他部分均顶格书写。

2. 证书类

证书通常非常简短，其格式一般由标题、正文、证书出具单位、署名、日期、印章、照片等部分构成。

证书的样式通常均为缩进型，用一段文字说明。

Layout of a Certificate

由于证明文书类型多样，因而不同类型的证明书格式也不尽相同。下面就常见的几种证明文书的简单格式作一简述。

1. 工作经历证明

This is to certify that _____ (Name), _____ (Sex), _____ (Birth Date), was employed as _____ (Post) in _____ (Company) from _____ (Date) to _____ (Date).

Sample of Experience Certificate

Certificate of Experience

To Whom It May Concern：

    This is to certify that Mr. Chen Hong was employed in our Sales Department as chief salesman from January 2013 to the end of October 2019. During the time he faithfully attended to his duties. He left us of his own accord.

From The Bell Co.
Henry Sun
(Manager)

证 明 信

敬启者：

兹证明陈弘先生从 2013 年 1 月到 2019 年 10 月底在本经销部担任总经销一职。在此期间工作诚实可靠。陈弘离职，系出于自愿。

贝尔公司

亨利·孙

（经理）

---

2. 学历、学业证明、毕业证书

This is to certify that _____ (Name), _____ (Sex), _____ (Birth Date), _____ (Birth Place), was a student of _____ (major) of _____ (Department) in _____ (School) from _____ (Date) and, having completed _____ (Number of Year) Study, graduated in _____ (Date).

Sample of Graduation Certificate

GRADUATION CERTIFICATE

I hereby certify that Zhao Hujun, male, born on May 2, 1999, was a student of the computer application major of the Department of Computer Science & Engineering and, having completed the four years' courses from September 2017 through July 2021 and fulfilled all the requirements prescribed by the Department, graduated from Jiao Tong University in July 2021.

（Signature）

President

Jiao Tong University

毕 业 证 书

学生赵虎君，男，1999 年 5 月 2 日生，2017 年 9 月至 2021 年 7 月在本校计算机科学与工程系计算机应用专业 4 年制本科就读，修业期满，成绩合格，准予毕业。

交通大学校长

（签名）

---

3. 奖状

可以用 Certificate、Certificate of Merit 或者 Certificate of Commendation 作为标题。

Sample of Certificate of Merit

Certificate of Merit

This is to certify that Ms. Xu Fang has won the title of Rising Star for her outstanding work in the Emulation Campaign of the year of 2019.

Sales Section
Nanjing Silk Import & Export Corporation
(Stamp)

Date: December 20, 2019

奖　状

徐芳同志在 2019 年度工作竞赛中成绩显著，荣获本公司"新星奖"，特此表彰。

南京丝绸进出口公司营销部
（公章）
2019 年 12 月 20 日

---

4. 学习成绩证明

　　This is to certify that ＿＿＿＿＿（Name）graduated from ＿＿＿＿＿（Name of School）on ＿＿＿＿＿（Date），and received the following results in examinations:

Sample of Certificate of Academic Record

School Record Certificate

　　This is to certify that Zhu Xiaoguang, male, born in September 1993, studied the English Language in the Foreign Language Department of Southeast University from September 2012 to July 2016, and then he was enrolled in September, 2018 to study in the Foreign Language Department of Nanjing University as a postgraduate in Linguistics. He had studied there for three years and finished the courses in July 2021. The following is the report of results in his examinations:

　　Linguistics: Excellent
　　English Literature: Good
　　Applied Linguistics: Excellent
　　Defense: Pass
　　Graduation Thesis: Pass

Nanjing University

学 历 证 明

　　朱晓光，男，出生于 1993 年 9 月。2012 年 9 月至 2016 年 7 月就读于东南大学外文系英语专业，2018 年 9 月被南京大学外文系录取攻读语言学研究生，就读 3 年，2021 年 7 月毕业。其学习成绩如下：

　　语言学：优秀
　　英国文学：良好

应用语言学：优秀
答辩：合格
毕业论文：通过

南京大学
---

5. 病假证明书

This is to certify that _____ (Name of Patient), _____ (Sex), _____ (Age), _____ (Symptom of Sickness). It is suggested that he need a rest for _____ (Number of Days).

Sample of Doctor's Certificate

CERTIFICATE FOR SICK LEAVE

This is to certify that Gao Fengjia, male, 30, has a high fever of 39℃ and a very bad pharyngolaryngitis. It is advised that he take a three-day rest, and if necessary, come back for a check by that time.

Date: March 15, 2020

Doctor
Wu Ji

病假证明单

兹证明高丰嘉，男，30岁，发高烧至39℃，患严重咽喉炎。建议休息3天，如有必要，到时须来复诊。

主治医生
吴极
2020年3月15日
---

6. 其他证明信

其他证明信的简单格式可依照上述证明信的格式，稍加改变即可。

Samples

1) 在职证明信

Certificate

To Whom It May Concern:

    This is to certify that Ms. Li Bofang, (born on Oct. 23, 1986, ID: 326174198610237264) has been employed as Assistant Manager in HL Company from Sept. 2016.

Yours truly,
(Signature)
(Stamp)
Date

证 明 信

敬启者：

兹证明李伯芳女士（1986 年 10 月 23 日生，身份证号：326174198610237264）自 2016 年 9 月至今，一直在我公司（HL 公司）担任经理助理职务。

特此证明！

（署名）
（印章）
（日期）

2）进修证明

Certificate

This is to certify that Wang Xiaofeng, from our college, male, aged 26, has been selected to take a refresher course at Oxford University.

Fudan University
August 28, 2019

证 明 书

兹有我院王晓峰，男，26 岁，现选送至牛津大学进修，特此证明。

复旦大学
2019 年 8 月 28 日

7. 公证书

公证书是由国家专门机构签发的证明文件，以 Notarial Certificate 作为标题，无须称谓部分。

Notarial Certificate

This is to certify that Wu Yunxia (female) was born on March 28, 1987 in Shanghai, China. Her father is Wu Guodong and her mother is Wang Fang.

Photo

Shanghai Notary Public Office
The People's Republic of China
(Sealed)
Notary Public：...
Dated 19th day of November, 20...

公 证 书

兹证明吴云霞（女），于 1987 年 3 月 28 日出生在中国上海市，其父吴国栋，其母王芳。

照片

中华人民共和国上海市公证处
公证员：×××
20××年 11 月 19 日

Sample Reading

【Sample 1】

下面是一则工作经历证明。这份证明值得肯定的地方在于其行文简洁明了，但也存在不足之处，即其对被证明人的工作情况说明过于笼统含糊。如果能稍加提及被证明人的工作表现，会使证明更有说服力。

CERTIFICATE

To Whom It May Concern,

  This is to certify that Miss Yang Ling has been an accountant in our company for the past 2 years and has been working to our complete satisfaction. She is now leaving our company as we have no further need of her service. Any enquiries concerning her will be answered.

Yours Sincerely
Wang Jiawei
Director of the J&Z Company

证 明 信

敬启者：
  兹证明杨玲小姐曾在我公司任会计两年之久，工作一直让我们很满意，现因我公司压缩人员而离职，如欲了解其他情况，乐于奉告。

J&Z 公司董事
王家卫

【Sample 2】

下面是一份进修培训证书，说明了持证人获得该证书的情况。

ADVANCED CERTIFICATE IN ENGLISH STUDIES (FOREIGN STUDENTS)

  We, the Dean of the Faculty of Arts and the Secretary to the University of Edinburgh certify that Rongmin Wan has duly conformed to the Regulations of the university defining the conditions upon which the advanced Certificate in English Studies (Foreign Students) is awarded, having attended the prescribed courses of instruction, and having passed the necessary examinations and tests.

  This Advanced Certificate in English Studies (Foreign Students) has accordingly been awarded this Thirteenth day of May, 2017.

(Signature)
Dean of the faculty of Arts
(Signature)
Secretary

Unit 2　Certificates（证书与证明）

爱丁堡大学
外籍学生英语研修高级证书

　　兹有爱丁堡大学艺术系主任及校秘书证明，万榕敏正式符合本校对外籍学生英语研修高级证书授予条件的规定并参加了规定课程的指导学习，通过了必要的考试和考查，为此于 2017 年 5 月 13 日授予（外籍学生）英语研修高级证书。

艺术系系主任（签名）
校秘书（签名）

【Sample 3】

　　下面是一份出国经济证明。

CERTIFICATE

Dear Sir,

　　I have the pleasure to give evidence that Mr. Wang Guanglie, an assistant lecturer in our university, has the ability to bear his expenses during his stay as a graduate student in the United States. This government of ours has given him permission to go abroad for further studies. The Ministry of Education of the People's Republic of China undertakes to bear all his expenses, including those for traveling to and back from our university. Therefore, he does not need any financial help from any other sources.

　　Thank you very much.

Respectfully yours,
Cheng Xuguang
Dean of Studies
Nanjiang University

证　明　信

尊敬的先生：

　　我非常高兴地向您证明，我校助教王光烈先生有能力支付他在美国攻读研究生期间所需要的全部费用，我国政府已同意他出国深造。中华人民共和国教育部将承担他的全部费用，包括来回旅费在内。所以他不需要其他任何经济资助。

　　谢谢。

南江大学教务处处长
程旭光

Useful Expressions

Useful Words & Phrases

academic performance	学业
be awarded ...	被评为……
chancellor/president	大学校长
complete all the courses	修业期满
contest	竞赛
cup	奖杯
decoration	奖章
diploma	文凭，证书
excellent student	优秀学生
first/second/third prize winner	一/二/三等奖
fulfill all the requirements prescribed	成绩合格
labor emulation	劳动竞赛
medal	奖章
outstanding	优秀的
principal	中学校长
qualification	资格
trophy	奖品

Common Expressions

(1) Certified that ...　　　　　　　此证明……
(2) This is to certify that ...　　　　兹证明……
(3) To Whom It May Concern：　　敬启者：
(4) I hereby certify that ...　　　　兹证明……

Useful Structures

(1) As requested by Miss Wang Min, my most outstanding secretary, I'm very glad to write this letter in support of her application to your department store for the position of secretary.
应我最优秀的秘书王敏小姐的请求，我很高兴地致函为她到贵公司担任秘书做出证明。

(2) At college, he was the best student; at the company, he is the most excellent technician.
他在校是最好的学生，在公司是最出色的技师。

(3) At your request, I take pleasure to provide you with some information regarding Mr. Yuan Lekai's employment at this company as an executive secretary.

应您的要求,我很高兴地向您提供袁乐凯先生在本公司担任秘书的情况。

(4) I offered to write this letter in support of Mr. Sun Fang's pursuing a position in your office.
孙方先生向贵公司求职,我主动为他写此证明信。

(5) He displayed his ability in cooperation and leadership, so he was promoted to vice director, and later director, of the Production Department.
他表现出了极强的合作精神和领导能力,所以他先后被提拔为生产部的副经理和经理。

(6) He is hardworking, sincere, and ambitious. He is always avid for knowledge. He reads widely and actively participates in all kinds of activities.
他工作努力、待人真诚、抱负远大、求知若渴、博览群书,积极参加各种活动。

(7) He is a very able man with a strong sense of responsibility and great enthusiasm for helping others.
他能力很强,有责任感,乐于助人。

(8) He is quite charming and humorous, and these are qualities of great importance in dealing with the public and building the corporate image.
他富有魅力,幽默风趣,这对公关工作和企业形象的建立非常重要。

(9) I feel confident that she will make contributions to your company if she is employed.
如果她被聘用,我相信,她一定能为贵公司做出贡献。

(10) I think Ms. Liu's education and character doubtlessly qualify her to serve as an administrator in your company. I recommend her without reservation and believe you will find her a helpful and responsible staff member.
毫无疑问,刘女士受过良好的教育,具有良好的素质,完全能胜任贵公司的管理工作。我毫无保留地推荐她,相信她一定会成为一名有用、负责的员工。

(11) Mr. Tian has been engaged in research and development for 10 years and has published several outstanding papers in leading journals. His paper entitled "A Study of Product Discrimination" won the top prize from *Management Science and Engineering* in 2000.
田先生从事研究与开发已有10年之久,在一流刊物上发表过数篇优秀论文。其中,题为"产品区别研究"的论文在2000年的《管理科学与工程》杂志上获得一等奖。

(12) She impressed me as courteous, pleasant, and well-motivated. Her excellent communication ability and her good command of the English language add a lot to her managerial skills.
她给我的印象是彬彬有礼,待人和蔼,有追求。她善于交流,精通英语,这使她的管理能力更强。

Writing Practice

I. Translate the following certificates from Chinese into English according to the given information.

(1) 上海市国际商务英语等级考试中心于2016年9月签发证书,证明蔡明辉先生已通过上海市国际商务英语等级考试（中级）。

（2）宋佳卫同学被共青团江苏对外贸易学院委员会于2019年12月评为2006年江苏对外贸易学院大学生社会实践活动先进个人，特颁发荣誉证书。

（3）苏州市易进进修学院于2016年5月20日给唐芳慧（女，27岁）完成了为期4个月的中级计算机培训，成绩合格，准予结业，颁发证书。

II. Translate the following certificate letters from Chinese into English according to the given information.

（1）旧金山州立大学海外学生定向培训部主任裘·安·克雷格于2017年10月23日授予上海—旧金山姐妹城市委员会主办的商务管理课程班访问经理王晓峰圆满结束中美跨文化培训计划的结业证书。

（2）喜天游公司总经理证明持证者王应京先生是我的一位熟人，我知道他完全可以信赖。

（3）证明大卫·布朗先生在本公司担任推销员4年，其间，勤勉努力在履行职责过程中显示出自身的聪明才智，获得同事和上司的敬重。

Unit 3

Application Letters（求职信）

- General Introduction
- Sample Reading
- Useful Expressions
- Writing Practice

General Introduction & Sample Reading

What Is an Application Letter?

求职信是说明求职者经历、能力的信函。它是突出求职者相关学历、经历、能力、业绩等的重要手段。一封好的求职信可以帮助求职者获得面试机会，并最终获得所谋求的职位。求职信可分为两大类：自荐信和推荐信，本章着重于自荐信。

Characteristics of an Application Letter

求职信不同于其他题材的英语书信作文，不要求辞藻华丽，而是既要简明有趣，与众不同，又不宜过于古怪。其特点如下。

① 清楚（Clearness）：要突出求职主题，直截了当，层次分明。

② 简练（Conciseness）：行文简洁，说清必要内容，不提与求职无关的事，以短句为主。

③ 准确（Correctness）：用语准确，避免过多使用形容词和副词。

④ 礼貌（Politeness）：语气要有礼貌，不卑不亢。

⑤ 客观（Objectiveness）：用语客观，多使用委婉语气。

⑥ 适度（Moderation）：不宜过度夸大自身能力，甚至凭空捏造。

The Layout of the Application Letter

求职信的格式虽有细微差别，但总体上是基本固定不变的。

1. 信头（Heading）

信头是求职者本人的地址，用作招聘单位的回信地址，因而应当准确无误。如信的样式为齐头型，信头每行均应顶格书写；如为缩进型或综合型，则信头应位于右上方，每行开头对齐。

2. 日期（Date）

日期在信头下方，与信头间隔一行。如信的样式为齐头型，日期应顶格书写；如为缩进型或综合型，则日期应位于右上方，与信头的开头对齐。

3. 信内姓名及地址（Inside Name and Address）

信内姓名及地址是收信人，即招聘单位或招聘负责人的名称或地址，应当具体准确，与信封上的写法一致，在日期下方隔一行处书写于左下方。

4. 称呼（Salutation）

称呼位于信内姓名及地址下方隔一行处，并顶格书写。

5. 正文（Body）

正文是求职信最重要的部分，各段间均宜间隔一行。如信的样式为齐头型或综合型，正文各段均应顶格书写；如为缩进型，则各段应空5格书写。

6. 结束问候语（Complimentary Close）

结束问候语与正文间隔一行书写。如信的样式为齐头型，应顶格书写；如为缩进型或综合型，则宜与日期的开头对齐。

7. 署名（Signature）

位于结束问候语下方，应为亲笔署名。

8. 附件（Attachment）

即所附简历等，应予以注明，并顶格书写于署名下方隔一行处。

Styles of the Application Letter

求职信一般分为3种：齐头型（Blocked Style）、缩进型（Indented Style）和综合型（Modified Style）。

齐头型求职信中的每个部分都是顶格书写，段落的开头也不空格，这样更便于编排。

缩进型求职信的信头和日期位于右上方，各段开头空5格，结束问候语及署名位于右下方，其他部分顶格书写。

综合型求职信的信头和日期位于右上方，结束问候语及署名位于右下方，其他部分均顶格书写。

Unit 3　Application Letters（求职信）　29

Sample Reading

[Sample 1]

　　下面这份求职申请中申请人经历不多，因而此份申请就显得平淡普通，较难令人一睹之下留下深刻印象，且陈述语气也较为平淡，令人难以提起兴趣阅读。

311 Shanghai Road
Tianjin 300013
June 11, 2020

Mr. William Darnley
Manager, Personnel Department
Novell Company
3 Jiefang Road
Dalian, Liaoning 116056

Dear Mr. Darnley,

　　Your advertisement in the July 7 issue of *21st Century* for an administrative assistant describes exactly the position for which my training and experience have prepared me. Please consider me an applicant.

　　While I was a student in Tianjin Commercial College, I completed a training program designed specifically for office assistant as well as my major in business administration. As part of this course, I worked part-time in the dean's office. I always finished assignments rapidly and efficiently in a careful way, thus winning the dean's good comments.

　　In addition, Mr. Darnley, I gained valuable experience by working at the Friendship Trading Corporation. There I did general office work for Mr. Li Nan, who was so satisfied with my performance that he, on hearing of my application to you, offers to be a reference. Please refer to the enclosed résumé for additional information concerning my qualifications.

　　When would it be convenient for you to meet with me? I will be in Dalian from July 12 through July 20. If a date before July 12 or after July 20 would be more convenient for you, I would be happy to return to Dalian for an interview. At any time you may telephone me at 13984873621.

Sincerely,
Ms. Qian Qian

Attachment: Résumé

辽宁省大连市 116056
解放路 3 号
Novell 公司人事部经理
威廉·丹尼先生（收）

亲爱的丹尼先生：

    我的教育情况和工作经历正适合你们 7 月 7 日在《21 世纪报》上征招的行政助理职位。请接受我在此提出的申请。

    我在天津商学院学习期间，除主修工商行政管理课程外，还修完了办公助理的专设课程。作为办公助理课程的一部分，我在系主任办公室做过兼职工作。我做事认真仔细、干净利落，受到了系主任的好评。

    另外，我在友谊贸易公司工作期间，获得了宝贵的经验。我为李楠先生做了一段时间的办公助理，他对我的工作非常满意，所以一听我说要求职，就主动提出要当我的证明人。丹尼先生，如果您想进一步了解我的素质和能力，请参阅我随函附寄的简历。

    您什么时候对我进行面试较为合适？我 7 月 12 日至 20 日都在大连。如果 7 月 12 日前或 20 日后对您来说更合适，我也会非常乐意来大连参加面试。您随时都可以拨打 13984873621 通知我。

    此致
    随信附上：个人简历

钱前
上海路 311 号
天津市，300013
2020 年 6 月 11 日

【Sample 2】

    下面同样是一位应届毕业生的求职申请信，由于申请人所学专业在校期间就可以拥有较多兼职工作的机会，所以申请人的工作经历相对更为丰富，因而申请人大部分篇幅都是在说明自己的工作经历，以强调自己的实际运用能力，是一份比较不错的求职信。

30 Daming Road
Shanghai 200012
12 February, 2018

Mr. Huang Haifeng
Manager, Personnel Department
CenturyCom Inc.
216 Anxi Road
Shanghai 200037

Dear Mr. Huang,

    I am interested in applying for a position as an electronic engineer at CenturyCom. I found the position advertised at the placement office at Fudan University. I will graduate in June with a degree in electronical engineering and hope to start my career at that time.

During the past four years I have had a good deal of academic experience in communication technology. As an active member of the Fudan Society of Computer Communication, I learned much about the practical challenges mechanical engineers face each day, and about the strategic significances of collaborating with fellow team members. In my position with Excelcom, I was able to test and sharpen the skills I was learning at school and use them on a regular basis. In addition to the responsibilities noted in my résumé, I designed an innovative software program that compiled data used by other firms and interpreted the results for the sales division at Excelcom.

My experience of working with others has given me confidence in my interpersonal skills and decision-making abilities, particularly in the area of computer communication. And I believe that making a contribution to a general goal goes much further than simply possessing skills; one must have the ability to work toward a consensus everyone can live with.

I am available for an interview at any time convenient to you. I can be reached by phone at 48202928. Thank you for your time and consideration.

Sincerely,
Pan Yanggang

Enclosure: Résumé

上海市大明路30号，200012
2018年2月12日

上海市安西路216号，200037
CenturyCom 合作股份有限公司
人力资源部经理
黄海峰先生（收）

亲爱的黄先生：

我非常希望能在贵公司谋取电子工程师的职位。我是在复旦大学的就业办公室看到你们的招聘广告的。我将于今年6月份毕业，并取得电子工程学士学位，然后开始我的工作生涯。

四年来，我掌握了丰富的通信技术专业知识。作为复旦计算机通信协会的一名会员，我积极参与协会活动，深悉电子工程师每天都面临挑战，也熟知和同事配合的战略重要性；我在优通公司任职期间，常把学校所学的知识技能应用于实际工作，对这些知识技能进行检验，得到了很大提高。除我在简历中提到的所承担的职责外，我还设计了一种颇具创新性的软件，能对其他公司的数据进行处理，而后把结果提供给销售部使用。

我有与他人相处的丰富经历，深信能协调好各种人际关系；同时，我也坚信自己的决策能力，尤其是计算机通信方面的决策能力。我认为，光有能力不一定就能为众人所奋斗的目标做出贡献，还必须和他人配合默契才行。

您认为方便的任何时间，我都可以来面试。我的联系电话是48202928。望能抽出时间考虑我的申请为荷。

此致

附：个人简历

潘扬刚

[Sample 3]

以下是一份申请培发部经理职位的求职信，申请人并未将全部经历列上，只是突出了与应聘职位最相关的内容，同时也是聘用单位最感兴趣的部分。

11 Yangqiao Road
Fuzhou, Fujian 350083
23 November, 2019

Ms. Helen Smiths
Director, Human Resource Department
Coopers Company
375 Lianjiang Road
Fuzhou, Fujian 350092

Dear Ms. Smiths,

My background makes me confident that I can creatively perform as the training and development manager for Coopers.

As my résumé indicates, I have four years of full-time experience in training and development. Perhaps my most notable accomplishment in this field was the extremely successful training and development program that I developed and implemented at Haida Corporation. By the time I left Haida, 75 percent of the managerial and professional employees were voluntarily participating in my program's training activities.

While studying for the MBA degree in management, I took some 100 hours of training and development courses, and I scored the highest among a grade of 30 students. Tsinghua University, the institution from which I earned my MBA degree, is well known for its excellent training and development courses.

Please call me at 666-1319 so that I can answer any of your questions concerning my qualifications. Sometime during this or next month I would like to meet with you at your convenience. I am eager to cooperate with you and make any possible contribution to Coopers'

Unit 3 Application Letters（求职信）

further development.

Sincerely,
Huang Ming

Enclosure

福建省福州市杨桥路 11 号，350083
2019 年 11 月 23 日

福建省福州市连江路 375 号，350092
Coppers 公司人力资源部主任
Helen Smiths 女士（收）
亲爱的 Smiths 女士：

  凭我的经历和能力，我相信自己完全能胜任贵公司的培训开发部经理一职。
  正如简历所示，我有足足 4 年的培训开发经验。我在培训领域取得的最大成就可能要数我在海达公司设计并实施的一个相当成功的培训开发项目。到我离开海达公司的时候，该公司已有 75% 的管理人员和技术人员在主动参加该项目的培训学习。
  我在攻读工商管理硕士学位期间，学习了约 100 学时的培训开发课程，在同年级 30 位学生中，成绩是最高的。授予我工商管理硕士学位的清华大学，培训开发方面的课程是相当有名的。
  关于我的素质和能力，如果您还有什么需要了解的话，请拨打 666-1319。我希望您能在方便的时候，于本月或下月对我进行面试。我迫切期望能早日和你们合作，共同为贵公司的进一步发展做出贡献。
  此致
  附函

黄明

Useful Expressions

Common Names of Positions

Accounting Supervisor	会计主管
Administration Manager	行政经理
Administrative Assistant	行政助理
Assistant Manager	副经理
Business Manager	业务经理

Buyer	采购员
Clerk Typist & Secretary	文书打字兼秘书
Deputy General Manager	副总经理
Financial Controller	财务主任
General Manager/President	总经理
General Manager Assistant	总经理助理
Manager for Public Relations	公关部经理
Market Development Manager	市场开发部经理
Marketing Manager	市场销售部经理
Marketing Assistant	销售助理
Marketing Executive	销售主管
Marketing Representative Manager	市场调研部经理
Office Assistant	办公室助理
Operational Manager	业务经理
Package Designer	包装设计师
Personnel Clerk	人事部职员
Personnel Manager	人事部经理
Production Engineer	产品工程师
Programmer	计算机程序设计师
Promotional Manager	推销部经理
Purchasing Agent	采购进货员
Real Estate Staff	房地产职员
Regional Manager	地区经理
Research & Development Engineer	研究开发工程师
Sales Assistant	销售助理
Sales Executive	销售主管
Sales Manager	销售部经理
Sales Representative	销售代表
Service Manager	服务部经理
Software Engineer	计算机软件工程师
Systems Engineer	系统工程师
Technical Worker	技术工人
Tourist Guide	导游
Trainee Manager	培训部经理

Useful Structures

(1) Are you looking for a dynamic salesperson?
你们需要充满活力的销售人员吗?

(2) Because I know my unique training would be an asset to your top-notch company, I am

eager to become a member of your staff.
我知道我所受的特殊培训对你们这样的顶级公司会很有用,我渴望成为你们中的一员。

(3) By referring to the enclosed résumé and contacting the people I list as references, you can acquire an overall picture of my specialized qualifications.
你可以从所附的简历及当中列出的证明人那里,全面了解我的专业才能。

(4) Five years of related work experience, and strong interpersonal skills have prepared me for a career in office administration.
我有5年相关工作经验和较强的人际交流沟通能力,能胜任高级管理工作。

(5) I am goal-oriented, creative, and able to identify and maximize the talent of subordinates.
我做事有目标,有很强的创造力,能够了解下属的能力并使之得到最大限度的发挥。

(6) I am very excited and delighted over the good news that you are recruiting a secretary.
获悉你们将招聘一名秘书的好消息,本人非常高兴。

(7) I look forward to talking further with you about the advertised position, and am enclosing a résumé for your information.
我希望能和您就招聘的职位进一步谈谈。我随函附上一份简历供您审阅。

(8) I shall bring to the job a willingness to work and an eagerness to improve. Let me prove this to you.
我乐于工作,渴望提高,希望能有机会向您证实这一点。

(9) I wish to apply for the job you are offering in today's *Yangtze Evening Paper*.
本人希望获得贵单位在今天的《扬子晚报》上所提供的工作。

(10) My education and experience is a match with the qualities you're looking for.
我的学历和经历正符合你们的要求。

(11) My internship at Huawei Industries proved my competency for challenging jobs.
我在华威公司的实习表明,我能胜任具有挑战性的工作。

(12) My management skills and ability to develop and implement business strategies have resulted in a successful track record of performance in tough operating environments.
我有很强的管理能力和制定并实施战略的才能,并因此在逆境下创造了成功的业绩。

(13) My strong sense of cooperation and intense kindness to people would fit me harmoniously into your organization.
我有很强的合作意识,对人友好,能和贵公司的员工融洽相处。

(14) My two degrees and my relative experience make me the right person, energetic, hardworking, and competent, for the position you advertised.
我取得了两个学位,并具有相关工作经历,精力充沛,积极肯干,能力较强,正是你们广告招聘的合适人选。

(15) You can contact me at my E-mail address, at 8473832, or at 8394712.
您可以发E-mail给我,也可以拨打电话8473832或8394712与我联系。

Writing Practice

I. Decide whether the following sentences are suitable or not in an application letter and try to explain which part is wrong.

(1) Qualifications: No education or experience.
(2) I am relatively intelligent, obedient and loyal as a puppy.
(3) My compensation should be at least equal to my age.
(4) Fired because I fought over lower pay.
(5) Please disregard the enclosed résumé — it is terribly out of date.
(6) Proven ability to track down and correct erors.
(7) I am a rabid typist.
(8) Work History: Performed brain wave tests, 1879 – 1981.
(9) Accounting cleric.
(10) Note: Keep this résumé on top of the stack. Use all others to heat your house.
(11) Also Known As: Mr. Productivity, Mr. Clever, Mr. Fix-it.
(12) Let's meet so you can "ooh" and "aha" over my experience.

II. Translation.

(1) 除了正常的助理工作，我还负责接电话和接待访客，安排约会时间表，处理文件和信函。
(2) 除了在我现在的工作职位上有7年的设计经验外，您还会满意地发现，在大学的学习给我提供了这个领域所必需的技术和知识，我可以确切地说，我现在一定能做好。
(3) 正如我所附寄的简历所述，我的工作经验，加上我的学历背景，应使我能胜任此职。
(4) 如果你们想了解更多的情况，我非常乐意在双方都方便时前去贵厂面谈。
(5) 我想你们会同意本人的看法，至少在你们所提供的职位上，我是个有实力的候选人。
(6) 我相信本人有能力满足贵公司所列的要求。

III. Write application letters according to requirements (the heading part can be omitted).

(1) 你要申请R&H公司上海代表处的行政秘书职位；曾担任过3年相同工作；本科毕业于华东理工大学，通过英语四、六级，熟悉计算机。
(2) 你向某信息技术公司总经理申请技术经理工作；毕业于上海交通大学；工作于一家计算机公司；申请是为了进一步施展自身才华。
(3) 你即将从江苏对外贸易大学毕业，向某外贸公司求职；专业是商务英语，学习成绩优秀。
(4) 你是南京大学国际商法硕士研究生，经导师介绍向江苏对外服务公司求职；掌握英语和日语；发表过论文。

Unit 4

Memorandums（备忘录）

- General Introduction
- Sample Reading
- Useful Expressions
- Writing Practice

General Introduction & Sample Reading

What Are Memos?

备忘录（Memorandum or Memo）大致可分两类。

第一类属于正式公文，常作为外交函件或商业合同的补充条款或事项，具有一定法律约束性，因此文体正规，措辞严谨。

第二类备忘录是一种非正式的商务文件、便条，多用于公司或机关内部，是以书面形式来交流内部事务的一种简便函件。它可以用来解释政策、程序和指示，发布通知，提出信息和行动要求，答复要求；也可以用来提醒事务，或对决定、电话交谈、会议提供书面记录。由于这类备忘录流通于一定单位内部，因此大多格式简明，语言通俗。

本单元主要介绍的是第二类备忘录，即商务备忘录（Office Memos）。

How Is a Memo Laid out?

备忘录的格式一般较为固定，通常分为开头（the heading）和正文（the body）两部分。开头包括"To:"（送交目标，即接受人the recipient），"From:"（发出者the sender），"Subject:"（主题）和"Date:"（日期）四项。顺序通常如上所示，但Date项的位置比较灵活，可以按书信格式置于正文右上方，也可以置于Subject项之前或之后。备忘录正文一般不超过一页，可以是一段或几段。正文后面往往没有签名，但个别的也有签名。

有些大公司或机构会备有打印好的备忘录纸笺。纸笺上端通常印有公司或机构名称和Memo字样，并印有开头部分：To, From, Date和Subject，在每次写备忘录时只需填入具

```
Memo
To:_____
From: _____
Subject/Ref:_____
Date:_____


_____
_____
_____

(Signature:_____)
```

体内容即可。

打印或书写备忘录时,通常有两种格式:每一行顶格左边对齐或每段首行缩进。

Sample Reading

[Sample 1]

这是一则在同事间送递的备忘录。理查·戴维斯将去欧洲做推销旅行。他给总经理助理米歇尔·道格拉斯写了一份关于日程安排的备忘录。该备忘录叙事简洁明了、条理清晰、语言规范、措辞得当,显示了发件人良好的职业素养,是一篇很好的备忘录范例。

Memo
To: Michelle Douglas
From: Richard Davis
Ref: European sales trip
Date: 16 May, 2016

During my forthcoming trip, I propose to visit the following companies:
Electrotechnic S. A., Barcelona, Spain   10 June
Klaus Cramer, Hamburg, Germany   11 June
MTB Thermoplastiques, Lyon   13 June

Unit 4 Memorandums（备忘录）

Please arrange for our agreed publicity material to go to each of these, seven days before the date of my visit. **Could you also please arrange** flights and hotel accommodation?

I estimate that I shall need about £300 in cash (£100 in each currency) and travelers cheques to the value of £300, to cover hotel bills, entertaining, etc., and **I shall be grateful if I can have this as soon as possible.**

备忘录

致：米歇尔·道格拉斯
自：理查·戴维斯
事由：欧洲推销旅行
日期：2016年5月16日

  在即将进行的旅行中，我计划参观下列公司：
Electrotechnic S. A., 巴塞罗那，西班牙　　　6月10日
Klaus Cramer, 汉堡市，德国　　　　　　　　6月11日
MTB Thermoplastiques, 里昂，法国　　　　　6月13日
  请在我拜访之前7天将我们的广告资料寄给这些公司。另外，能否请你安排航班和旅行住宿？
  我估计，这次旅行将需要300英镑的现金（每种货币100英镑）和300英镑旅行支票，以支付旅馆账单、商务招待等。请尽快安排，谢谢。

【Sample 2】

  这则备忘录是关于公司销售经理 Mr. Johnson 的退休通告。公司总经理以备忘录的形式号召全体员工出席公司为 Mr. Johnson 饯行的告别宴会，并表示希望大家慷慨解囊，为 Mr. Johnson 的告别礼物积极募捐。该备忘录是以总经理的名义发送给所有员工，叙事清晰，语言简练，正式中却不乏亲切。

Memo
To：All Members of Staff
From：Managing Director
Subject：Retirement of Mr. Johnson
Date：18 Oct., 2018

  As you will know, Mr. Johnson, the Sales Manager, is retiring next week after working for our company for 40 years.
  I am arranging a farewell dinner in his honor at the Hilton Hotel on Friday, 20 October, at 7:00 pm. I hope that as many members of staff as possible will be present to give Mr. Johnson the warm farewell that he deserves; **not only has he been a loyal member of**

our staff for so many years but in addition his friendliness and generous personality have endeared him to all those with whom he has worked.

Mr. Smith is making a collection for a parting gift to Mr. Johnson and I hope you will all make a generous contribution.

备忘录

致：全体员工

自：总经理

主题：琼森先生退休事宜

日期：2018年10月18日

如大家所知，我们的销售经理琼森先生，在为公司效劳40年之后，将于下个星期退休。

本周五（10月20日）晚7点在希尔顿饭店安排了琼森先生退休告别晚宴。希望大家尽可能前往，为琼森先生饯行。琼森先生应当得到我们温暖的告别，不仅因为琼森先生这么多年一直对公司忠心耿耿，更因为他友爱和大度的个性值得所有和他共事过的人爱戴。

史密斯先生正在为琼森先生募捐告别礼物，希望大家慷慨解囊。

[Sample 3]

下面这则备忘录相当于一份内部通知，用来宣布单位新规定。规定涉及办公室禁止吸烟及员工自行车摆放问题。备忘录由人事部门Paul Smith签发，送交单位所有员工备忘。

Memo   04/08/17

To：All Members of Staff

From：Paul Smith, Personnel Dept.

Subject：Smoking and Bicycles

SMOKING

All members of staff are reminded that the office is a NO SMOKING AREA and that smoking is restricted to the coffee lounge and terrace.

BICYCLES

Members of staff who cycle to work leave their bicycles behind the office building.

备忘录

致：所有职员

自：保罗·史密斯，人事部

事由：吸烟与自行车

Unit 4　Memorandums（备忘录）

> 吸烟
> 所有职员应记住，办公室是无烟区，吸烟请到咖啡休息室或平地上。
> 自行车
> 凡骑车上班的职员请将自行车存放在办公楼后面。
>
> 　　　　　　　　　　　　　　　　　　　　　　　　　2017 年 4 月 8 日

Notes & Analysis

（1）由于备忘录主要流通于单位内部，发件人和收件人对其背景都有一定了解，因此备忘录的写作往往直接、开门见山，语言通俗简洁。

（2）备忘录可以是由上级对下级作出指示或要求行动，如例 2 中公司总经理对其员工提出行动要求；也可以是同事间的信息交流或事务备忘，如例 1。

（3）备忘录的主题广泛，可以是关于老员工退休宴会的安排（如例 2），也可以是业务汇报和公司发展建议等。

（4）备忘录一般来说属于非正式文件，因此往往不使用问候和结束敬语。但注意基本的办公礼节。

Useful Expressions

（1）Please note that . . . ; Please remind . . . that . . .	请注意……
（2）It has come to my attention/notice that . . .	我注意到……
（3）I'd like you to . . .	我希望你……
（4）Would you please . . .	你能否……
（5）May I remind you that . . .	可否提醒您注意……
（6）This is the reminder of . . .	此函用来提醒……
（7）Be sure to . . .	务必……
（8）Thank you for your attention and cooperation.	感谢您的关注与合作。
（9）I should appreciate your understanding and cooperation.	对于您的理解和合作，我深表感激。

Writing Practice

I. Read the following memos and give appropriate subject headings.

（1）SUBJECT ＿＿＿＿＿＿

There will be a meeting on Wednesday, Jan. 14, at 2:30 pm in Room 503 to discuss the Education Leave Request. Jiang Ming, Division Chief, will be there to provide information and answer questions.

(2) SUBJECT _____

We need an update on those employees in your department who are participants (参与者) in the company stock option plan. Please list the names of those who are currently participating and their years of service. Also list anyone who will be eligible (有资格的) for participation next year. Be sure to turn in this information to me by 28 October.

(3) SUBJECT _____

We've long talked of the need for a manual to help train our new receptionists (接待员). At Sue's suggestion, I've written the attached (附着的) draft. I'd appreciate your reviewing it and suggesting any changes that would make it clearer and more helpful. Since Sue wants the manual by Dec., could I have your reaction by the end of this week? If that's too soon, please let me know.

II. Look at the memo below and decide how it can be improved; rewrite it in your own words.

MEMORANDUM

To: All members of staff, Northern Branch.
From: K. L. J.
Date: 3 December, 2017

As you know, one of the reasons for the introduction of PCs in Northern Branch was to provide us with feedback (反馈) before we decide whether to install (安装) PCs in other departments. The Board has asked me to submit a report on your experiences by the end of this week. I talked to some of you informally about this last month. During my brief visit I noticed a junior member of staff playing some kind of computer game in the lunch hour, and a senior manager told me that he used his for writing letters—a job for a secretary, surely? So that I can compile a full report, I would like everyone to let me know what they personally use the PC for, what software they use and how long per day they spend actually using it. It would also be useful to find out how their PCs have not come up to expectations, and any unanticipated (没有预料到的) uses they have found for their PCs, so that others can benefit from your experience.

III. Draft memos according to the notes given.

(1) 全体部门负责人备忘:

总经理徐大亮将于9月10日去欧洲出差,因此本周(9月12日)公司例会取消。有重要事务须在9日前向其汇报。

在徐总出差期间,副总经理赵星将暂时接管其日常工作并主持下周(19日)例会,例会时间、地点不变。

(2) You work for Foley Press, publisher of school and college textbooks. Your office manager, Mary McMahon, leaves the following message for you.

We've had several complaints from customers saying that some of them received the books they ordered with the wrong invoices, and some were sent the correct invoices with the wrong books. This has never happened before. The Managing Director, Mr. Augustus Foley, is very concerned about this. Will you please draft a memo, under his name, a copy of which can be sent to all workers in the Dispatch Department, expressing his concern and asking them to give them full attention to their work and to double-check that the correct invoices are sent with orders? I know they have had several new workers starting there during the last six months but that they must take them to the Dispatch Department Manager, old Harry Hawke. Oh yes, write it in a friendly, helpful tone and not a threatening one.

Unit 5

Notes (便条)

- General Introduction
- Sample Reading
- Useful Expressions
- Writing Practice

General Introduction & Sample Reading

What Is a Note?

便条（Note）是书信的一种形式，它内容简短，格式简单。由于便条常常是临时的通知、留言，或是询问、要求等，涉及的又是将要发生的事情，因此大多言简意赅，一两句话就可以结束。当我们有事要告诉别人却在某一情形下无法与之会面时，我们就可以留个便条。

便条多用于朋友、同事等熟悉的人之间，往往是委托别人办理某事或是某人在某场合下的直接留言。它一般书写在纸条上，书写形式没有书信那么严格，通常不用写开头语、写信人地址、收信人地址、结尾语等项目。但如果要求对方回复，而对方又不知你的地址，就有必要留下地址了。便条用词比较口语化，通俗易懂。比如"要让某人知道某事"可以用"When you receive this note, please..."开始整个留言而不必用"This is to announce..."。前者较为随意，而后者是比较正式的说法。

常用的便条有"假条"和"留言条"两种。

How Is a Note Laid out?

	DATE
SALUTATION	
	SIGNATURE
(ENCL)	

Unit 5　Notes（便条）

便条的格式一般较为简单，通常分为日期（Date）、称呼（Salutation）、正文（Body）、署名（Signature）等项。

日期部分位于便条右上角。可以将年、月、日完整写上，也可以只写星期几或星期几上午、下午，或者写几日、几点钟也行。一般来说，日期为几月几日的比较普遍。因便条的内容大多是最近要发生的事，所以年份可以省去不写。

称呼部分位于正文的左上角，其后紧接正文。由于便条多用于熟悉的人之间，称呼用语可以不必很正式，如：Mary，Wang，Comrade Wang，Mr. Clark，Dear Frank，Miss Hobart，Dr. Zhang，Professor Albert.

正文要求简短精要，用词通俗易懂，将内容讲清楚即可，以便让对方一眼就能明了。

署名部分位于正文右下角，一般写上留言人的姓名。如果是熟人之间的留言，也可以只写姓，或只写名字，如 Harper，Bill，Tom，Alice，Anna 等。

Sample Reading

1. 假条（Request for Leave）

假条包括病假条（Asking for Sick Leave）、事假条（Asking for Business Leave）和续假条（Asking for an Extension of Leave）等。

【Sample 1】

下面这则便条是一份病假条。学生约翰因患胃病不能到校上课，向老师史密斯小姐请假4天。全文语气委婉，字里行间流露出对老师的抱歉，并不忘附上相关证明，让人读来觉得情有可原，是一则写得不错的假条。

　　　　　　　　　　　　　　　　　　　　　　　　　　　　　　　　05/12

Dear Miss Smith,

　　I am very sorry that I am unable to go to school today **due to** a bad stomachache. I **enclosed**① **a certificate**② from my doctor and **ask you for sick leave** of four days.

　　I should be very obliged③ if you grant my leave. Considering the lessons missed during my absence, I will try my best to make them up.

　　　　　　　　　　　　　　　　　　　　　　　　　　　　　　Yours respectfully,

　　　　　　　　　　　　　　　　　　　　　　　　　　　　　　　　　John

Encl: doctor's certificate for sick leave

---

① enclose（Encl）：附上　　② certificate：证明　　③ obliged：感激不尽的

　　　　　　　　　　　　　　　　　　　　　　　　　　　　　　　　5月12日

亲爱的史密斯老师：

　　很抱歉，由于严重的胃病，我今天不能到校上课了。我已附上医生证明并向您请假四天。

如您准假，万分感谢。请假期间落下的功课，以后一定努力补上。

尊敬您的学生

约翰

附：医生的病假证明

【Sample 2】

下面是一则事假条。黄明的爷爷病重，家里来电让他赶紧回去探望，因此黄明给系办公室的陈辅导员递交了一份事假条，要求请假一周。假条中，理由陈述恰当，但语气不够委婉，如修改后再将家中电报作为证明附上，则不失为一份好的假条。

July 21, 20＿＿

Dear Miss Chen,

I have just received a telegram from my home **saying that** my grandfather is seriously[①] ill and **urging me to** go home. So I ask for one week's leave of absence from 21st to 27th in order to go home at once to see my grandfather.

Your student,

Huang Ming

① seriously：严重地

20＿＿年7月21日

亲爱的陈老师：

刚收到家中发来的电报，信中讲我的祖父病得十分严重，并催促我立即回家。我打算立即回家探望，故请假一周，从7月21日至27日。

您的学生

黄明

【Sample 3】

这是一则续假条。伍德因患重感冒未好，还需卧床休息3天，为此他向经理续请3天的假。

Oct. 12, 20＿＿

Mr. Benson,

I am still not feeling very well with the bad cold and unable to get up. The doctor came to see me this morning and **suggested a rest of** another three days. Please **give an extension**[①] **of leave for three more days**. The doctor's certificate of advice is enclosed.

Yours cordially,

Wood

Encl：Doctor's Certificate of Advice

① extension：延长，延期

Unit 5   Notes（便条）

20＿＿年10月12日

本森先生：
　　我患的重感冒未见起色，仍卧床不起。今早请医生看了一下，他建议我再休息三天，请准予续假。另附医生证明。

您诚挚的
伍德

附：医生证明

Analysis

（1）写假条时务必将请假缘由及请假日期表述清楚。注意理由要表述充分，措辞一定要恰当。如例1中的"sick leave of four days"和例2中的"absence from 21st to 27th"都是对日期的清楚表述。

（2）针对不同的阅读对象，考虑是否运用一些委婉的说法。如例1是给老师的假条，因此用了"I am very sorry that ..."和"I should be very obliged ..."等委婉句式。而例3是递交给公司经理的假条，所以使用了"Yours cordially"等更为礼貌一些的表达方式。

（3）如果有医院出具的或是其他有关请假原因的证据，也应附于假条之后一起递交。如例1中的"Encl: doctor's certificate for sick leave"和例3中的"Encl: Doctor's Certificate of Advice"。

2. 留言条（Notes Left）

留言条是便条的另一种常用形式，它使用范围较广，大多是某一场合下直接的、简短的留言，往往用于熟悉的人之间。

[Sample 1]

下面一则便条是专访不遇留言（Message to One Who Is Out）。

王翔因故来到这个城市想顺道拜访一下刘先生，刘先生刚好不在，因此王翔留了张便条，请刘先生和他联系。行文条理分明，并不忘留下相关信息，是一则用词得体的留言条。

4:15 p.m., Thursday

Dear Mr. Liu,
　　You **happened to be out** when I **called on** you. I arrived here the day before yesterday on business and will stay here for another two days. Please come over and have a talk. I'm staying at the Hilton Hotel, Room 301. Give me a call before coming. My telephone number is 84539641, extension① 301. **I shall be glad if you find time to favor me with a visit** as soon as possible.

Cordially,
Wang Xiang

---

① extension：分机

> 周四下午4时15分
>
> 亲爱的刘先生:
>   我来拜访您时,您恰好外出。我因公出差于前天来到此地并且还将停留两天。请前来一叙。我住在希尔顿酒店301房间。来前请给我电话,我的电话号码是84539641,分机号为301。如您有空来此一聚,我将十分高兴。
>
>   您诚挚的
>   王翔

[Sample 2]

　　下面一则便条是有关邀请医生就诊的留言(Asking a Doctor to Come)。李老师的母亲得了重病急需治疗,小程代他们给胡医生留了便条,请胡医生看到留言后立即前往诊治。由于是在紧急情况下留言,便条省去了委婉和客套,让人一目了然。

> 　　　　　　　　　　　　　　　　　　　　　　8:45 a.m., Friday
> Doctor Hu,
>   Please come to Room 306, the Northern Building as soon as you receive this note. Miss Li's mother **is suffering that a necessary treatment is needed immediately**.
>
>   Xiao-cheng

> 星期五上午8点45分
>
> 胡医师:
>   请接到此条后即来北楼306号房间。李小姐母亲的病痛又犯了,急需必要的治疗。
>
>   小程

[Sample 3]

　　下面这则便条是有关会议延期的留言(Informing the Meeting Put off)。由于有外校老师来参观,曹洋通知张华原定明天召开的党组织会议将推迟。

> 　　　　　　　　　　　　　　　　　　　　　　Tuesday Afternoon
> Dear Zhang,
>   **Just a line to tell you that** tomorrow afternoon's Communist Party members' meeting should be postponed① because of a visit paid by the teachers from other schools. Please set another time for the meeting and inform② the other members in time.
>
>   Cao Yang

① postponed:延迟　　② inform:通知

Unit 5 Notes（便条）

星期二下午

小张：
　　因外校老师来参观，原定于明天下午举行的党员会议将被延迟。请另定开会时间并及时通知其他成员。

曹洋

Useful Expressions

（1）I am very sorry that...　很抱歉……
（2）I enclosed a certificate from my doctor and ask you for sick leave of...
　　　附上医生证明一份，向您请假……
（3）Encl: doctor's certificate for sick leave　附：医生的病假证明
（4）I beg to apply for...　我请求……
（5）I should be very obliged if you...　如您……我将不胜感激
（6）The doctor came to see me this morning and suggested a rest of...
　　　医生今早来看了我，建议我再休息……
（7）Please give an extension of leave for...　请允许我再休息……
（8）You happened to be out when...　当……时，您碰巧外出。
（9）Give me a call before coming.　来之前给我来个电话。
（10）be requested to contact...　要求您与……联系
（11）feel so regretful that...　对……感到非常遗憾
（12）couldn't attend the evening party tonight because of something urgent
　　　因为一些急事，不能参加今晚的晚会
（13）should be postponed because of.../be put off to... because...
　　　由于……，……被延迟了
（14）Please notify...　请通知……
（15）Thank you for your entertainment　感谢您的招待
（16）I wonder if...　我想……
（17）I shall be most grateful if you.../I shall be greatly obliged if...
　　　如您……我将不胜感激
（18）Sorry to bring inconvenience to you.　很抱歉给您带来不便。

Writing Practice

I. Read the following notes and judge the subject of each one.

(1) SUBJECT _____

Thank you very much for the loan of your notebook computer. It is most useful for my completion of my thesis because it saved me a lot of time and trouble as well.

(2) SUBJECT _____

I am still lying in bed with the bad headache, unable to go to school. The doctor was called in this afternoon. He advised me to stay in bed for another two days. Please give me an extension of leave.

Encl: Doctor's Certificate of Advice

(3) SUBJECT _____

Shall we go to see the Minority Report Sunday night? Ring me when you are back so that I can arrange it ahead of time.

(4) SUBJECT _____

Please accept this book as a small gift of my congratulation for your birthday. I hope you will enjoy having the gift.

(5) SUBJECT _____

I have just received a letter from my father, saying that my old grandmother is dangerously ill. I hope to go back home to see her as soon as possible. I would be very obliged if you will send me a ticket from Beijing to Changchun at five tomorrow morning.

(6) SUBJECT _____

I am going to Tianjin to negotiate the business with the company there tomorrow. Will you please give me a letter of introduction to Tianjin Huashi Company, from whom I expect to get some help in my trip?

II. Look at the note below and decide how it can be improved; rewrite it in your own words.

Jiangning Road
5 Feb.

Dear Fei Ming,

    I am conducting an experiment on computer and in badly need of the software you borrowed from me last month. I shall appreciate it very much if you will return it at once to me.

Sincerely yours
Li
3:00 p.m.

III. Draft notes according to the hints given.

（1）杨宇从体育老师处得知消息后给周妍留言：由于阴雨连绵，原定于星期四举行的日语专业三年级对英语专业二年级的足球赛将推迟至下星期举行，请转告你班同学。

（2）许自强急需用钱，他给张为留言向他借两百元钱，并允诺下周五就归还。

（3）张为同意借钱给许自强，并给他留言。

（4）艾丽思因患感冒生病而不能去上课，她的妈妈替她向老师请病假一天，并提及如果第二天她感觉好点，就让她到校上课。另附医生证明一份。

（5）查尔斯因急事需明日早晨赶往福建，他给小倪留言将本周五的见面延迟至下周三，并对造成的不便表示歉意。

（6）史密斯先生初来这座城市，他完全不熟悉这边的情况。向导小张给他指了路，史密斯留言表示感谢并说他明早将乘飞机回国，以后会和她保持联系。

Unit 6

Notices & Announcements (通知及公告)

- General Introduction
- Sample Reading
- Useful Expressions
- Writing Practice

General Introduction & Sample Reading

What Is a Notice?

通知（Notice）是书信的一种形式，常常是告知别人某件事或某个要求的文件。它的内容可长可短，格式可分为正式和非正式，可口头表达，也可书面传达。

正式的通知是一种公告性文体。企业、政府、机关、团体或个人如有什么事情需向公众声明，或对往来对象、群众有什么要求，可以将要传达的意思简短地写成启事、公告等，张贴于布告栏、广场、路口等引人注目之处。特别需要通告的内容往往还要登在报纸、杂志、公文簿、电视、网络等大众媒体上。

一般性的通知除用于单位、学校、工厂等，也可用于熟悉的人，如朋友、亲戚之间，往往是通知别人某事，如一般的结婚通知、班级通知、搬迁通知等。它一般书写在纸条上，书写形式没有书信那么严格，通常不用写开头语、写信人地址、收信人地址、结尾语等。但如果要求对方回复，而对方又不知你的地址，就有必要留下地址了。

通知要求用词简洁，内容清晰而有条理。

常用的通知有商业通告、市政通告、广播通知和一般性通知或启事。前两类通知较正式，后两类相对来讲非正式些。

Unit 6 Notices & Announcements（通知及公告）

How Is a Notice Laid out?

```
                ANNOUNCEMENT（NOTICE）
（××），
    Your attention, please. _____


                                                （Yours,）
                                                  （××）
```

通知的格式较为简单。一般来说，正文上方往往有 Notice 或 Announcement 的字样，来引起公众的注意。正文的右下方写明发出通知的单位。日期通常写于通知正文的右上角或左下角。而单位、日期有时也可以省略。有时出于方便、醒目，发出通知的单位名称和发布时间也可以直接在通知正文前、Notice 标题下注出。

正文要求简短精要，将内容讲清楚就可以，以便让对方一眼就能明了。

Sample Reading

通知和通告区别不大。一般的通知可以比较随意，而通告则较正式一些。根据写作意图，可将通知类分为商业通告（Business Notice）、市政通告（Municipal Notice）、广播通知（Broadcast Notice）和一般通知（General Notice）等。

1. 商业通告（Business Notice）

商业通告属于商业书信的一种。它虽较一般通知正式些，却又不如商业信函那么正式。通常是采用书信的方式。目前不少公司、银行为求简便快捷、经济实用，直接将通告内容印于明信片或卡片上，送达顾客。凡是有关开业、合并、迁址、人事变动、财务办理等方面的通告都可以采用这种形式。

【Sample 1】

下面是一则公司合并通告（Notice Announcing to Form a New Firm）。原公司将和伦敦的 Nimida 有限公司合并，并改名 Latt 贸易有限公司。新建公司迁至伦敦大树街 150 号后继续营业。行文流畅，措辞正式、得体，符合公文文体，是一则写得不错的通告。

                                                Oct. 12, 2018

Dear Sirs,

　　We are pleased to announce that from January 1, 2019 our firm, with which you have had dealt over many years, **will amalgamate**[①] **with** Nimida Co., Ltd. of London to form the new firm of Latt Trading Co., Ltd.

The new firm will **carry on business** at No. 150 Big Tree Way, London City, to which address you should send all communications after December 31.

Yours cordially,

① amalgamate：合并

2018 年 10 月 12 日

各位：
　　由于与您有多年贸易合作关系，现欣然奉告，自 2019 年 1 月 1 日起，我公司将和伦敦的尼米达有限公司合并，称为拉特贸易有限公司。
　　新建公司迁于伦敦大树街 150 号继续营业。凡 12 月 31 日后来函，务必请寄至上述新址，谢谢。

您诚挚的

【Sample 2】

下面是一则公司更名通告（Change of Name）。

1）书信式

C. M. 公司现更名为 B. W. 股份有限公司，发出通告。通告主旨清晰，但语言不够正式、简练，如能将之改为 "We inform you that the business hitherto① carried on the name of C. M. & Co. will be continued under the style of B. W. & Co., Limited." 就更能体现它的正式性。

June 20, 2017

Dear Sirs,
　　We **inform you that** the name of C. M. & Co. will be changed into B. W. & Co., Limited. All the business carried on the former will be continued under the latter.

Yours faithfully,

① hitherto：到目前为止

2017 年 6 月 20 日

各位：
　　兹特奉告，C. M. 公司现更名为 B. W. 股份有限公司，并将继续营业。

您真挚的

2）明信片式

位于美国芝加哥公园大街 21 号的 LG 有限公司更名为 LG Frank 贸易有限公司，发出通告。

Unit 6 Notices & Announcements (通知及公告)

LG Frank Trading Limited

21 Park, Chicago.

U. S. A.

CHANGE OF NAME

Please be advised that the name of

LG & Co., LTD. will be changed into

LG Frank Trading Limited

with immediate effect[①].

Our telephone number is also

changed: 624-7825637.

① immediate effect：即时生效

更名通告

美国芝加哥公园大街21号的 LG & CO. LTD.（LG 有限公司）更名为 LG Frank Trading Limited（LG 弗兰克贸易有限公司），自即日起生效。电话号码已改为：624-7825637。特此奉告。

LG 弗兰克贸易有限公司

美国芝加哥公园大街21号

2. 政府通告

政府通告一般是向群众解释某一项新的措施、方案、决定等，以便遵照办理。市政通告相对来说较正式，尤其时间的标注很重要。这类文体的重要特点是尽量避免带有个人感情色彩的词语出现。

[Sample 1]

下面是一则放假通告（Notification of Holiday）。主旨清晰，语言简洁，全文不带有个人感情色彩，是一篇得体的正式通告。

NOTIFICATION

In celebration of Spring Festival, all municipal parks, with the exception of Sea Park, **will be admission free** for three days, February 24 to 26, inclusive[①].

Visitors are requested not to step on lawns newly mown.

City Parks Administration,

Nanjing

February 22, 2019

① inclusive：包括的

> 通　告
>
> 为庆祝春节，除海洋公园外，所有市政公园将从 2 月 24 日至 26 日免费开放三日。
>
> 游人请勿践踏新修剪的草坪。
>
> 南京
城市公园管理处
2019 年 2 月 22 日

【Sample 2】

下面是一则禁行通告（Notice to Inform Road is Closed）。

> NOTIFICATION
>
> The northern sector of Nanjing Road between Hunan Road to the west and Qinghai Road to the east **will be closed to vehicular**[①] **traffic** for five days from April 10 to 14 inclusively as road repair **is in progress**.
>
> City Transportation Bureau
>
> March 3rd, 2017

① vehicular：交通的

> 通　知
>
> 由于道路维修，南京路北段（位于湖南路西部和青海路东部的路段）将在 4 月 10 日至 14 日这五日内禁止通行。特此通告。
>
> 城市交通局
2017 年 3 月 3 日

3. 广播通知（Broadcast Notice）

【Sample 1】

下面是一则紧急开会通知（Urgent Announcement of a Meeting）。由于情况紧急，通知开头直接称呼了通知对象，时间、地点分明，行文紧凑，足以引起人们的关注。

> URGENT ANNOUNCEMENT
>
> **Comrades, attention, please**. An urgent announcement of the College Party Committee is as follows:
>
> An important meeting **has been decided to be held** in Conference Room 201 at 3:00 this afternoon to study some documents of the Central Committee of the Party. All Party Committee members in our college and secretaries of the Party branches of all the schools **are requested to be present** on time.
>
> The College Party Committee
>
> Sept. 18, 2016

Unit 6 Notices & Announcements（通知及公告）

紧 急 通 知

同志们，请注意。下面播报院党委的一个紧急通知：

定于今天下午3时在201室召开重要会议，学习党中央有关文件，请院党委全体委员和各系总支部书记准时出席。

院党委
2016年9月18日

[Sample 2]

下面是一则列车晚点通知（Notice to Inform Train Is Late）。语言简洁，意思表达完整。因为是站台通知，对象为普通人，所以运用了一些带有个人情感的词，显得更有人情味。

ANNOUNCEMENT

Ladies and Gentlemen,
　　The Train T318 is **behind time because of** the bad weather. **Please wait** in the waiting room. **We will inform you as soon as** the train arrives.

Beijing Railway Station

通　知

女士们、先生们：
　　因天气恶劣，T318次列车晚点。请在候车室等候。火车一到达，我们立刻通知您。

北京火车站

[Sample 3]

下面是一则商场寻找顾客的广播通知（Announcement to Customers）。

ANNOUNCEMENT

　　Customers, your attention, please.
　　Just now two young boy students wearing the school clothes with the words "Foreign Language School" bought two basketballs at the athletic products counter. But when they left after paying, they forgot to take their books. Will they please come back to take them?

通　知

　　顾客们，请注意！
　　刚才两位穿着印有"外国语学校"字样校服的年轻男学生在体育用品柜台购买了两只篮球。但他们在付款离开后，把书遗忘在此处。烦请回来取走。

4. 一般通知（General Notice）

一般通知也有正式与非正式之分。如结婚通知、出生通知、死亡通知等都属于较正式一类。

【Sample 1】

下面是一则结婚通知（Wedding Announcement）。Lam Dickson 先生和 Cathy Chen 小姐将于 2015 年 3 月 6 日星期四在加拿大举行婚礼，特此通知。用词虽简单，但格式上令人一目了然，是一份正式的结婚通知。

NOTICE

Miss Cathy Chen

and

Mr. Lam Dickson

announce their marriage

on Thursday, the sixth of March

Twenty Fifteen

Canada

启 事

凯西·陈小姐与兰姆·迪克森先生将于 2015 年 3 月 6 日星期四在加拿大举行婚礼，特此通知。

【Sample 2】

下面是一则死亡通知，即讣告（Obituary）。
Bart K. Stone 先生于 2011 年 7 月 6 日因脑出血去世，特发此讣告。

Obituary

Bart K. Stone, 89, died at 5:00 a.m., Wednesday, July 6, 2011, of a brain attack at his home, 245 Olive Street. **In addition to** his wife and three children, **he is survived by** two brothers, Rex and Hans, in Chicago.

讣 告

巴特·K·斯得恩，因脑出血于 2011 年 7 月 6 日（星期三）凌晨 5 点在橄榄树大街 245 号的家中去世，享年 89 岁。他太太和三个孩子以及在芝加哥的两个兄弟，雷科斯和汉斯特发此文，以示悼念。

【Sample 3】

下面是一则工厂布告（Factory Notice）。工厂机械检修，故发出调休通知。

Unit 6　Notices & Announcements（通知及公告）

NOTICE

　　The Thursday off-day (March 8) this week is **to be shifted to** next Tuesday, March 13, as the mechanical devices of this factory will **be suspended for** some 18 hours on that day for the repair of some cables, to be conducted by the Fujian Power Supply Company.

　　Engineers and workmen of the engineering division, however, will carry on work as usual on next Tuesday and **are expected to** give full cooperation to the city repair gangs upon request. **They are to** have their day off on Friday this week.

General Management Office,
Fujian Steel & Iron Works

March 7, 2018

通　知

　　福建电力公司将于 3 月 13 日（下周二）来我厂检修电缆，届时我厂机械设备将停用 18 小时。因此原定于 3 月 8 日（本周四）的调休日调至 3 月 13 日。

　　但工程部的工程师和职工务必协助市修理队，因此下周二正常工作，调休调至本周五。

总经理办公室
福建钢铁厂
2018 年 3 月 7 日

Analysis

（1）写订婚、结婚通知时，按西方习惯一般由女方家长出面登报。如果父母都健在，则由父母具名发出，而且通知上先写新娘的姓名再写新郎的。
（2）出生通知一般是用一张卡片印上婴儿的姓名和出生日期发给亲朋好友。
（3）死亡通知一般应说明死者的年龄、工作、死亡原因、死亡地点、日期以及死亡者的家属等。如例 2。
（4）书写通知时注意一般采用第三人称记叙方式，写给熟悉的人时也可采用第一人称。

Useful Expressions

（1）We inform you that...　我们通知您……
（2）Please be advised that...　我们建议您……
（3）This is to announce...　……宣布……
（4）for the purpose of/in the matter of/owing to　因为
（5）A lecture meeting will be held...　将于……召开报告会
（6）be reminded to　提醒您……

(7) Comrades, attention, please.　同志们，请注意。
(8) Residents in this district, your attention, please.　小区居民，请注意。
(9) Your attention, please./Attention, please.　请注意。
(10) behind time　晚点
(11) Now here is...　现在是……
(12) excessively regret to announce...　谨以极大悲痛告诸……
(13) have the honor of announcing...　荣幸地宣布……
(14) be requested to...　务必……

Writing Practice

I. Read the following notice and judge the subject of each one.

(1) SUBJECT _____

Comrade passengers, your attention, please. No. 16 Express is departing for Wuhan, Zhengzhou and Beijing. All aboard, please. Final call.

(2) SUBJECT _____

We have the honor to announce that effective on 12th April, 2015, the Huse's Company will become associated with the Hui Hong Company into the new H & H Company Limited. The merger gives the new strength in terms of the promotion of sales and operative capital, and we hope to be able to serve you more effectively than ever before.

The new company will thereafter carry on business under the new name at Room 301 Jingle Hotel, New York.

(3) SUBJECT _____

The engagement announcement is of Lucy Margaret Chen, the eldest daughter of Mr. and Mrs. B. M. Chen, to G. P. Lee, the eldest son of Mr. and Mrs. D. J. Lee, Singapore.

(4) SUBJECT _____

Dr. and Mrs. Holand Walshman of No. 1 Willow Street, Hong Kong, announce the birth of a son, Joseph Walshman, in the Beach Hospital on Friday, October 15.

(5) SUBJECT _____

Freed Russell passed away peacefully at St. Louses Hospital on 26th December, 2017. Funeral at Red Cape Cemetery, Greenville, at 3:00 p.m, December 29.

II. Draft notices according to the hints given.

(1) 董飞先生和谢璇小姐将在2015年6月8日星期五在香港Hilton饭店举行婚礼，请帮他们写一封请柬式的通知。
(2) 美术活动小组2018年12月25日宣布，元旦晚会将于12月28日（星期五）晚六点在音乐厅举行，节目有唱歌、朗诵、讲故事、越剧和话剧等。可以去办公楼304李老师处领取入场券。请写一份通知。

（3）比利时大街87号的Bill Black先生及夫人于2月23日（星期一）上午10:00得一女，取名Evelyn，产于市立医院。请写一份通知。

（4）接待处于2014年6月6日发出通知，定于6月16日（星期六）参观南京长江大桥等名胜古迹。凡愿参加的人请于当日早7点在南京大学前门集中，7:20乘车出发。请写一份通知。

Unit 7

Meeting Minutes（会议记录）

- General Introduction
- Sample Reading
- Useful Expressions
- Writing Practice

General Introduction & Sample Reading

What Are Meeting Minutes?

  会议记录（Meeting Minutes）是一种将开会时与会者的发言和会议内容记录下来的文字材料。由于一次会议的决议不一定能当场通过，所以需要记录下来以备将来参考和修改。
  会议记录用途广泛，内容往往涉及政府、公司、学校等场合的会议。会议记录与报告的书写不同，它只是如实记录会议情况，不需要像写报告书那样加入自己的分析和建议。
  会议记录大致包括以下几个方面：
① 会议记录的名称；
② 开会的具体日期、时间和地点；
③ 参加会议的人员及主持人；
④ 对会议流程和内容的详细描述及最终决议的记录；
⑤ 会议结束的时间和下次会议时间的确定。
  会议记录一般采用过去式。最后往往经主持人和记录人签字后保存。会议记录一般有两种形式：摘要记录和全文记录。

How Are Meeting Minutes Laid out?

MINUTES OF MEETING ON . . .
TIME, PLACE & NATURE OF THE MEETING
PRESENT: _____

Unit 7　Meeting Minutes（会议记录）

```
APOLOGIES FROM: _____

SUMMARY OF THE MEETING:
_____
_____
_____

ANY OTHER BUSINESS
1) _____
2) _____
NEXT MEETING: _____
_____
ADJOURNMENT: _____


                                    SIGNATURE
```

  会议记录的格式较为正式，通常分为会议名称（Title）、开会时间（Time）、地点（Place）、出席人（Persons Present）、缺席人（Persons Absent）、讨论事项（Items）、通过决议（Resolution）和记录人等几部分。

  记录名称一般标于文章开头部分，可以居中，也可以按时下流行的书写格式一律居左。

  接下来的日期、时间和地点部分往往用一两句话表述清楚。为确保准确性以便日后引用或查找，会议记录中的时间常常准确到年、月、日甚至几时几分。如 "A meeting was held at 9:00 a. m. on 24 December 2018 to evaluate the reform of the education system of high schools which is to be carried out in January of next year." 会议记录中的地点如没有特殊要求可以不予交代。如有必要，也要写清楚。如 "... will be held in Conference Room 108 of the Company ..."。

  出席人和缺席人一般另起一行。出席人一栏中，首先注明的是会议主持人。如 "Mr. ××, Chairman"，"Mrs. ××, Chairperson"。缺席人如无须交代，也可以省去。如要注明，则可续上缺席原因等。不管是出席人还是缺席人，一般都应该给全名，必要时续上职务名称。如 "Mr. John Black, Personnel Manager"。

  正文要求用词精确，条理清晰，内容精要，以便于让参看记录的人一眼就能明了会议的整个流程和主要内容。

  如果涉及下次会议的时间，一定要记录清楚。最后还可记上会议结束的时间。

  署名部分一般位于正文的右下角，写上记录人的姓名，有时加上主持人的签名，也可以参照计算机版格式一律左起顶格，但不管采用哪种方式，签名都尽可能用全称，以便日后查找。

Sample Reading

1. 摘要记录（Summary Minutes）

摘要记录即将发言的概要、发言人的基本观点、问题的主要事实、会议的结论等记录下来。

【Sample 1】

下面这则是一份市场营销会议的摘要记录（Minutes of the Marketing Meeting）。会议发言人为营销部经理，生产部经理及广告代理人。会议内容为对营销计划的讨论。摘要准确记录了时间、地点和参会人，并按照发言的先后次序对发言进行了记录。由于是记录讨论，内容稍有琐碎，如稍加整理则效果更好。

Minutes of the Marketing Meeting

A meeting was held on 12/06/14 to evaluate the marketing strategy for the new range of Dawoo mobile phone which the company is to launch① in October this year.

Present: Mr. Grant, Marketing Manager; Mr. Salve, Product Manager; Ms. Green, Advertising Agent; Miss Chen, Sales Secretary.

The meeting began with a discussion of the budget② proposals for the product launch. Ms. Green pointed out that the proposed allocation③ was too low. She was of the opinion that it was necessary to spend a high percentage of anticipated sale revenue④ on marketing. Mr. Grant supported this view and also thought that they should be prepared to consider a situation where first year sales revenue was not sufficient to cover costs. However, Mr. Salve disagreed with these arguments.

Next, Mr. Grant pointed out that Dawoo needed to make a reasonable compromise⑤ between three important factors, namely: impact, frequency, and coverage. It was obvious, Mr. Grant went on to say, that they could not achieve an ideal combination of all three. Ms. Green suggested that it was much better to restrict spending geographically, given the constraints of the budget. She explained that a full advertising campaign against half the market would be more effective than half a job against the whole market. Both Mr. Salve and Mr. Grant agreed with this approach.

Mr. Salve said he would provide facts and figures for the design of the marketing plans.

Finally, various aspects of promotional policy were considered. Mr. Salve pointed out that the company used to favor coupons⑥ as a means of encouraging sales, but Ms. Green was not all in favor of using this method. The latter said that she preferred a combination of price cuts, trade discounts, and consumer special offers. Mr. Grant's feelings on the matter were that it would be better to use the available resources on package, design and display. Owing to the lack of agreement on this subject, a decision on promotion methods would be put forward to the next meeting.

  Mr. Grant is to arrange a further meeting as soon as possible.

Miss Chen
Sales Secretary

① launch：发行　② budget：预算　③ allocation：细分　④ revenue：收入　⑤ compromise：折中　⑥ coupon：优惠券

市场营销会议记录

  公司预备今年10月在新的范围内上市Dawoo手机，为此于2014年6月12日召开会议，评估行销策略。

  参加者：Grant先生，营销部经理；Salve先生，生产部经理；Green女士，广告代理人；陈小姐，销售秘书。

  因产品上市，会议首先讨论了预算草案。Green女士指出草案中营销预算分配太低。她认为必须提高预期销售收入用于营销支出的百分比。Grant先生对这种看法表示支持，他认为应该考虑到第一年销售额不足以收回成本的情形。然而，Slave先生的观点与他们的并不一致。

  接着，Grant先生指出Dawoo需要建立三个重要因素之间的合理协调关系，即：效果、频率和覆盖面。Grant先生继续说道，他们显然无法达成三者的理想组合。考虑到预算限制，Green女士建议，好一点的做法是根据地理区域限制预算开支。她解释说，针对半个市场的全面的广告活动将比针对整个市场的一半的工作有效。Slave先生和Grant先生同意了这个方案。

  Slave先生说，他会为营销计划的设计提供论据和数据。

  最后，他们考虑了促销策略的不同方面。Slave先生指出，公司过去一直使用折扣券作为促进销售的方法，但是Green女士对使用这个方法不是很赞成。她说，她觉得融降价、优惠和顾客特别服务为一体的组合更好些。Grant先生认为，在实物的包装、设计和陈列上利用既得资源比较好。由于在这一点上没能达成一致，促销方式于下次会议再议。

  Grant先生将负责尽快安排进一步的会议。

销售秘书
陈小姐

[Sample 2]

  下面这则是董事会会议记录（Minutes of the Directors' Meeting）。会议分为六部分：报告、决议、分公司建立、投资计划、选举经理和提供担保。记录总结了会议内容，但有美中不足之处。首先，开头部分没有提及会议的主持人，记录结尾也没有署名。其次，各分段没有次标题，使人感觉凌乱。

Minutes of the Directors' Meeting

  A Directors' meeting was held at 9:00 a.m. on Tuesday, May 22, 2019 at the meeting room of the company.

Presentees： Mr. C. K. Dong   Mrs. P. R. Chen
     Miss. H. L. Fee   Mr. D. W. Xian
     Mr. J. M. Hung   Mrs. L. M. Wong
     Mr. L. N. Wong

The notice of convening① this meeting and the manager's report on the state of business of the Company were read by the secretary.

The manager's report having, with the content of the meeting, been regarded as read, the Chairman made a speech and proposed that a gold medal be given to Mr. Chew Chi Zhi as a reward for his loyal and successful service in the past ten years. Mr. J. M. Hung seconded the motion, which was then put to the meeting and carried unanimously②.

Mrs. P. R. Chen proposed that two branches be established in Taiwan and New Zealand. The motion was seconded by Mrs. L. M. Wong and carried unanimously.

The Chairman proposed that an amount of HK＄800,000 be invested in Ho Ya Shipping Co., Ltd., which will make up 65% of the capital. This motion was opposed by Mr. D. W. Xian, who in turn proposed that a smaller amount of HK＄500,000 be better. The Chairman agreed to this and Mr. Xian's motion was carried unanimously.

Miss. H. L. Fee proposed that Mr. Y. C. Cheng be selected as the successor to Mr. Chew. The motion was seconded by Mr. D. W. Xian and carried unanimously.

The Chairman made an introduction of Mr. Lee Fang's status and his relations with the Company since the foundation③ of the company and proposed that the guarantee be offered. The motion receives no objection and was carried unanimously. However, Mr. C. K. Dong proposed that a term of one year be fixed for the guarantee. The motion was carried unanimously. The meeting closed at 12:00 a.m. and the next meeting was scheduled④ for next month.

① convene：召集   ② unanimously：无异议地   ③ foundation：成立   ④ schedule：将……列入计划

董事会会议记录

董事会会议于2019年5月22日星期二上午9点在公司会议室举行。

出席者：C. K. Dong 先生，P. R. Chen 女士，H. L. Fee 小姐，D. W. Xian 先生，J. M. Hung 先生，L. M. Wong 女士和 L. N. Wong 先生。

秘书宣读了召集会议的通知和经理提交的关于公司业务情况的报告。

作为会议内容之一，大家审议了经理的报告。主席作了讲话，并建议授予 Chew Chi Zhi 先生金奖以回报他过去十年来忠诚且成功的服务。J. M. Huang 先生赞成这一提案。大家在会上也一致同意。

P. R. Chen 女士建议在台湾和新西兰建立分公司。提议受到 L. M. Wong 女士的支持，随后大家一致通过。

主席建议在 Ho Ya 船坞有限公司投资80万港币。这笔投资将占总资产的65%。这个提议受到 D. W. Xian 先生的反对。他提出投资额应减少，以50万港币为宜。主席同意了这提议，Xian 先生的提议被一致通过。

H. L. Fee 小姐提议推选 Y. C. Chen 先生继任 Chew 先生的职位。提议得到 D. W. Xian 先生的赞成。全体无异议通过。

主席介绍了 Lee Fang 先生的情况以及自公司建立时他与公司的关系。主席提议向他提供担保。提议没有异议，被一致通过。但是，C. K. Dong 先生提出，担保期限应以1年为限。此提议被一致通过。会议在中午12:00结束，下次会议定于下个月召开。

2. 全文会议记录（Verbatim Meeting Minutes）

全文记录即将与会者的发言与涉及的问题完整地记录下来。全文记录只需按照发言顺序将发言完整记录整理即可，无须添加自己的评价或观点。

【Sample 1】

下面是一则执行委员会的全文会议记录（Executive Committee Meeting Minutes）。会议讨论了章程的修改、目标的制定以及下次会议的时间。

A MEETING OF THE EXECUTIVE COMMITTEE OF THE YOUNG WRITER'S ASSOCIATION WAS HELD IN THE CONFERENCE ROOM AT 56 OLIVE ROAD, AT 3：00 p. m. ON TUESDAY, JULY 17, 2017.

Present：Reve A. C. Huge, in the chair
　　　　Miss H. L. Guo　　　　Mr. J. K. Zhang
　　　　Mr. Jack Cheng　　　　Mr. Cary Guan
　　　　Mr. Ivan Luke　　　　 Mr. Henry Brest
　　　　Mrs. B. Y. Cao, Secretary

Absent：Miss Ada Miller

The contents are as follows：

Huge：After the discussion, the minutes of the meeting of the Executive Committee held on Monday, January 15, 2017, should be approved. The "young readers" in Para 3, Line 2 should be revised into "all the readers"; the "＄30,000" in Para 5, Line 4 should be "＄35,000". Miss Zou will resign soon. Will Elizabeth Chen replace her?

Cao：Yes. Miss Elizabeth Chen has accepted the post of Public Relation officer and will assume her duties on August 1, 2017.

Huge：The Association will organize a number of social gatherings in the near future. It is necessary to co-opt a Social Convener[①] into the Committee.

Guo：We have considered the choice in detail. We agreed that Miss Janet Yang be co-opted as Social Convener.

Hugh：Our Association will launch a fund-raising campaign in the form of Gala Premiere in September, with a target of ＄10,000. What is your opinion?

Zhang：I am afraid the target is a little low. We need to spend more on marketing in order to attract more readers. I think ＄15,000 will be enough.

Guan：I don't agree with you completely. Now, we are facing fierce[②] market competition. We need to cut down the cost to gain benefits.

Huge：I am in agreement with Mr. Guan. Mr. Ivan Luke and Mr. Henry Brest, please form a Sub-committee and work out a plan for the next meeting. Mrs. Cao, do you have anything else to say?

Cao：Yes. NEW WEEK magazine has donated 200 books to our Association.

Huge: That's great. Please write a letter to thank the company on behalf of the Association.

Cao: OK.

Huge: I announce that the next meeting of the Committee will be held at 3:00 p.m. on Jan. 16, 2018, in the Conference Room.

(The meeting was closed at 4:30 p.m.)

Prepared by: B. Y. Cao, Secretary

① convener: 召集人　　② fierce: 激烈的

青年作家协会执行委员会会议于2017年7月17日星期二下午3点在橄榄树路56号会议室举行。

参加人: Reve A. C. Huge, 主持人; H. L. Guo 小姐; J. K. Zhang 先生; Jack Cheng 先生; Cary Guan 先生; Ivan Luke 先生; Henry Brest 先生; B. Y. Cao 女士, 秘书

缺席人: Ada Miller 小姐

会议内容如下:

Huge: 经讨论,执行委员会2017年1月15日星期一的会议记录第三段第二行的"年轻读者"改为"所有读者";第五段第四行的"$30,000"应改为"$35,000"。Zou 小姐不久后将辞职。Elizabeth Chen 将会代替她吗?

Cao: 是的。Elizabeth Chen 小姐已经接受公关部主管的职位并且于2017年8月1日任职。

Huge: 协会将在不久的将来组织若干社会性集会,必须选出社会集会召集人参加执行委员会。

Guo: 我们已经详细考虑过人选。经过会员选举,我们同意 Janet Yang 小姐成为社会集会召集人。

Hugh: 我协会将在9月份以节日公演的形式发起一个筹款活动,预期筹款10 000美元。你们有什么意见?

Zhang: 恐怕目标定得低了一点。为了吸引更多的读者,我们需要在销售方面花费更多。因此,我认为要筹集15 000美元才够。

Guan: 我不完全同意你的看法。现在,我们正面临激烈的市场竞争。我们需要减少成本来获利。

Huge: 我同意 Guan 先生的意见。Ivan Luke 先生和 Henry Brest 先生,请组织一个下属委员会,拟出下次会议的计划。Cao 小姐,你还有别的事要说吗?

Cao: 是的。"新周刊"向我们协会捐赠了200本书。

Huge: 那太好了。请代表协会向该公司写一封感谢信。

Cao: 好的。

Huge: 我宣布,委员会的下一次会议定于2018年1月16日下午3:00在会议室召开。

(会议于下午4:30结束。)

此记录由秘书 B. Y. Cao 进行整理。

【Sample 2】

下面是一则讨论会的会议记录（Minutes of a Discussion）。

Minutes for the Discussion of Cloning

The meeting was held at 8:00 a.m. on Monday, March 25, 2002 in the Conference Hall, National Health Center.

Unit 7　Meeting Minutes（会议记录）

Participants: Priest Donald, Chairman　Prof. Robert Lanza (RL)
　　　　　　　Prof. Charles Griffin (CG)　Prof. Rock Oscar (RO)
　　　　　　　Eve Hogen, Assistant and Secretary
　　　　　　　Other research fellows

Chairman: Ever since a lamb named Dolly came into the world in 1997, there have been endless arguments about whether we should clone human beings. Should cloning[①] be banned by law or not?

RL: Though many people are fascinated by the idea, I insist that the cloning of human beings should be immediately banned by law; otherwise society will fall into chaos.

CG: The technology of human cloning is one of the most sensational scientific developments in recent years. It stirs up fierce controversy in the world, largely because it greatly changes our traditional concepts of life, which, in some people's point of view, can only be produced through sexual reproduction, and some even appeal to ban it. However, I firmly believe that this technology should not be banned by law, and that its legalization[②] can by all means be fairly justified.

RO: I agree with Prof. Lanza. There is the risk brought about by immature[③] technology. Cloning an adult sheep was extremely difficult; over 270 attempts were needed before Dolly was born. Many fetal lambs did not survive the early stages of development. And other experiments show that cloning may result in abnormal clones. Many attempts at animal cloning produced disfigured[④] monsters[⑤]. Worse is that some abnormalities may not appear till after birth. A cloned COW recently died several weeks after birth with a huge abnormality in blood cell production. These immature technologies should not be put on human beings.

CG: I am afraid that I couldn't agree with you. To ban human cloning is undoubtedly to restrict the freedom of scientists. Research in the field of human cloning will help people produce discoveries that will push the study of genetics, cell development and human growth. Many scientists believe that cloning may produce a better understanding of the nature of genetic diseases and thus it is an aid in the production of embryos[⑥]. Cloning could provide the opportunity to some infertile[⑦] couples to have children of their own. And in case of fertile couples in which one member carries a gene for a disease, cloning using a cell from the other member could assure that the couple has a healthy child.

RL: But there are emotional risks. How would you treat your mother's clone, who might be ten years younger than you? How will a person face the fact that he or she is just a duplicate of an older individual? If the creation of a child through sexual reproduction is replaced by a non-sexual reproduction, what could the future of human beings be? They will become identical copies with no individuality at all. Even if different environmental factors create some individuality, we still can't neglect the genes they inherit—they are identical!

Human cloning will distort the relationship between human beings.

RO: Yes. It is true that human cloning might benefit the world in some way, but it's not worthwhile to sacrifice too much for the limited benefits. Suppose Hitler or Bin Laden's cells were obtained by fascists or terrorists and hundreds or thousands of copies of Hitler or Bin Laden were produced. What would the world be faced with? Remember the cloned baby can neither be destroyed nor be returned to the cells' owner.

CG: I don't exactly agree with you. People who are against human cloning say that clones would have less of a sense of individuality, since they are just copies of an adult person. However, just like identical twins, clones made from the same cell may also have different moral values, academic achievements, occupations or even tastes in music. Because various environmental factors are more important in molding a person than inherited factors. A person might, for example, inherit genes for a large body size, but those genes will not be fully expressed unless the person receives proper nutrition. So it's groundless to worry that human cloning will interfere with human distinctiveness or individuality⑧.

Chairman: But how to deal with the action of cloning terrorists or fascists?

CG: Human cloning might be used, we admit, by some people for questionable purposes like breeding a superior race, but this shouldn't result in the prohibition of human cloning. The technology itself is not faulty. What we should do is to work out rules and laws to regulate these people's actions and punish them for their deeds. After all, the technological benefits of cloning clearly outweigh the possible harmful consequences. So obviously it's not wise to outlaw human cloning.

Chairman: The cloning of human beings is not only a technology; it is a great step forward toward an understanding of the evolution of human beings. We believe people should develop science and technology to make our lives better; but we also believe there must be an area in nature that human beings should always avoid disturbing.

...

Chairman: The meeting is closed now and the next meeting for the discussion of laws to regulate⑨ will be scheduled for next month.

Prepared by Eve Hogen (Secretary)

① cloning: 克隆　② legalization: 合法性　③ immature: 不成熟的　④ disfigured: 使变丑　⑤ monsters: 怪物
⑥ embryos: 胚胎　⑦ infertile: 不育的　⑧ individuality: 个性　⑨ regulate: 调节

克隆讨论会会议记录

会议于2002年3月25日星期一上午8点在国家卫生中心的会议大厅举行。

参加者：Priest Donald，主席；Robert Lanza 教授（RL）；Charles Griffin 教授（CG）；Rock Oscar 教授（RO）；Eve Hogen，助理兼秘书；其他研究人员

主席：自从一只叫"多利"的小羊在1997年来到这个世界，关于我们是否应该克隆人类，已引起不断的争论。克隆应该被法律所禁止吗？

RL：虽然很多人对这个想法着迷，但我坚持认为，克隆人类应立刻被法律禁止，否则社会将会陷入混乱。

CG：人类克隆技术是最近几年来最为突出的科学发展之一。它在世界上引起强烈争议主要是因为它极大地改变了我们对生命持有的传统观念。在一些人的传统观念中，生命只能通过有性繁殖而产生，所以一些人甚至恳求禁止克隆。然而，我坚信，这种技术不应该被法律禁止，而且无论如何，都应该公正地赋予它合法性。

RO：我同意Lanza教授的看法。不成熟的技术会引起危险。复制一只成年羊极其困难；多利的出生经过了270多次尝试。许多处于胚胎期的小羊没能平安度过早期发展阶段。而且其他实验表明，克隆可能造成不正常的复制品。许多克隆动物的尝试生产出了畸形物。更糟糕的是，一些反常现象直到出生后才会显现。一只出生数星期的克隆牛，因血细胞制造的极大反常于最近死亡。这些不成熟的技术不应该用于人类。

CG：恐怕我无法同意你的意见。禁止克隆人类无疑是在限制科学家的自由。人类克隆领域的研究将有助于人类的发现，这些发现将推动遗传研究、细胞发展研究和人类生长研究。许多科学家相信，克隆有助于更好地理解遗传基因疾病的本质，因此它有助于胚胎的培养。克隆可以为一些不育夫妇提供机会，使他们拥有自己的孩子。同时，即使对可以生育的夫妻而言，一旦夫妻一方携带有病基因，通过使用另一方的细胞进行克隆仍可以保证这对夫妇拥有一个健康的孩子。

RL：但是有情感危机。你将如何对待可能比你年轻十岁的你母亲的克隆人？一个人将如何面对他/她自己只是年长个体的复制品的事实？如果有性繁殖被无性繁殖所替，人类的未来会如何？他们将会变成没有个性也没有任何差别的复制品。即使不同的环境因素塑造了一些个性，我们仍然不能忽视他们的遗传基因——基因是同一的！克隆人类将扭曲人与人之间的关系。

RO：是的。克隆人类可能在某些方面对世界有益，但不值得为这些有限利益牺牲太多。假设希特勒或本·拉登的细胞被法西斯分子或恐怖分子获得，然后希特勒或本·拉登的数百个或数千个复制品被制造出来，世界将面对什么？请记住，复制的婴儿既不能被摧毁也不能再回到细胞捐献者体中了。

CG：我不太同意你的意见。反对人类克隆的人会说，克隆体缺乏个性，因为他们只是成人的复制品。然而，正如同卵双胞胎一样，生于同一细胞的克隆儿们也可能有不同的道德观念、学术成就、职业，甚至对音乐有不同的品味。与遗传因素相比，不同的环境因素对塑造人类更重要。因此，举例来说，一个人可能遗传身材高大的基因，但除非他获得充足的营养，否则那些基因特征将不会被完全表现。因此对人类克隆将扰乱人类特殊性和个体性的担心是毫无根据的。

主席：但是该如何应对克隆恐怖分子或法西斯分子的行为呢？

CG：我们承认，人类克隆可能会被一些人用于可疑的目的，例如培养优秀的种族，但是这不应是禁止克隆人类的理由。技术本身没有过错。我们应该做的是制定出准则和法律管理这些人的行为，让他们为自己的行为受到处罚。毕竟，克隆的科技利益显然超过可能产生的有害结果。因此，很明显，取消克隆的合法性是不明智的。

主席：对人类的克隆不仅是一种技术；它是迈向理解人类进化的一大步。我们相信，人们应该发展科技使我们的生活变得更好；但我们也相信，自然界必定有一个区域是人类不应去扰乱的。
……

主席：会议现在结束，下个月召开下次例会讨论法律调控问题。

会议记录由Eve Hogen（秘书）整理

Useful Expressions

(1) convene the ... meeting at ... , at ... 于某时某地召开……的会议
(2) ATTENDING: (PRESENT:) ... 出席人:……
(3) ABSENT: (APOLOGIES FROM:) ... 缺席人:……
(4) began the discussion by outlining ... 通过概述……开始讨论
(5) presided at this study session which began at ... p.m., and concluded at ... p.m.
主持了这次工作例会,会议于……开始,……结束
(6) Last month's meeting minutes were amended and approved.
上个月的会议记录经修正予以通过。
(7) The contents are as follows: ... 内容如下:……
(8) report on 就……作了报告
(9) point out that .../propose that ... 指出……/提出……
(10) suggest that .../explain that ... 建议……/解释说……
(11) announce that ... 宣布……
(12) The motion is seconded by ... and carried unanimously. /Motion carried. /Motion passed.
提案由……附议,一致通过。/提议通过。/提议通过。
(13) ask for ideas for 征求对……的意见
(14) be nominated and elected as ... 被提名并被任命为……
(15) Other business raised at the meeting include: ... 会议中提出的其他商务问题有:……
(16) adjourn the meeting at ... a.m. 于……时宣布会议结束
(17) Minutes were submitted by .../recorded by ... 会议记录由……递交/由……记录

Writing Practice

I. Look at the minutes below and change it into a summary.

Minutes of the Annual General Meeting of Education and
Training Committee
Minutes of the Annual General Meeting held at 2:40 p.m. on Tuesday, 22 May, 2007 at 21 Century's Hotel, Bukstock.

Unit 7 Meeting Minutes (会议记录)

PRESENT: R. P. Norman, Chairperson
   W. M. Noel Chalmers W. Robin Watson
   H. R. Waller   T. K. White
   C. Nigel Rye   A. E. Belly
   M. Hunt Joes   Miss H. Newduck
   E. P. Arnold, Secretary Miss J. Crown, Secretariat

The content is as follows:

Chairman: Welcome. First I announce the apologies for absence from two Committee members: H. Y. West and J. N. Nigel. Now let's start with the previous minutes of the meeting of 20 April, 2007. What do you think of the resolution of that meeting?

Chalmers: Last time it was not passed because of some small issues. After correction, the minutes are available now.

Waller: I agree with you. Minutes are available for approval.

Chairman: And I announce that the minutes of the meeting of 20 April, 2007 have been approved by General Meeting.

Chairman: Are there any matters arising?

Secretary: None.

Chairman: Let's move to the next.

Chairman: The Committee has met five times during the year. Principal matters dealt with have included liaison with the local education authority. Both the Secretary and I are serving on the Joint Committee to establish closer contact between schools and industry.

The Business/Teacher Liaison Scheme has continued, and ten visits for teachers have been arranged.

In March the Committee assisted with the Careers Week Exhibition during which a panel from the Committee held advice sessions on careers for school leavers.

Chairman: Mr. Arnold, could you please report on the financial statement?

Secretary: Yes, it's my pleasure. The financial statement was delivered on 25 October, 2006 in respect of the fund held for the payment of medals and prizes.

Belly (accountant): Mr. M. Hunt Joes donated £10 for prizes to the Bukstock College of Commerce. The capital sum now stood at £199.28.

Chairman: It's pleasing. Please write another letter to him to express our gratitude.

Chairman: I have served my term of office but the Vice Convener, Mr. W. Dania, is unable to accept the position because of illness. What we need to do next is to appoint a new Chair.

Newduck: I nominate W. Robin Watson, Principal of the Scotland College of Technology, who has served the Committee for so many years and made great achievements.

Watson: Yes. In my opinion, he is the ideal one.

Chairman: After discussion, we appoint W. Robin Watson to serve as chairman of our committee. This was approved via Unanimous Vote.

Chairman: Next issue is Joint Liaison Committee. Ten teacher visits have been organized during the year. Head teachers have written to the secretary commenting on the success of these team visits.

The scheme for work experience for pupils has been started. The first response from firms and industry was encouraging.

We have found difficulty in placing teachers for work experience. We will appoint an ad hoc committee to examine the reason for this.

White (Youth Employment Service): The committee has recruited five committeemen. They show an excellent performance. This is an encouraging result of the Liaison Committee.

Watson (Scotland College of Technology): I also found that. What's more, we have contact another six companies that are willing to accept teacher visits.

Chairman: It is a great success. Any other business?

Chairman: I announce that the meeting is closed now. The secretary will inform the time for the next meeting in the due time after arrangement.

Meeting terminated at 4:20 p.m.

E. P. Arnold,
Secretary

II. **Look at the minutes below and decide how it can be improved; rewrite it in your own words.**

The meeting was held on Friday.

Present: Robert   Bess
          Max   Peter

The minutes were taken as read and approved. Mr. Robert Debbie requested the secretary to send copies of the minutes to all previous members of the association. After brief discussion it was resolved that Mr. Debbie's request serves as a motion at the next general meeting.

Mr. Max Smith reported that the European Association had been approached on the matter of affiliation. This was noted. A letter would be written to the association to express gratitude for its consideration.

> The chairperson's report was read and accepted with thanks.
>
> The following members were elected to the new committee:
>
> Mrs. D. Maxine and Mr. L. Hady
>
> On a motion by Mr. Max Smith, seconded by Mrs. Bess Ivy, it was resolved that two stands, numbers 12 and 14, would be purchased as new building sites on which three boathouses could be erected. It was further resolved that the building contractors would be approached for a quotation.
>
> The treasurer informed the meeting that the accounts for the coming term would be discussed much sooner than the proposed date. This was unanimously accepted.
>
> The following correspondence was noted:
>
> 1) Municipality: water pollution
>
> 2) Farmers' Association: Gala
>
> Mr. Peter Madson moved that a new siren be bought. Mr. Robert Debbie seconded the motion. After deliberation it was resolved that a new model would be bought during the next financial year.
>
> The meeting closed at 6:00 p.m. with a vote of thanks to the chairperson.

III. Draft meeting minutes according to the hints given.

这是一个办公会议。会议在 2017 年 2 月 14 日（星期二）召开。主持人为吴强，出席人有郑剑、罗纹、马可和 J. K. Roberts。张金缺席。

会议纪要

主席于下午 4:00 宣布开会。大会的第一项议程是通过 2016 年 11 月 15 日的会议记录。除做下述两项变更外，到会代表一致签名通过了上次的会议记录。

① 第三段第二行中的"marketing"应改为"advertising"。

② 张金的报告部分第二行中的"all"应改为"most"。

关于本次会议的议题，主席首先请人事经理郑先生向大会通报人事变动。郑先生说公司会计江珊已于 12 月底退休，其职已由罗纹先生接任。郑先生还说公司财务经理已送辞呈，将于三月底离任，目前打算在本公司内部招聘一名财务经理以接替他，欢迎部门领导推荐。

新任公司会计罗纹接着汇报了本公司第一季度的财务规划（见附件）。经过讨论，与会者签名通过了这项财务规划。

销售经理马可向大会简要汇报了最近的市场动向。他说目前本公司正面临着来自一家新近建立的日本电子生产厂家"Dawoo"的激烈竞争。他提出可以从几个方面采取措施与"Dawoo"的销售策略抗争。

在会上提出的其他问题还有：

① 总经理 J. K. Roberts 强调必须重视对新员工的在职培训；

② 总经理解释奖金的发放原则。他强调应该根据职工的贡献大小而不是根据其服务时间长短来发放奖金。

由于春交会，原定3月20日举行的下个月例会将延期，具体日期议定后另行通知。

会议于6点结束。

（由公司秘书 Morphy Cai 记录整理。）

Unit 8

Itineraries & Agendas (行程表和议程表)

- General Introduction
- Sample Reading
- Useful Expressions
- Writing Practice

General Introduction & Sample Reading

What Are Itinerary and Agenda?

行程表和议程表（Itinerary and Agenda）都属于时间表（Schedule）一类。

行程表（Itinerary）是将活动进程按照时间顺序一一列出的一种文件。行程表多用于商业往来、旅行出差、会议安排等。它可以用来解释指示，提出信息和行动要求，它还可以使活动内容一目了然，以便相关人士做好充分的事前准备。行程表可以用于提醒单个人的行程，也可以用于公司或单位内部交流，还可以用于政府、机构的集体规划。

会议议程（Agenda）原意为"将要做的事"。议程专指会议上各项内容的安排，是一种正式的商务文件、政府文件，多用于对外交流的大型会议，是以书面形式来交流会议事务的一种简便函件。它可以用来解释会议政策，发布会议程序，提出会议的各项要求，也可以用来提醒会议事务使参会人员在了解会议流程的同时做好相关准备。由于会议议程流通于部门之间或直接公布于网上，因此大多格式简明、语言简洁。

How Is an Itinerary or Agenda Laid out?

```
              ITINERARY (AGENDA)
                   (PLACE)
                   (DATE)


      TIME                          ACTION
      ... - ...                     _____
      ... - ...                     _____
      ... - ...                     _____
      ... - ...                     _____
      ... - ...                     _____
```

行程表的格式一般较为固定，通常分为开头（Heading）和正文（Body）两部分。开头包括主题（Subject）、地点（Place）、日期（Date）三项。顺序通常如上所示，但日期的位置比较灵活，可以按书信格式置于正文右上方，也可以置于主题之前或之后。行程表的书写可以使用书信形式或表格形式。大部分公司或机构倾向于后者，因为表格形式更为正式、清晰。

议程表的写法与行程表相似，也是包括上述几部分。由于议程表往往是一个或一系列会议的活动安排，它的时间长度明显短于行程时间，所以正文部分比行程表要详细一些，有时会给出会议的提要，必要时需写出各项活动的起止时间。

由于大多数行程表和议程表的发送对象都不限于单个人，所以开头不用像写信一样加上称呼，而正文后面往往也不需要签名，但个别情况下也有。

打印或书写行程表或议程表时，通常有两种格式：每一行顶格左边对齐或每段首行缩进。

1. 行程表（Itinerary）

行程表将活动内容按时间顺序排列，内容应简洁明了。

【Sample 1】

下面是一份详细的北京之行的旅程表（Itinerary in Beijing）。文中不仅列出了旅行的时间和地点，还列出了具体的景点路线，即使不了解北京的读者也能从中获得一定信息。

Unit 8 Itineraries & Agendas（行程表和议程表）

Itinerary in Beijing（March 26 – 30）

Day 1: **Take flight from Shanghai to** Beijing. **Visit** Tian'anmen Square—one of the largest city squares in the world. After lunch visit the Forbidden City—the imperial palace of Ming and Qing dynasties, and go to Silk Factory to see the process of making silk. **After dinner enjoy** the Chinese Traditional Acrobatics.

Day 2: Go to Great Wall（Badaling Section）, and visit Jade Factory. After lunch go to Ming Tombs. In the evening enjoy the Chinese Foot Massage.

Day 3: Visit the Summer Palace—the largest imperial garden in the world. After lunch go to Pearl Factory.

Day 4: Visit the Temple of Heaven—the place where the Emperors of Ming and Qing dynasties performed their worship to the God of Heaven. After lunch taste traditional Chinese Tea and visit Beijing Enamel Factory.

Day 5: Visit Tongrentang—a very famous Drug Store in Beijing. Go to Silk Street or Russia Street. **Take flight back to** Shanghai.

在北京的旅程（3月26—30日）

第一天：从上海飞往北京。游天安门广场——世界上最大的城市广场之一。午餐后游览紫禁城——明清时期的帝王宫殿，去丝绸厂参观造丝过程，晚餐后欣赏中国的传统杂技。

第二天：去长城（八达岭区），参观制玉厂。午餐后去明陵，晚上体验中国足部按摩。

第三天：参观颐和园——世界上最大的皇家花园，午餐后参观珍珠厂。

第四天：参观天坛——明清时皇帝朝拜天地的场所，午餐后品尝传统的中国茶，参观北京瓷釉厂。

第五天：参观同仁堂——北京一家著名的药店，去丝绸一条街或俄罗斯一条街。乘飞机返回上海。

[Sample 2]

下面是一则表格形式的会议日程表（Conference Itinerary）。

Conference Itinerary	
Monday, June 16th, 2014	Tuesday, June 17th, 2014
Arrival and Welcome	Diplomacy Day
14:00	**8:00 – 9:00**
Check-in:	Breakfast
∗ Room Registration	**9:30**
∗ Personal Meetings with Instructors	United Nations Security Council Crisis Simulation
18:30 – 19:30	**11:30 – 12:00**
Dinner	Lunch
19:45	
Meet in Classrooms	
20:00 – 21:00	**12:15**

Opening Ceremonies: * Welcoming Addresses 21:30 First Planning, Development and Strategy Session: * Getting to Know Everybody * Parliament Introduction * Preparation for the United Nations Crisis	Buses Depart for Embassies 13:30 – 14:30 Embassy Visits 15:00 – 17:00 Visit the Senate or European Commission and Ministry of Regional Development 17:30 Return to Conference Venue 19:00 Dinner 20:30 PDS Session: * Preparation * International Law Day Briefing 22:00 Evening Mixer
Wednesday, June 18th, 2014 Media, Business & International Law Day 8:00 – 8:45 Breakfast 8:45 Meet for Bus Boarding 9:00 Buses Depart for International Business Center Arrive at International Business Center 10:00 – 12:00 Special Guest Speaker Presentation (TBD) 12:00 – 13:00 Lunch 13:00 – 14:30 Guest Speaker Presentation: Human Trafficking 14:30 – 15:30 Mixer with Sponsors, Panel, Speaker and Politicos 15:30 Buses Depart for Conference Venue 16:30 – 18:30	Thursday, June 19th, 2014 Model Parliament Preparation 8:00 – 9:00 Breakfast 9:00 Regional Presentations Topic: Issues Facing the Former Yugoslavia 10:30 – 12:00 Parliament Preparation and Party Strategy Meetings 12:00 – 13:00 Lunch 13:00 – 14:00 Regional Presentations Topic: Issues Facing Palestine 14:00 – 18:00 Group Debate Lobbying Amendment Writing and Posting 18:00 – 19:00 Dinner 20:00 Parliamentary Hearings

Downtime and Prep **19:00** Dinner **20:00 – 22:30** International Criminal Court Simulation **23:00** Open Culture Night	
Friday, June 20th, 2014 Parliament Day **8:00 – 9:00** Breakfast **9:00** Final Classroom Preparations for the Parliament **10:00** Buses Depart for Prague **11:30 – 13:30** Parliament Proceedings and Lunch **13:30 – 19:00** Time to See More of Prague's Beauty **19:30** Buses Depart for Conference Venue **21:00** Closing Ceremonies and Farewell Party with DJ	Saturday, June 21th, 2014 Goodbye and Farewell until Next Year **8:00 – 9:00** Breakfast **10:45** End of Week Wrap-up Evaluations **12:00** Check-out time **13:00** Buses Depart for Airport

会　议　日　程	
2014年6月16日，星期一 到达欢迎会 14:00 登记： ＊房间登记 ＊与讲师的私人见面 18:30—19:30 晚餐 19:45 教室见面 20:00—21:00 开幕式： ＊欢迎致辞 21:30　第一次计划、发展与策略会议： ＊熟悉每一个人	2014年6月17日，星期二 外交日 8:00—9:00 早餐 9:30 联合国安全理事会危机模拟 11:30—12:00 午餐 12:15 乘巴士前往大使馆 13:30—14:30 参观大使馆 15:00—17:00 到参议院或欧洲委员会和地区发展部参观 17:30 返回会议举行地点 19:00 晚餐

* 国会介绍 * 联合国危机的准备	20:30 PDS 会议： * 准备 * 国际法律日简报 22:00 晚间见面会
2014年6月18日，星期三 媒体、商务和国际法律日 8:00—8:45 早餐 8:45 集中乘车 9:00 乘车前往国际商务中心 　　　到达国际商务中心 10:00—12:00 特殊嘉宾发言 12:00—13:00 午餐 13:00—14:30 特殊嘉宾发言：人口贩卖 14:30—15:30 与赞助商、会议参加人、发言人和政治活动家见面 15:30 乘车前往会议举行地点 16:30—18:30 休息，准备 19:00 晚餐 20:00—22:30 国际刑事法庭模拟 23:00 露天文艺晚会	2014年6月19日，星期四 议会准备 8:00—9:00 早餐 9:00 地区性发言 　　　论题：前南斯拉夫问题 10:30—12:00 国会预备和党战略会议 12:00—13:00 午餐 13:00—14:00 地区发言 　　　论题：巴勒斯坦问题 14:00—18:00 分组讨论会 休会 修正书面文件和布告 18:00—19:00 晚餐 20:00 国会听证会
2014年6月20日，星期五 国会日 8:00—9:00 早餐 9:00 最后一次国会预备会议 10:00 乘车前往布拉格 11:30—13:30 国会会议和午餐 13:30—19:00 观赏美景 19:30 乘车前往会议举办地点 21:00 与主持人一起参加闭幕式和告别会	2014年6月21日，星期六 辞别，明年再会 8:00—9:00 早餐 10:45 结束一周的综合报道、评估 12:00 退房结账时间 13:00 乘车前往飞机场

2. 议程表（Agenda）

议程表与行程表的写法相似，即按照会议进程将会议活动、内容一一列出并注明具体时间。如有必要，议程表应包括会议的内容摘要。

【Sample 1】

下面是一所大学董事会的会议议程表（Agenda of Board Meeting）。该议程表列出了会议进程，并对各项讨论内容做了简单陈述，使与会者参会前就能了解会议步骤，以便适时作出回应。

Final Meeting Agenda (Distributed February, 2013)
Agenda of the University of Colorado
University of Colorado at Denver and Health Sciences Center

(Day 1 of 2)
Wednesday, January 14, 2015—Board Study Sessions
12:00 p.m. Strategic Planning Study Session Immediately **Followed by** the Intercollegiate Athletics Study Session
(Day 2 of 2)
Thursday, January 15, 2015—Board Business Meeting
8:00 a.m. Executive Session

Board will reconvene in public session to vote to go into executive session for specified matters; public session will reconvene[①] immediately following executive session but no earlier than 10:00 a.m.

The Contents

A. APPROVAL OF MINUTES OF THE BUSINESS MEETING HELD DECEMBER 8 – 9, 2014 (no earlier than 10:00 a.m.)

B. REPORTS
- President Hoffman
- Host Campus Chancellor
- Board of Regents Ad Hoc Committees and Liaison Activities
- Colorado Commission on Higher Education (Vice President Burns)
- Governance
  - Faculty Council Chair Rod Muth
  - Staff Council Chair Pat Beals Moore
  - Intercampus Student Forum Chair Joseph Neguse

C. ACTION ITEMS

    1. **Approval of** Department Name Change from Department of Rehabilitation[②] Medicine to Department of Physical Medicine and Rehabilitation—APPROVED

    2. **Selection of** the Engineering Firm to Perform Quality Assurance for the Chilled Water Expansion of the Central Utility Plant—APPROVED

    3. Mid Year Faculty Salary Adjustments for Academic Year 2014 – 2015 (School of Nursing) —APPROVED

    4. **Amendment to** the Program Plan for the University of Colorado at Colorado Spring Parking Garage and Office Space—APPROVED

    5. **Creation of** the Institute for Science and Space Studies—APPROVED

6. **Establish** the Christopher and Catherine Fund, a Quasi-Endowment in the University Endowment of the University of Colorado—APPROVED

7. **Establish** the Helen Geneva Smith Scholarship Fund, a Quasi-Endowment in the University Endowment of the University of Colorado—APPROVED

D. Next board meeting is **scheduled on** February 23–24, 2015, at University of Colorado.

① reconvene：重新召集　　② rehabilitation：复原

最终会议议程（2013 年 2 月发布）
科罗拉多大学会议议程
丹佛科罗拉多大学和健康科学中心

（第一天）
星期三，2015 年 1 月 14 日——校董事会研究会议
中午 12:00　战略性计划研究会议以及之后的大学间体育研究会

（第二天）
星期四，2015 年 1 月 15 日——校董事会事务会议
上午 8:00　执行会议

　　董事会召开全体大会投票处理具体事项，行政会议后全体大会将立刻再次召开，但不会早于上午 10:00。

内容

A. 核准 2014 年 12 月 8 日—9 日召开的会议的记录（不早于上午 10:00）
B. 报告
　　□ 主席 Hoffman
　　□ 主办学校的名誉校长
　　□ 董事会特别委员会和联络活动
　　□ 科罗拉多高等教育委员会（副主席 Burns）
　　□ 管理
　　　　○ 教师委员会主席 Muth
　　　　○ 职员会主席 Pat Beals Moore
　　　　○ 校际学生论坛主席 Joseph Neguse
C. 动议
　　1. 核准将"康复医学部"更名为"物理理疗与康复部"的动议。
　　2. 核准选择工程公司为中央公用事业厂的冷水延伸工程提供质量保证的动议。
　　3. 核准 2014—2015 学年，调整护理学院全体教员年中薪水的动议。
　　4. 核准修正科罗拉多大学关于科罗拉多斯普林车库和办公室空间的项目计划的动议。
　　5. 核准成立科学空间研究学院的动议。
　　6. 核准建立克里斯多夫和凯萨琳基金（类似科罗拉多大学捐助基金）的动议。
　　7. 核准建立海伦日内瓦史密斯奖学金基金（类似科罗拉多大学捐助基金）的动议。
D. 下次董事会定于 2015 年 2 月 23—24 日在科罗拉多大学举行。

Unit 8　Itineraries & Agendas（行程表和议程表）

【Sample 2】

　　下面是一则表格式董事会会议议程（Agenda of Board Meeting）。该议程采用了表格形式，简单明了。

<table>
<tr><td colspan="3" align="center">Board Meeting Agenda
(9th September, 2017)
(Conference Room 1)
(9:00 a.m. – 11:00 a.m.)</td></tr>
<tr><th>Time</th><th>Activity</th><th>Action</th></tr>
<tr><td>9:00 – 9:20</td><td>Minutes from previous meeting</td><td>Approval</td></tr>
<tr><td>9:20 – 9:40</td><td>Chief Executive's Report</td><td>Discussion</td></tr>
<tr><td>9:40 – 9:50</td><td>Finance Committee's Report</td><td>Approve Budget Changes</td></tr>
<tr><td>9:50 – 10:00</td><td>Development Committee's Report</td><td>Approve Fundraising Plan</td></tr>
<tr><td>10:00 – 10:20</td><td>Board Development Committee</td><td>Approve Plans for Retreat
Adopt Resolution to Change Bylaws[①]</td></tr>
<tr><td>10:20 – 10:40</td><td>Other Business
—Old
—New
—Announcements</td><td></td></tr>
<tr><td>10:40 – 10:55</td><td>Roundtable Evaluation of Meeting
Review of Actions from Meeting</td><td></td></tr>
<tr><td>10:55 – 11:00</td><td>Adjourn</td><td></td></tr>
</table>

① bylaws：次要法规

<table>
<tr><td colspan="3" align="center">董事会会议议程
(2017年9月9日)
(第1会议室)
(上午9:00—上午11:00)</td></tr>
<tr><th>时间</th><th>活动</th><th>决议</th></tr>
<tr><td>9:00—9:20</td><td>先前会议记录</td><td>通过</td></tr>
<tr><td>9:20—9:40</td><td>首席执行官报告</td><td>讨论</td></tr>
<tr><td>9:40—9:50</td><td>财务部报告</td><td>通过预算变动</td></tr>
<tr><td>9:50—10:00</td><td>发展部报告</td><td>通过融资计划</td></tr>
<tr><td>10:00—10:20</td><td>董事会发展委员会会议</td><td>通过撤销计划
采用制度变更决议</td></tr>
</table>

续表

时间	活动	决议
10:20—10:40	其他事务 —以前的事务 —新的事务 —通告	
10:40—10:55	圆桌评估会议 会议活动回顾	
10:55—11:00	闭幕	

Useful Expressions

(1) Arrive in Shanghai. 抵达上海
(2) Transfer to the hotel, and the rest of the day is free. 转往宾馆，其余时间自行安排。
(3) Depart from the Chongqing Harbor 从重庆港出发
(4) Chengdu to Beijing by flight, stay in a four-star hotel.
 乘飞机从成都至北京，入住四星级宾馆。
(5) The tour will be finished after breakfast. 早餐后旅行结束。
(6) Return to Conference Venue 返回会议中心
(7) Buses depart for 乘巴士前往……
(8) After dinner enjoy... 晚餐后欣赏……
(9) Check-In 入住登记
(10) Room Registration 登记房间
(11) Getting to know everybody 认识大家
(12) Preparation for... 为……的准备
(13) Lobbying 休会
(14) Time to see... 看……的时间
(15) Overview of.../Report on.../New policy on.../Speech of...
 对……的回顾/关于……的报告/……的新政/……的发言
(16) Introduction and Welcome Remarks/Welcome Reception 介绍和欢迎致辞/欢迎接待会
(17) Coffee Break/Working Lunch/Pre-dinner Drinks 休息/工作午餐/饭前餐酒
(18) Keynote address 演讲致辞
(19) Close and Departure 闭幕离开

Unit 8　Itineraries & Agendas（行程表和议程表）

 Writing Practice

I. Draft an itinerary according to the notes given.

总经理 John Black 将去日本出差，由秘书制定行程表，具体内容如下：
星期二，4月4日：东京总部
　　上午9:20　　分公司经理会议
　　下午2:00　　销售经理会议
　　下午5:30　　公司餐会　希尔顿饭店
星期三，4月5日：东京—名古屋
　　上午9:30　　与东京分公司经理比尔在希尔顿饭店见面后乘他的车去羽田机场
　　中午12:00　乘日航95次飞机离开羽田机场（头等舱，包括午餐）
　　下午1:10　　抵达名古屋
　　　　　　　　名古屋分公司经理汤米去接机
　　　　　　　　下榻新名古屋酒店（双人标间带浴室）
　　下午3:00　　分公司办公会议
　　下午5:30　　公司餐会　新名古屋酒店
星期四，4月6日：名古屋—北京
　　上午9:30　　与汤米在新名古屋酒店见面后乘他的车去名古屋国际机场
　　上午11:40　办理登机手续
　　中午12:40　乘日航117次航班飞机离开日本去北京（头等舱，包括午餐）

II. Draft an agenda according to the hints given.

公司将召开一个董事会会议，请按下列提示撰写一份会议议程：
　　会议将于2017年7月6日星期四下午1:30在2号会议室召开。
会议安排：
　　1:30—1:50　　讨论2017年5月8日会议的会议记录
　　1:50—2:30　　讨论在纽约与新加坡建立分公司的可行性
　　2:30—3:00　　决定在日本分公司的投资额
　　3:00—4:00　　威尔·史密斯先生将做一个公司2018年销售策略的报告
　　4:00—4:30　　从候选人中选出新任人事经理来代替辞职的刘杨先生
　　4:30　　　　　会议结束

Unit 9

Business Reports (商务报告)

- General Introduction
- Sample Reading
- Useful Expressions
- Writing Practice

General Introduction & Sample Reading

随着国际商务环境日益复杂，有效的交流越来越成为事业成功的关键因素。在进一步丰富收集信息、调查研究等手段的同时，将信息有效传达给同事、商业伙伴及主管部门十分重要。要达到这一目的需要有技巧地撰写商业报告。本章将介绍撰写商业报告的目的与报告的基本特征，着重讲解报告的格式、主要内容及写作技巧，并提供一些商业报告的范例分析和写作练习。

How Is a Business Report Laid out?

1. Structures of Reports

报告的种类多样，非正式报告可能以多种形式出现，只需写明收件人、报告撰写人、时间、标题（书信式不需标题）即可；而事实上，报告一般都是机构、企业、政府部门内部或之间非常正式的公文。这类文本的共同特点在于篇幅无论长短，体例必须规范；内容可繁可简，格式非常关键。这类文件的英语版本对内容和形式往往格外讲究。

报告的格式类似于商品的包装。不夸张地说，许多情况下格式和体例是不是正式、规范，要与内容是不是翔实等量齐观。

这里首先介绍的是一般报告的通用型结构形式。所谓"通用型"并非一个类别，而是说这种框架属于一种基本型，根据具体场合和用途，只需稍加修改题目和体例，即可制作成一份得体的报告书。无论篇幅长短、用处尊卑，各类报告均能以此为基本模式。

报告文体的通用型结构主要包括以下部分：

- 题目/标题；
- 报告传达书（包括作者姓名和单位、呈送对象、日期）；

- 总结/提要/摘要/概要；
- 鸣谢；
- 目录（可将使用的图表单列一项）；
- 前言/引言/导言/导语/序言（可将研究方法单列一项）；
- 正文/调查结果/研究结果；
- 结论；
- 建议（结论和建议可合并为一部分）；
- 参考资料/参考文献/书目；
- 附录/附件。

如果报告比较长或者比较重要或者应用场合比较庄重，上面所列的前五个部分有必要各占一页。如果报告比较短或者使用目的不那么正式，前四个部分可以合并成为一页甚至更短，相互之间拉开一定距离即可。

前面的四个部分中，各部分的详略程度可变。除了题目之外其余项目的位置可以互换。正文之后的"参考文献"和"附录"两个部分根据情况可要可不要；如果附录比较多，还可以有列表和小标题。

1) Title Page

The title page's appearance should get the attention of the reader and its layout plays an important role. Prominence should be given to certain information such as the title, the author's name and the position on the page, the area allocated to the information, the size of the typeface and the font used. You should provide the following:

- a clear concise title that indicates the subject matter exactly;
- author's name and the Position or Department;
- date of completion.

And, in accordance with local requirements:

- use the company's or business's template;
- provide clients' names/details where appropriate;
- reference number;
- signatures of authorising officers if this is company practice;
- classification e.g. confidential.

2) The summary

The summary is prepared last and is the most influential section of the whole report—it is sometimes the only part a busy manager will read. The summary should therefore be self-contained and self-explanatory. It is placed at the beginning of the report and is usually about one page long and certainly not more than two pages in length.

The summary should state:

- the problem;
- essential evidence;
- conclusions;

- recommendations.

3) Acknowledgments

Any significant help received should be acknowledged in this section, especially if someone has given it from outside the organisation that commissioned the report. If other people's research, results or ideas are quoted or used in the text of the report, they should be referenced by bibliographic citation.

Typically the author of a report will acknowledge the following:
- the name(s) of person(s) with whom they have had useful or stimulating discussions;
- those who have provided financial support;
- those who have loaned you equipment;
- software specialist(s) who helped to process data.

4) Contents list

The contents list is simply a list of the various sections in the report together with their associated page numbers. The most helpful reports have sections with succinct but meaningful headings.

The contents list:
- gives a detailed structure of the report;
- shows all section numbers, headings and associated page numbers;
- provides a separate list of diagrams and their page numbers if necessary.

Main sections usually include subsections in a hierarchy, which are usually distinguishable by using a numbering system. For example, Section 1 of your report may have 4 subsections that should be numbered 1.1, 1.2, 1.3 and 1.4.. Section 1.3 may have subsections which should be numbered 1.3.1, 1.3.2 and 1.3.3.

5) Introduction & terms of reference

The introduction aims to set the scene for the report and to describe what was known at the start of the project. It should be brief, concise and address issues such as:
- why the report has been written;
- the general problem under investigation;
- the importance of this problem to the individual or to the company;
- definitions of uncommon terms/symbols (if many of these glossaries should be included);
- states the main aim(s) of the project;
- outlines the approach used;
- states the most significant result.

6) Methodology

The reader will want to know what methodology was used. Some typical questions, which the reader might wish to have been answered, include:
- What equipment and software were used?

- What were the operating conditions?
- What assumptions have been made (if any)?
- What statistical techniques have been used?
- Can their validity be justified?

7) Results

The results are included only to support the arguments that lead to the conclusions. The results should be complete but manageable and presented in summary form as tables or graphs depending on the use the reader will have for them.

The presentation of results means choosing the clearest means of communication. Words, tables, graphs, and drawings are visual representations of meaning. In designing the presentation of results you should ask yourselves:

- What is the precise function of this table or graph?
- Is the reader likely to make use of the actual data?
- Will the reader understand this information more easily in verbal, visual, tabular or diagrammatic form?
- How can I make this easy for the reader to understand?

There are many software packages, such as Excel or SPSS, that manipulate data and aid graphical visualization.

8) Discussion and analysis of results

This is the core of your report. The results in the preceeding section should not simply be repeated, but features of these results should be explained in terms of theory and, where possible, compared with the findings of others. This is the section in which arguments are made which form the route from the original question to the conclusions.

Gaps in your argument may become evident while writing this section and you may well identify additional work that must be done. For this reason you should write your analysis of results section early while there is still time to obtain more data.

You should aim to answer the following questions:

- What were the main results?
- What are the implications of the data I've presented?
- What conclusions can be drawn?
- What recommendations for changing future practice can be made?

Additionally, in your discussion you should aim to:

- ensure your discussion leads logically to conclusions and recommendations;
- present the content of your discussion as objectively as possible;
- organise your discussion into an orderly sequence;
- divide and label your discussion into numbered sections and subsections.

9) Conclusions

Your conclusion should be a short section which suggests the answer(s) to the questions

posed in your introduction. Your conclusion should:
- briefly summarize discussions/results in the main body i.e. list the points you now know as a result of having done the investigation;
- assess the implications of evidence already presented.

There should be no arguments or new evidence presented in your conclusions—these should all occur in the discussion. A reader should be able to pick up your report and grasp the most significant points by reading only the summary and the conclusions.

10) Recommendations

Recommendation should be clear and given without discussion. Recommendations should:
- present one of possible courses of action to be taken as the result of conclusions;
- expand on the recommendations given in summary.

Recommendations may be subjective since, in certain jobs (e.g. solicitor, surveyor, financial adviser, business analyst), your professional credibility may be on the line.

11) References

Most academic work is not carried out in isolation but built upon the ideas and efforts of other people. It is important to give credit to other people when you cite their books, reports, journal papers as references. References also help the reader track down the source material for further investigation if required.

12) Appendices

Appendices may contain detailed, lengthy or supplementary information. Removing this material from the text allows the reader to concentrate on the main issues without distraction—it keeps your report concise and enables the reader to locate key information quickly and efficiently. However, the details are nevertheless there in the appendix to be followed up at the reader's discretion. The sorts of material you might place in your appendices could include:
- raw data;
- computer printouts;
- calculations;
- sample questionnaire(s);
- supplementary diagrams.

2. Outlined Structures of Major Types

1) Short Reports

Now we are using this space for a few words on reports that are brief in subject matter and short in length. Short reports serve business purposes in their own right. Shortness does not imply any surrender to quality or utility. If anything, they are more organized and "distilled", so to speak. We might as well have a look here at the structure and organization of two typical short reports, before we talk about the structures of other and formal types.

这里我们对主旨精练、篇幅短小的报告做一简要介绍。短篇报告在商业运作中起着不可替代的作用。

短小并不代表质量差或没用处。如果说它们有什么特别的话，那就是结构清晰、精练。在讨论其余的和正式的报告前，我们有必要首先看看两种短报告的组织结构。

Figure 1　Skeleton of a short and informal report
短篇非正式报告纲要

```
              To:      × × × ×
              From:    × × × ×
              Date:    × × × ×
              Subject: × × × ×

Content:
```

Figure 2　Highlights of a short but formal report
短篇正式报告纲要

```
                     Title
              Transmittal information

State the Problem to be dealt with
Explain the Background and Methods used
Present Research Results and other data
Provide your Analysis of the available data
Give your Conclusion or Conclusions
```

2) Long Reports

A long report may contain many reports of varying lengths and types. Unlike the "Small Reports", a big report is not a type by itself. Rather, it is a collection of documents necessary for a big economic project. The format outlined below is one of the most frequently adopted structures for long business reports. It is important that readers have a clear idea of the components it contains. Also important to note is that this outline below can be identical to the contents page of a formal report. For that purpose, all readers have to do is to add page numbers on the right to each item in the major framework. Also, if needed, readers can alter or replace most of the items in this outline to suit your actual report requirements.

一份长篇报告可以涵盖很多篇长度不同、种类各异的报告。与"小汇报"不同，大报告并不自成一类。它更应被认为是为一个大型经济项目进行的文献汇编。读者有必要了解它包含的成分。需要说明的是下面的提纲也可以用作正式报告的目录。那时，读者只需在主要框架中每一栏的右边加上相应的页码。必要时，读者也可改变这一提纲中的大部分项目以适应具体的报告要求。

Figure 3　Basic structure of long reports
长篇报告基本结构

```
                          CONTENTS
Executive summary
I    INTRODUCTION
     1.1    Purpose
     1.2    Background
     1.3    Methodology
     1.4    Scope
II   FINDINGS
     2.1    Heading 1
            2.1.1    Sub-heading
            2.1.2    Sub-heading
            2.1.3    Sub-heading
            2.1.4    Sub-heading
     2.2    Heading 2
            2.2.1    Sub-heading
            2.2.2    Sub-heading
            2.2.3    Sub-heading
            2.2.4    Sub-heading
     2.3    Heading 3
            2.3.1    Sub-heading
            2.3.2    Sub-heading
            2.3.3    Sub-heading
III  CONCLUSIONS
IV   RECOMMENDATIONS
Bibliography
Appendix
Survey Form
```

　　As we have seen in past discussions, there are many types of reports and they tend to follow different structures. And the number of inclusions within different reports can also vary greatly. For these reasons we are here showing the basic formats of one of the most complex reports in practical business operations—the research report and the marketing report. Please note there is plenty of space for variety and change in the formats.

　　在前面的讨论中我们已经看到，报告的种类繁多，结构各异，包含的内容也不尽相同。因此，我们在此提供一种在具体商务实践中最为复杂的报告的基本形式——研究报告和营销报告。请注意，在基本形式基础上还有很大的变化空间。

Figure 4 Structure of a detailed research report
具体的研究报告结构

A RESEARCH REPORT

EXECUTIVE SUMMARY

I. INTRODUCTION
—Brief statement of the report
—Purpose and context of the report
—When and how it was prepared
—Name(s) and title(s) of the writer or writers
—Sponsors and funding for the report

II. METHODOLOGY
—Description of the project
—Narration of the procedures
—Scope and focus of the research
—The research instruments used
—Other factors related to the process

III. MAIN FINDINGS AND DISCUSSION
—Main findings of the report
—Description of the analysis
—Supporting details and evidence
—Appropriate explanations

IV. COSTS (or BUDGET)

V. CONCLUSIONS AND RECOMMENDATIONS
—Summary of the main points and their importance
—Recommendations for action or further investigation

VI. APPENDICES
—Sampling instruments
—Investigation techniques
—References

Sample Reading

[Sample 1]

以下是正式商务报告的两种主题页样文。分别以"三点式"和"四点式"结构排版，读者在具体操作中可根据个人喜好进行选择。注意样文中对版式的注解。

1）三点式主题页

FEMALE MANAGERS'
DIFFERENT STYLES AND
DIFFERENT PROBLEMS

Prepared for
Ms. J. ELLIS
Professor of Office Administration
Lamar University
Beaumont. Texas 77710

Prepared by
Craig Smith
August 14, 2018

> This three-spot title page has a wider top and bottom margin (16 spaces) than most title pages, but it looks attractive on the page

---

2）四点式主题页

---

2 inches
(12 blank lines)

**FEMALE MANAGERS' DIFFERENT STYLES
AND DIFFERENT PROBLEMS**

(10 – 12 blank lines)

Unit 9 Business Reports（商务报告）

Prepared for John Whigman
Publisher, Plain Talk Daily Herald

（10 – 12 blank lines）

Prepared by Mary Alice Brown, Consultant
Winning Communications

（10 – 12 blank lines）

August 2018

（2 inches）

【Sample 2】

以下是正式商务报告的传递信（Transmittal）样文。

Winning Communications

Suite 112, Plaza Center
Spokane, Washington 999204

October 18, 2018

Mr. John Whigman
Plain talk daily herald
Bangor, ME 04401

Dear Mr. Whigman,

  The report that you asked me to prepare on female managers has revealed some interesting facts.

  My research indicates, as you thought, that male and female managers do have different management styles. However, some of the qualities female managers exhibit—empathy, listening and conciliation skills—make them particularly suited to management.

  Basically, the abilities of career-oriented males and those of career oriented females do not show a gender correlation. I have found greater differences among individuals within each group than between the male female groups.

  Thank you for your confidence in selecting the firm of Winning Communications. I hope that this information will be valuable to you and that you put your faith in us again in the future.

Cordially,
WINNING COMMUNICATIONS
Craig Smith
Consultant

成功传播

999204 华盛顿 斯波凯恩
普拉泽中心 112室

2018. 10. 18

约翰·惠格曼先生
每日简报通报员
班戈，ME 04401

亲爱的惠格曼先生：

您要求我准备的关于女性管理人员的报告显示出一些有趣的现象。

正如您的观点，我的调查显示，男性和女性管理人员之间确实存在管理风格上的差异。但是，女性管理人员展示出的某些特质——设身处地、倾听和抚慰的技巧——使她们更适合管理工作。

总的来讲，事业型的男性及女性的能力并未显示出与性别的关系。我发现在每个团队中个人的差异大于男性团队和女性团队间的差异。

感谢您有信任并选择成功传播公司。希望这是对您有价值的信息。期盼未来您能再次惠顾。

诚挚的
成功传播
顾问 克雷格·史密斯

[Sample 3]

以下是正式商务报告正文前的目录表（Content）样文，这一部分对于长篇报告尤其重要。

```
                        TABLE OF CONTENTS

                                                                    Page
I    INTRODUCTION
     A Purpose                                                         1
     B Background and report preview                                   1
II   MANAGEMENT STYLES                                                 2
III  PROBLEMS WHICH FEMALE MANAGERS FACE                               8
     A Male resentment                                                10
```

B Nonverbal barriers	14
C Sexual problems	20
IV SUMMARY	24

LIST OF TABLES AND FIGURES

TABLE

I THE BASES OF POWER	5
II JOB SATISFACTION OF MALES IN NONTRANSITIONAL JOBS	12

FIGURE

1. Relation of family role/organization role	19
2. Qualities of career-oriented males	22
3. Qualities of career-oriented females	23

目   录

	页码
Ⅰ 导言	
A 目的	1
B 背景与报告预览	1
Ⅱ 管理风格	2
Ⅲ 女性管理人员面临的困难	8
A 男性的怨恨	10
B 无声的障碍	14
C 性别问题	20
Ⅳ 总结	24

表格与图形列表

表格

Ⅰ 权力的基础	5
Ⅱ 担任长期职位的男性工作满意度	12

图形

1. 家庭角色与组织角色的关系	19
2. 职场男性特质	22
3. 职场女性特质	23

Analysis

(1) 三点式安排的主题页其三点分别为标题、呈送对象、报告作者，日期与作者写在一起

（如例1的1））。而四点式主题页将日期单独列为一点（如例1的2））。

(2) 正式商务报告正文前的标题、传递信、目录多数应单列一页（如例1、例2、例3）。如果报告十分简洁、结构清晰，则目录这一部分可以省略。

 Useful Expressions

由于商务报告的种类繁多、内容各异，很难将其可能用到的表达方法一一列举，现仅根据一般的报告结构将有些部分常用的句型列举如下。

Title/Heading

(1) Report on ...　就……报告
(2) Proposed ...; Suggestions for ...　提议……

Introduction & Terms of Reference

(1) The purpose of this report is to ...　本报告的目的是……
(2) The aim of this report is to ...　本报告旨在……
(3) Mr. X has asked me to report to ...　某先生要求本人就……做出报告

Findings

(1) It was found that ...　已发现……
(2) It was generally the case that ...　多数情况下……
(3) Many members of staff suggested that ...　许多员工建议……
(4) A number of people mentioned that ...　一些人提到……
(5) It was proposed that a series of changes could be made. For instance, ...
　　有建议认为有必要进行一些改变，比如……
(6) Both A and B have ...　甲与乙均已……
(7) A is similar to B in that there is ...　甲和乙同样的……
(8) Despite the fact that A is not quite as good as B in terms of ..., it is just as ... as B.
　　尽管事实上在……方面甲不如乙，甲和乙也一样……

Recommendations

(1) The policy would mean a greater level of ...　这一政策意味着更高水平的……
(2) This should allow for ...　这应考虑到……
(3) This might lead to a shortage of ...　这可能导致……的短缺

 *Writing Practice*

I. Rewrite the conclusions below.

The present market of English-training in the county is big and it has a great potential. The research shows that with more than 4,000 teachers and more than 10,000 young people, it can be a giant market for the center.

The center has a lot of advantages with its rich teacher resources and well-equipped facilities. With its good public relations and advertisement strategies, it has a bright prospect in the market of English-training in the county.

II. Based on the findings presented below, write logical conclusions and make appropriate recommendations to complete the report below.

2. FINDINGS

2.1 Distribution Difficulties

Mr. Zhang, the Area Manager in China, has reported distribution difficulties in the south of the country, an area affected by floods in the last few months. There have been 22 truck breakdowns, resulting in complaints about poor delivery time. On the other hand, there have been no problems with delivery time in the north. In fact, there is evidence that the warehouse there is overstocked and over-manned.

2.2 Payments

Another problem which the Area Manager has reported is difficulty obtaining prompt payment for goods delivered. The annual accounts indicate that $25,000 were owed to the company at the end of the year. Small customers are largely to blame. In two cases, customers have gone bankrupt and this has resulted in bad debts of $45,000.

2.3 Production Problems

The District Manager, Mr. Li, has reported production problems in the west of the country, an area which has been affected by water supply shortage during the past years and most severely early this year. There have been daily stoppages, leading to production falling by 30 percentage below target. In the east, however, there is evidence that the factory has over capacity since they were 15% above target.

2.4 Personnel Problems

Mr. Kang the Human Resources Manager reported difficulty in recruitment. Evidence of this can be found in the personnel budget in which $10,000 was allocated for job advertisements. Low salary rates are largely to blame. For example, maintenance and electrical technicians are paid only $100 per month on average.

III. Read the following report carefully and decide how it can be improved, then rewrite it.

Reduce the price of car

   Yesterday an article run in newspaper named Cankao Xiaoxi said that Hoda, the Jpanese car company expended six years entering into the car market in China, now it wants to expend five years for producing economy and family car and expanding their chare of the car market in China. Since 1980 we began to negotiate with China, we produced a first car in Shanghai in 1990, for entering into the car market in China we expanded for ten years. Now the annual output is very optimistic, in 1997 our net profit reached at 20 billion, in 1998 at 40 billion, in 1999 at 80 billion, in this year from January to June our output are 28000 units, the total Sales attained at 60 million. In the end of 2000 China will join in WTO, more international automobile companies will enter in China. We will face more competitors, but I believe firmly that in the following years, Hoda is one of few of most dangerous competitors for us. So the longer that we would delay taking some right stratagem, the more we risk being shut out of growing car market in China.

   In 1997, our company started to develop marketing research plans. We focus on price, buyers, quality, capability and the other car companies in China. We find that the most factor influence on buyers is the price of car. So I advice that we could depreciate in large the price of cars, at the same time, we want to apply $100 million for building another product line, and raising our annual output to 150 billion units. Forming mass production could reduce the cost.

   Today the economy of China is developing so quickly that the hot spots of consumption focus on car, mobile telephone, and so on, especially the car is the most favorable items in the eyes of white-collar. It is a fad. How do the Chinese consumers look on the sales promotion of Chinese car? According to our marketing research which concerns to 3000 families in Beijing, among them there 2000families want to buy cars within three years coming, showing that the price of car influences directly the buying behavior of Chinese consumers. This research tells us that 68 percent expressed that they decided to buy cars in term of price. How about the price of cars is? Now let us look at the following list of price car and we divide it into three levels: Top grade car, Medium-price, Low-price.

The price of top grade car
Shanghai GM Bieke-360 000
Guangzhou Honda ~ 250 000
Audi 250 000
Red flag 260 000
Medium-price cars
Fukang 140 000

Unit 9　Business Reports (商务报告)

Jieda 130000
Low-price cars
Xiali 90000
Aotuo 60000

　　Our marketing research shows that some articles pointed that the car industry profits reached at billions. Some media publish following numbers: in last year the sales of Jieda is 70000 units, earned 12 billion RMB, Bieke 23000 units, earned 6 billions RMB, 20000 (RMB) per unit. No wonder the boss of GM exclaimed that you could not earn so large money in every industry except in Chinese car market and in gambling house. Our Sangtana 230000 per unit earned 40 billion (RMB). Why we don't want to reduce the price to attract the purchasers, and hold this market.

　　Chinese families need to buy cars. If we read the above list of price of car, we could understand that the lower income is the main fact affects the buyer's behavior. Taking a governmental official for example, is about 20000 - 30000, the high-salaried class is little in our society, if he or she wants to buy a car, he or she must spend several decade's saving or deposit. Although according to Engle's laws, as family income rises, the percentage spent on food declines, and the percentage on saving increases. The another factor that will push the sales of car is the construction of cities. Now the China government is constructing in force its old cities, for example Beijing, Shanghai, Guangzhou, Tianjing and so on. A lot of new apartment buildings are built in the suburb of cities. Thousands upon thousands of local residents moved from the center of city to the suburban colony, they need to buy car for going to work because of lack of transportation.

　　Our marketing research expanding for two years shows that if HQ could input 100 million into our company for building a new product line. Our annual output could raise and our cost could decline, the depreciation could be available.

　　Regarding to the source of capital and the range of depreciation, we have following suggestions: About the source of capital: we advice that HQ offer 40 million, the rest of the capital we could loan from the Bank of China and the Construction Bank of China. And the range of falling price, we think that it is best to place price under 100000 (RMB) per unit. During five years we would fall our price 50000 (RMB) per unit stage by stage. I am sure this price is favourable for salariats and accepted by them.

　　According to the latest news in the car market of China, the price of Fukang reduces, its range is from 10000 to 5000.

　　The above dates come from the www.chinacar.online.com, Beijing Evening News, (*Beijing Daily*).

Unit 10

Business Letters (商务书信)

- General Introduction
- Business Letters for Different Purposes

General Introduction & Sample Reading

What Are Business Letters?

商务书信是公司或企业间保持商务联系的重要手段。公司或企业可以通过商务书信的方式进行一定的商业活动，比如询价、报价、还价、订货、交货、支付、索赔、理赔、代理等。与口头商务联系相比，商务书信作为文字记录，在双方发生业务纠纷或争执时，能提供重要的法律证据。近些年随着网络技术的迅速发展，电子商务逐渐流行，商务书信也大多不再通过传统的邮寄、电传方式收发，取而代之的是快捷又便利的E-mail的盛行。而信函语言尽管仍遵循一定的原则，但因信函传递方式的变革而呈现出随意和口语化的倾向。

How Are Business Letters Laid out?

1. The Essential Parts

尽管不同的商务书信目的不同，但一般都包括以下几个必要部分。

1）信头（The Heading or Letter-head）

信头部分通常包含这些项目：发信人的公司名称、地址、电话号码、传真、电子邮箱、网址、主要经营业务、公司标志等。大部分公司的信笺都印有信头，以方便收信人辨别。

2）日期（The Date）

日期通常按日、月、年的顺序打印，如13th April, 2005; 13 April, 2005。日以基数词或序数词表示均可。但有时也将月置于日前，如April 13, 2005。要注意的是，月份最好不用数字表示，以避免误解，如04/03/2005在英国人看来是指2005年3月4日，但美国人会认为是2005年4月3日，因为各个国家标示日期的习惯不同。日期的位置一般在信头下方两三行处，可以紧左页边写，也可以将最后一个数字紧右页边写。

3）信内地址（The Inside Name and Address）

信内地址是收信人所在公司的名称和地址，一般从距日期两行信纸左页边写起。其写法类似于信封的写法，地址按从小到大的顺序书写：

- 收信人姓名、职务；
- 收信人公司名称；
- 收信人公司所在大楼或街区名称及门牌号；
- 所在城市/城镇、州名称及邮编；
- 国家名称。

如：Personnel Manager
　　Great Western Publishing Co., Ltd.
　　7777 State Street, Room 456
　　Chicago, IL60606
　　U.S.A.

4）称呼敬语（The Salutation）

称呼敬语位于信内地址下两行。如知道对方姓名，就用 Dear Mr./Mrs./Miss/Ms. 加上姓，如不知道对方姓名，可用 Dear Sir, Dear Madam, 也可用 To whom it may concern。如对方职务较高，则最好用其职务名称，如 Dear Prof. Smith, Dear Dr. Henson 等。称呼一家公司就用 Dear Sirs 或 Gentlemen。

5）正文（The Body）

正文是信函的主体部分。其书写通常遵循"7C"原则，即准确（correctness）、清晰（clearness）、简明（conciseness）、具体（concreteness）、体谅（consideration）、礼貌（courtesy）和完整（completeness）。根据信函的具体目的，正文部分可长可短。但是，无论长短，一封正式的商务书信都包括开头、主体和结尾三部分。

6）结束敬语（The Complimentary Close）

结束敬语往往和称呼语相呼应。如称呼用 Dear Sir/Dear Sirs/Dear Madam, 结束敬语就用 Yours faithfully；称呼用 Dear Mr. John/Dear Mr. Smith, 结束敬语就用 Yours sincerely, Yours truly, 或 Yours cordially。

7）署名（The Signature）

署名一般是手写体签名，署名和结束敬语对齐，通常紧左页边写，相隔两行间距。署名包括名字和职务，起首字母都要大写。有时也会签上公司的名称。

2. The Optional Parts

上述 7 项构成商务书信的必要部分，除此以外，特定的商务书信还可以包括其他的一些选择部分。

1）致收信人（The Attention Line）

当发信人希望将信件递交给对方公司的某个特定收信人时，可在信内地址之下两行称呼之上两行处添加这一项，并加以底线以引起充分注意。如 For the attention of Mr. Blair 或

Attention/Attn：Mr. Blair。

2）主题（The Subject Line）

主题一项用来简要介绍信件正文的内容，以使收信人能快速获得关键信息。主题项一般在称呼下两行处，前加 Subject 字样或以黑体字打印。

3）经办人代号（The Identifying Initials）

经办人代号由书信口述人或撰写者和秘书或打字员姓名首字母组成，通常打印在署名下两行紧左页边处。口述者或撰写者姓名首字母在先，秘书或打字员姓名首字母以冒号或斜线隔开。可全部大写或小写，或仅前者首字母大写。如 JB/GS，JB：GS 或 JB/gs，JB：gs。

4）附件（The Enclosure）

当信函中包含附件（如支票、账单等）时，应在信函左下角署名下两行处印上 Enclosure 或 Encl. 字样。如有必要，还应注明具体的附件内容和份数。如：

Encl. Commercial Invoice（3 copies）
      Insurance Policy

5）抄送（The Copy Notation）

有时商务书信除了递送给对方，也同时抄送给第三方。通常的做法是，在署名或附件下两行紧左页边印上 cc 或 CC 及要抄送的第三方名称。如 CC：Mr. George Blair, Sales Manager。但要注意的是，在美国等一些国家的商业界，现在基本上是用影印件来抄送，所以也用 Xerox 代替 CC。

3. Two Styles of Layout

商务书信有两种格式：混合式（The Indented Style）和平头式（The Block Style）。

1）混合式（The Indented Style）

按混合式撰写的信函中，每段第一行缩进一定距离（通常是 4～6 个空格），封内地址各行紧左页边书写，日期、结束敬语及署名置于右下角处。这是一种较为传统的书写格式。

The Nile Trading Co. Ltd.
161 Pyramid Street，Alexandria，Egypt
Tel：（20 - 3）4900000 Fax：（20 - 3）4900001

11th May，2019

The Export Manager
China Motorbike Co. Ltd.
34 Fazhan Street
Jinan，Shandong
P. R. C.

Dear Sir or Madam,

  We are interested in importing mopeds and would be grateful if you would send us a copy of your latest catalogue, your price list and export terms. Could you also let us know the name of your import agent in Egypt?

  We look forward to hearing from you.

Yours faithfully,
Abdul Aziz
Marketing Manager

  2) 平头式 (The Block Style)

  按平头式撰写的信函中，所有各行包括日期、封内地址、结束敬语、署名等均紧靠左页边书写，无首行缩进。现在的商务书信大部分都按平头格式打印。

H. Woods & Co., Ltd.
Nesson House, Newell Street
Birmingham B15 3EL
Tel: (44-121) 4560000　Fax: (44-121) 4560001

1 March, 2019
The Manager
Shanghai Textile Trading Co. Ltd.
72 Zhongshan Rd.
Shanghai 200001
China

Dear Sir or Madam,

We are interested in tweed lengths suitable for skirt-making and would like to have details of your prices and terms.

It would be helpful if you could supply samples.

Yours faithfully,
Larry Crane
China Trade Manager

Business Letters for Different Purposes

开头已经提到，企业或公司可以利用商业书信的方式从事不同的商业活动。本章将根据不同的商业目的逐一介绍最常见的7种商业书信。

1. Establishing Business Relationships（建立商业关系）

1）What are letters for establishing business relations?

在国际贸易中，要保持或扩大业务就必须巩固和发展已有的业务关系，并且不断物色新的贸易伙伴以建立新的业务关系。新的业务关系可以通过银行、报纸广告、因特网、驻外商务机构、国外商会、商品交易会等多种渠道建立。

2）How to write a letter for establishing business relations?

To write a letter for establishing business relations, you had better follow the steps below:

- to inform of the source of the information you get about your addressee;
- to state your intention of establishing business relations;
- to give a brief introduction of your business scope, products, etc.;
- to show the reference to your firm's credit standing;
- to express your expectation for cooperation and an early reply.

【Sample 1】

这是一家中国丝绸出口商向一家经营丝织品的英国公司发出的要求建立业务关系的信函。写信人首先说明了他们获得信息的来源——对方驻北京使馆商务处，接着提出要建立贸易关系的要求，然后用一句话介绍了自己公司的主要业务，并告知对方信函中附有一份公司出口项目单，请其阅读并尽快回函。

Dear Sirs,

We have obtained your address from the Commercial Counselor of your embassy① in Beijing who has informed us that you are in the market for silk fabrics②.

We avail③ ourselves of this opportunity to approach you for the establishment of trade relations with you.

We specialize④ in the exportation of Chinese silk cloth, which has enjoyed great popularity in world market. We enclose a copy of our export list covering the main items suppliable⑤ at present and hope that you would contact us if any item is of interest to you.

We look forward to receiving your reply soon.

Yours faithfully,

Encl. Export List

① the Commercial Counselor of your embassy：使馆商务处　　② silk fabrics：丝织品　　③ avail...of...：利用
④ specialize in：专门（生产）　　⑤ suppliable：可供应的

敬启者：
　　我们从贵方驻北京使馆商务处得知贵公司经营丝织品业务，并获悉贵公司地址。
　　我们希望能利用这个机会与贵公司建立贸易关系。
　　我公司专营中国丝绸出口业务，我们的产品在很多国家备受欢迎。现附寄一份我公司出口商品目录，其中涵盖了目前我们能提供的主要产品。若贵公司对其中的产品感兴趣，望能接洽我们。
　　早复为盼。

敬上
附录：出口商品目录

[Sample 2]

　　这是一家南京电器用品进口商向波士顿电子公司提出进口业务要求的信函。写信人首先说明他们从因特网上得知对方的业务范围碰巧和自己公司相同，因此写信想要建立合作关系。接着简单介绍了其公司的业务状况并给对方提供了资信调查途径。最后提及对对方无绳电话的兴趣及对回复的期待。

Gentlemen,

Having obtained from the Web that your business scope① coincides② with us, we are writing to you in the hope of establishing business relations with you.

We have been in this line for many years and now we are one of the largest importers of electric goods in Nanjing. As to our credit standing③, we are permitted to mention the Bank of China, Nanjing, as a reference.

At present we are interested in your cordless phone④ and we look forward to hearing from you soon.

Yours truly,

① business scope：业务范围　　　　　② coincide...with...：与……巧合
③ credit standing：资信状况　　　　　④ cordless phone：无绳电话

> 先生们：
>   我们从网上了解到贵公司与我公司业务项目相同，故致函贵方希望建立贸易关系。
>   我公司进军电器行业多年，现在是南京电器业界的最大进口商之一。关于我公司的资信状况，贵公司可向中国银行南京分行咨询。
>   目前，我们对贵公司的无绳电话感兴趣，盼望尽快收到回函。
>
>   敬上

3) Notes & Analysis

(1) 大部分旨在建立商业关系的信函都不是写给特定的某个人，所以一般都称呼 Dear Sirs 或 Gentlemen，结束敬语用 Yours faithfully 和 Dear Sirs 呼应。

(2) 简洁是商务信函的重要特点。从上述几例可以看出，除了必要信息之外，每封信中都没有不相关的累赘信息。

(3) 由于旨在建立商业关系的信函其收信人是从未有过合作关系的潜在客户，因此信函语言较为礼貌正式。如在例1中，写信人用了 We avail ourselves of this opportunity to...，而非 We make use of this opportunity to....。

4) Useful Expressions

(1) Chamber of Commerce　商会
(2) Commercial Counselor's Office　商务参赞处
(3) business scope　业务范围
(4) in the line of/in the market for　在……行业
(5) specialize in　专营……
(6) enclose　附有……
(7) catalogue　商品目录
(8) On the recommendation of ..., we have learned that...　经……推荐，我们得知……
(9) Being specialized in the export/import of ..., we express our desire to trade with you in this line.
   我公司专营……进/出口业务，愿与贵公司建立业务关系。
(10) We enclose in this letter a copy of ..., if any item is of interest to you, ...
   随函附上一份……，若贵方对其中的任何一款感兴趣，……

5) Writing Practice

I. Fill in the blanks with the proper forms of the given expressions.

　　be of interest; refer to; enter into; fall within; enclosed; in the line of

(1) We are pleased to find that the articles you require _____ our lines.
(2) We have been _____ chemicals for more than ten years and now one of the largest exporters in China.
(3) Should any of the items _____ to you, please let us know.
(4) We desire to _____ mutually beneficial business relations with you.

(5) The _____ is a copy of our latest catalogue.
(6) As to our credit standing, you can _____ the Industrial and Commercial Bank of China, Guangzhou Branch.

II. Translate the following sentences into English.

(1) 我们从我方在荷兰代理人处得悉你们的地址，现特去函希望能与贵公司发展合作关系。
(2) 我们公司专营各种家用电器的进口业务。
(3) 信内附有我公司最新的带插图商品目录。如有兴趣，请即与我公司联系。
(4) 我们的开户银行是中国银行南京分行，该行可向贵公司提供我们公司的资信情况。

III. Translate the following letter into Chinese.

> Gentlemen,
>
> You were recommended to us by the Standard Chartered Bank, which told us that you are a prospective buyer of Chinese textiles and cotton piece goods. And these items fall within the business scope of our corporation.
>
> We are now in position to accept orders against customers' samples specifying design and packing requirements.
>
> In order to give you a rough idea of our products, we enclose a copy of our latest catalogue for your reference. If you find any of the items interesting, please let us know. And we shall be glad to send you quotations and samples upon receipt of your specific inquiries.
>
> We look forward to your early reply.
>
> Truly yours,

2. Making Enquiries（询盘）

1) What are letters for making enquiries?

询盘亦称询价或索盘，是买卖双方交易磋商的开始。按询问的内容划分，询盘有一般询盘和具体询盘。前者是指关于商品目录、价格单和样品的一般询问；而后者则是买方在有了比较明确的意向后关于某种具体商品的价格、包装、交货期、付款方式等的询问。按询盘双方的交易历史划分，询盘有首次询盘和非首次询盘。顾名思义，首次询盘信的写信方和收信方之间没有交易历史；而非首次询盘发生在有交易历史的买卖双方之间。询盘信的写信人有时将询盘信抄送给多个收信人，目的在于比较各收信人的报盘，以选择其中最优惠的报盘。

2) How to write a letter for making enquiries?

Since letters for making enquiries fall into two categories, the procedures to write them are somewhat different.

When writing a letter to a potential seller for making a general enquiry, you should follow similar steps to those in writing a letter for establishing business relations, that is, first you have to state how you came to know about the company, and provide some brief information about your firm, and then express your desire to establish trade relations and enquire about the catalogues, price list and so on.

However, if the receiver of your letter is already one of your established business partners, you can start directly with the specific information you would like your seller to send you. For example, you may want to know about the discounts your seller can offer regarding a particular piece of goods, method of payments, delivery time, etc. And when stating your enquiries, make sure that they are easy and clear to read.

Besides, the language you use in writing such a letter is comparatively informal and casual though polite also.

[Sample 1]

这是一封一般询盘信函。信中买方向卖方提出进口塑料玩具的意向，要求其提供产品范围特别是一些尚未进入中国市场的新产品信息。

Dear Sir or Madam,

We learn from the Web that you are a leading manufacturer[①] and sales agent[②] of plastic products in Hong Kong. We are much interested in importing plastic toys from Hong Kong. We should be obliged if you will let us have detailed information about the toy range you produce[③].

Please indicate any new items not yet introduced into the Chinese mainland and send some samples if possible.

We await your early reply. Thank you.

Yours faithfully,

---

① a leading manufacturer：主要制造商　　② sales agent：销售代理
③ We should be obliged if you will let us have detailed information about the toy range you produce.：若贵公司能给我们提供详细的玩具产品信息，我们将不胜感激。

××先生或女士：

我们从网上得知贵公司是香港塑料产品主要制造商及销售代理。我公司很有兴趣从香港进口塑料玩具。若贵公司能给我们提供详细的玩具产品信息，我们将不胜感激。

烦请标出其中尚未在内地引进的新款，且可能的话，希望能寄送一些样品。

此致谢意。候复。

敬上

Unit 10 Business Letters（商务书信）

[Sample 2]

这是一封具体询盘信函。询盘信的发信人向收信人询问了若干事项，如货样的发货期、FOB报价、织物面料、最小订货数量等。发信人将询问事项逐条列出，显得条理清晰，一目了然。

Dear Linda,

Could you please take some time to read this email very carefully and answer the following questions ASAP?

1. Please advise if there are any more sales samples to be sent? If so, when will you send the samples?
2. Please complete the attachment and return by Friday this week. I need the following information completed on my spreadsheet and then return to me.
A. FOB COST. (We will supply all labels and tickets.)
B. FABRIC USAGE. (This can be approximate.)
C. FABRIC GROUP MINIMUM. (Please be realistic, our orders are never very large but we will do our best to give you good orders all the time.)
D. MINIMUM QUANTITY PER STYLE. (I need to know what is the smallest quantity you can make in a style, for example, we may have three styles in a fabric group, the first has sold very well so we order 1,000 units, the second style has sold average so we will order 500 units and the last has sold poorly so we want to know what is the smallest qty that you are happy to make, for example 200 units.)
3. Following is a list of information I need for each fabric group. Please study each group carefully and send the fabric information in the same format as the example below.
Fabric Group：COTTON SPANDEX TWILL
Styles Numbers：T5W2244102 /T5W2457102 /T5W2726102
Construction：WOVEN 125X50 20X20 +40D
Composition 98% COTTON 2% SPANDEX
Finish：REACTIVE DYED AND PRINTED
Width：48/50″
Weight (g/m^2)：210
Weight (oz/yd^2)：5.2

I look forward to your reply.

Best regards.

George Petheriotis
Production & Logistics Manager

亲爱的琳达：
　　能仔细读一下这封邮件并尽快答复下列问题吗？

1. 是否会寄送更多的售卖样品？如是，什么时候寄送？
2. 请在本周五前填好附件表格并发回。我希望你在我的试算表上填写以下信息并发回。
   A. FOB 报价（我们将提供所有的标牌和票据）
   B. 织物面料（可以是大概）
   C. 最小订购量（请注意我们的订单一直不是太大但会尽量多订购）
   D. 每款最小订购量（我需要知道每一款可能生产的最小数量。举例来说，某一类织物有三款，第一款卖得很好，因此我们欲订购 1 000 件；第二款卖得一般，我们欲订购 500 件；最后一款卖得很糟，所以我们想要知道能订购的最小数量，比如 200 件。）
3. 以下是我需要知道的各织物类别的信息。请仔细核实并按相同格式回函。

   织物类别：棉花 斯潘德克斯弹性纤维 斜纹织物
   款号：T5W2244102/T5W2457102/T5W2726102
   编织：针织 125X50 20X20 +40D
   成分：98% 棉花 2% 斯潘德克斯弹性纤维
   涂层物：反应性染制及印花
   宽度：48/50″
   重量（g/m²）：210
   重量（盎司/yd²）：5.2

   望尽快回函。
   祝顺利。

   制造与物流管理经理
   George Petheriotis

[Sample 3]

这封询盘信的写信人从《新千年贸易指南》得知，英国全球贸易有限公司是经营办公用品的出口大户。由于希望与该公司建立贸易往来，现发函询问该公司出口行情，索要其经营出口的产品目录与价目表，并简要介绍了自己的业务范围。

Dear Sirs,

We are a trade company specializing in import and export of various commodities[①]. We learned from *Trade Guide for the New Millennium* that you are a leading exporter of office equipment[②], and are now writing to seek more information about the types of equipment that you can offer.

Would you please send us your latest catalogue and price-list[③]? We hope that this will be a good start for a long and profitable relation between us.[④]

Yours faithfully,

---

① various commodities：各种各样的商品　　② office equipment：办公设备
③ latest catalogue and price-list：最新的（商品）目录和价目单
④ We hope that this will be a good start for a long and profitable relation between us.：我们希望这会成为和贵公司长久互惠关系的良好开端。

敬启者：
    我们是一家专门从事各种货物进出口业务的贸易公司。我们从《新千年贸易指南》得知，贵公司是办公设备出口大户。遂去函希望了解贵公司更多的产品详情。
    能否给我们寄来最新的（商品）目录和价目单？我们希望这会成为和贵公司长久互惠关系的良好开端。

敬上

3）Notes & Analysis

（1）非首次询盘信的买卖双方由于之前有一定交易历史，相互间已经比较熟悉，信函的语气相对比较随意。如例 2 中信函开头发信人直接提出 "Could you please take some time to read this email very carefully and answer the following questions ASAP"，少了客套和拘谨。而且，非首次询盘信的发信人和收信人不再是泛指的 Dear sirs 和 Yours faithfully，而是具体的 Dear Linda 和 George Petheriotis。

（2）首次询盘信的买卖双方由于是初次联系，目的在于建立起贸易关系，因此信函语气更为礼貌和正式。如例 3 既是一封一般询盘信函，也可看作是一封要求建立商业联系的信函。另外，这封信充分体现了商业信函的效率原则。

4）Useful Expressions

（1）We are interested in your ... and shall be pleased to have your quotation for ...
我们对贵公司的……感兴趣，很希望得到贵方对……的报价。

（2）Please quote your best price for ... and state your best terms and discount allowable.
请贵方给我方报最优惠的价格，并告知最好的优惠条款和折扣。

（3）Would you send us your (lowest) quotation for ... ?
能否请贵方寄给我们关于……的最低报价？

（4）Please quote us your prices CIF/FOB/CFR London, ...
请给我们报伦敦 CIF/FOB/CFR 价。

（5）Should your price be found competitive and delivery date acceptable, we intend to place an order for ... with you.
若贵方报价具有竞争力并且到货日期合适，我方将打算订购……。

（6）When replying, please state delivery period, discounts and terms of payment.
请在回函中说明到货日期、折扣及付款方式。

（7）Will you please send us your catalogue and full details of your export prices and terms of payment, together with any samples you can let us have?
能否烦请贵方寄给我们一份产品目录及出口产品价格、付款方式详细资料，并尽可能附上相关样品？

（8）Details regarding specifications and designs will also be much appreciated.
如能附上产品规格、设计等详细资料，我们将不胜感激。

（9）We should be grateful/obliged if you could ...
若贵方能……，我们将非常感激。

5) Writing Practice

I. Translate the following expressions into English.

(1) 询盘　　　　(2) 价目单　　　(3) 供应商　　　(4) 付款条件
(5) 大宗折扣　　(6) 运费　　　　(7) 订货　　　　(8) 不可撤销信用证
(9) 报伦敦成本、保险加运费价　　(10) 佣金

II. Arrange the following sentences into the coherent body of a letter for making enquiries.

(1) Besides, we have confidence in the quality of Chinese products.
(2) It would also be appreciated if samples or brochures could be forwarded to us.
(3) We are interested to buy large quantities of Iron Nails of all sizes and should be obliged if you would give us a quotation per metric ton C. F. R. Lagos, Nigeria.
(4) We look forward to hearing from you by return.
(5) We used to purchase this article from other sources but we now prefer to buy from your corporation because we are given to understand you are able to supply large quantities at more attractive prices.

III. Compose the body of letters for making enquiries according to the situations below.

(1) 你公司拟进口4 500支"好朋友"牌铅笔，得知对方是文具经销大户，故致函询问FOB上海到岸价并索要具体目录及样品。
(2) 你公司经营各种纺织品进口业务，最近接到不少顾客关于全棉床单的询盘，因此致函供应商，希望对方提供有关全棉床单产品系列的详细情况，包括可供应的产品花色、尺寸及包装与装运计内的价格，并索要产品彩色图示（如目录或手册等）。

3. Making Offers and Counter-offers（报盘函和还盘函）

1) What are letters for making offers and counter-offers?

报盘函（Offers）是指卖方在接到买方询价函后，向买方报价、介绍商品情况、提出交易条件（如商品数量、价格、付款方式、交货日期等）时所写的一种商务书信。

根据报盘时有无规定期限来分，报盘有实盘（Firm Offer）和虚盘（Non-firm Offer）。实盘函中报盘人提出一定的交易条件，并规定报盘的有效期限，如"This offer is firm, subject to the receipt of your reply before 29th March."等。在有效期内报盘人不得随意改变和撤回报盘内容，报盘一经买方接受，买卖立即敲定。而凡是报盘时没有规定期限的都称为虚盘，虚盘对买卖双方都没有约束力。

另外，报盘函也分为主动报盘和非主动报盘。主动报盘是不经买方询价卖方主动提出的交易愿望和条件；而非主动报盘则相反，大部分的报盘都属于这一类，是应买方询价要求而作出的回应。

还盘函（Counter-offers）是指买方接到卖方的报盘以后，对其提出的交易条件感到不能接受或不能完全接受，为了进一步磋商交易而对不接受的条款提出修改意见的信函。有

Unit 10 Business Letters（商务书信）

时一笔交易的达成会经过报盘、还盘的多次往来才能成功。

2）How to write a letter for making offers and counter-offers?

To open a letter for making offers, you express your thanks for the enquiry and a mention of the exact date of the enquiry is usually preferred.

In the body part of an offer, list clearly the price and conditions upon which your are willing to sell your goods, such as prices of the different items, terms of payment, discounts, the least quantity of an order, shipment date, etc.

To conclude an offer, you can stress the quality of your commodities to build up confidence in your potential buyer as well as the advantages of your quotation. And you express your wish for an early order.

Besides, if you want to encourage further business, you can provide information about the other products available in your company apart from those they enquired about.

When making counter-offers, you first thank the person who made the offer, and repeat the exact conditions offered. Then you state the reasons why some of the conditions should be revised if an order is going to be placed. And then you suggest your desired conditions. At last, you express your wish of a successful business.

【Sample 1】

这封报盘函是卖方收到买方询价函后的回复。信中卖方先分别对茶杯、茶托、茶壶（2品脱容量）进行了报价，并提出付款要求——不可撤销即期信用证，然后说明可能的优惠及承诺发货日期。这封报盘函没有规定确定的期限，因而是虚盘函。

Dear Mr. White,

Thank you for your enquiry dated 8 January for teacups and teapots. We are pleased to quote as follows:

    Teacups: USD 1,200 per hundred

    Tea saucers: USD 1,000 per hundred

    Teapots (2-pint):   USD 15 per piece

    (The prices quoted include packing and delivery.)

We will allow you a discount of 20% if the order exceeds 100 items (100 inclusive)[①].

We require payment by irrevocable sight Letter of Credit, and we can guarantee delivery within 15 days after we receive the L/C[②].

Please contact us if you need any further information.

We look forward to receiving your order.

Yours sincerely,
Kevin Chou

① We will allow you a discount of 20% if the order exceeds 100 items (100 inclusive).：若贵方订单超过 100 件（包括 100 件），我们将给 20% 的折扣。
② We require payment by irrevocable sight Letter of Credit, and we can guarantee delivery within 15 days after we receive the L/C.：我们要求以不可撤销即期信用证付款，并承诺在收到信用证后 15 天内发货。

亲爱的怀特先生：
　　感谢贵公司 1 月 8 日来函询购茶杯和茶壶。我们很高兴做以下报盘：
　　茶杯：　　　　　　每 100 件 1 200 美元
　　茶碟：　　　　　　每 100 件 1 000 美元
　　茶壶（2-品脱）：　每件 15 美元
　　（以上报价包括包装和运费）。
　　若贵方订单超过 100 件（包括 100 件），我们将提供 20% 的折扣。
　　我们要求以不可撤销即期信用证付款，并承诺在收到信用证后 15 天内发货。
　　若贵方欲知更多详情，请联络我们。
　　盼早日收到贵方订单。

凯文·周
敬上

[Sample 2]

　　这封报盘函是一封实盘函，发盘人除具体规定了此项交易的商品真空吸尘器的牌号、数量、单价、发货期、付款方式外，还规定了报盘的有效期，即对方收到报盘后的五天内。最后，发盘人告知对方所报价格为最优惠价格，不再接受任何还盘。

Dear Sirs,

Referring to your letter of September 12 enquiring for our vacuum cleaner①, we are offering you 32,000 "Bright Moon" Brand vacuum cleaners, at USD 22 per piece CIF Vancouver for shipment in November, 2015. Payment is to be made by D/P at sight and we hope that it will be acceptable to you②. The offer is firm, subject to your reply to us within 5 days③.

The illustrated catalogues④ enclosed will show you the exact sizes and designs of our goods. In view of⑤ our long and friendly relations, the price we have quoted you is already the most favorable price and no counter-offer will be entertained⑥.

Your immediate confirmation of our offer is anticipated⑦.

Yours faithfully,

① Referring to your letter of September 12 enquiring for our vacuum cleaner,...: 鉴于贵公司9月12日来函询购真空吸尘器,……

② Payment is to be made by D/P at sight and we hope that it will be acceptable to you.: 我们要求以即期付款交单方式付款,希望贵方能接受。

③ The offer is firm, subject to your reply to us within 5 days.: 此报盘为实盘,以贵方5天内回函确认为准。

④ illustrated catalogues: 彩页目录

⑤ in view of: 鉴于……

⑥ ... no counter-offer will be entertained.: 我方将不接受还盘。

⑦ Your immediate confirmation of our offer is anticipated.: 期望贵方能尽快对我们的报盘进行确认。

敬启者:
　　鉴于贵公司9月12日来函询购真空吸尘器,我们现提供32 000台"明月"牌真空吸尘器,每台22美元,CIF温哥华价,2015年11月装船。我们要求以即期付款交单方式付款,希望贵方能接受。此报盘为实盘,以贵方5天内回函确认为准。
　　在附寄的彩页目录中,贵方将能看到产品确切的规格和设计。鉴于我们之间长久友好的业务关系,我方给出的已是最优惠报价,将不接受还盘。
　　期望贵方能尽快对我们的报盘进行确认。

敬上

[Sample 3]

　　这是一封还盘函,买方在接到卖方报盘后,不能接受童装夹克和裤子的报价,要求对方给出10%的折扣。

Dear Stephen,

We thank you for your offer of March 26 and for the samples you kindly sent us.

We appreciate the remarkable designs and the good quality of your products, but the prices you quote about kids jacket (USD 10.80/pc) and kids pants (USD 8.00/pc) are too high and will deprive us of any profit①.

So we suggest that you make some allowance, say 10% on your quoted prices②. We believe your allowance would help to introduce your goods to our customers.

Hope to hear from you soon.

Yours sincerely,
Cherry Wang

---

① ...deprive us of any profit: 我们将毫无利润　deprive...of: 剥夺(某人)……

② So we suggest that you make some allowance, say 10% on your quoted prices.: 因此我们建议贵方能给予一定的优惠,比如在原报价基础上给10%的折扣。

亲爱的史蒂芬：

  感谢你 3 月 26 日给我们发来报盘及相关样品。

  虽然我们很欣赏你们产品的非凡设计和良好品质，但是，你们儿童夹克（每件 10.80 美元）及童裤（每件 8.00 美元）的报价太高了，如果按此价格销售，我们将毫无利润。

  因此我们建议贵方能给予一定的优惠，比如在原报价基础上打 10% 的折扣。我们相信你们的折扣会让我们更好地向客户推荐你们的产品。

  盼早复。

切瑞·王
敬上

[Sample 4]

  这是卖方就例 3 的还盘作出的再报盘。例 3 中，买方要求卖方给出 10% 的折扣，但卖方认为 10% 的折扣将使其无利可图，而建议各让一半——5% 的折扣，并且条件是童装夹克和裤子各 500 件以上。

Dear Cherry,

Upon receipt of your counter-offer of March 28, we have made a very careful study.

As we two companies have done business with each other for so many years, we should like to grant your request to lower the price by 10%[①]. However, such practice will mean nil profit[②] to us. So let's meet half way[③]. We suggest a reduction of 5% on orders of 500 pieces for each. That is as follows:

Kid jacket: US $10.40/pc

Kid pant: US $7.70/pc

We hope our counter-suggestion will be acceptable to you and look forward to your orders.

Thanks and best regards,

Stephan Gerspach

---

① we should like to grant your request to lower the price by 10%.：我们很希望能同意贵方要求，降价 10%。
② nil profit：零利润　　③ So let's meet half way.：那就各退一步吧。

亲爱的切瑞：

  收到你方 3 月 28 日的还盘，我们就进行了仔细的研究。

  我们双方进行贸易多年，很希望同意你方要求，降价 10%。然而，这么大的降价幅度将使我们毫无利润可言，因此各退一步吧。我们建议在订单为 500 件的基础上每件降价 5%。具体价格如下。

  儿童夹克：10.40 美元/件

> 儿童长裤：7.70 美元/件
> 希望我们的提议能为你方所接受，盼收到你方订单。
> 谢谢并祝顺利。
>
> 史蒂芬·吉斯派克

3) Notes & Analysis

（1）准确的信息是报盘函的最重要特征。在进行报价时，要保证所报商品价格、品名、数量等条款的准确性，因为一个小错误很可能酿成大损失。如所报的商品价格单位是美元，报盘人往往应注明是美国美元还是加拿大美元，因为这两者的汇率是不一样的。上述几例均有注明是 US $。另外，在例 1 中，报盘人在商品的报价后说明 "The prices quoted include packing and delivery." 这一备注很重要，如果少了它，则有可能会在交易结款时引起纠纷。

（2）报盘还盘是交易能否达成的最关键步骤。讨价还价本是商家常事，因此无论报盘还盘，在直接清楚说明交易条件的同时，也仍要注意显得友好真诚，避免过于强硬冰冷的态度。不能因为一笔交易不成功而影响到以后的商业往来。举例说明，如例 2 中报盘方在说明不接受还盘时，先以 In view of our long and friendly relations, the price we have quoted you is already the most favorable price and … 作为铺垫，而不是冷冰冰地直接说 no counter-offer will be entertained。

还有，在例 3 中，买方在提出还盘条件后，接着说 We believe your allowance would help to introduce your goods to our customers。这就给对方一种感觉，还盘不仅是为了买方自己的利益，也可以增加卖方产品对顾客的吸引力。这正符合了商务书信的体谅原则。

（3）除了应买方询价要求发出的报盘，也有类似于推销信性质的主动报盘（Voluntary Offer）。

4) Useful Expressions

（1）Thank you for your enquiry of … and we are pleased to offer as follows, …
感谢贵方询购……，我们很高兴作出以下报价……

（2）We were pleased to receive your enquiry of … and we now offer you …
贵方……询购函已收悉，我方深感荣幸，现报盘如下。

（3）In view of our long and friendly relations, we have quoted you the most favorable price.
考虑到我们长久友好的业务关系，我方已给予最优惠的报价。

（4）You will find our price most acceptable if you compare it with that from others.
若贵方比较我们的报价与其他同类产品报价，会发现我们的报价是最优惠的。

（5）We will allow you a discount of … if your order exceeds …
若贵方订单超过……，我方将给予……的折扣。

（6）Please note that we offer special discounts on the following basis: …
请注意在以下情况下，我们将给予特别优惠。

（7）We guarantee delivery/shipment within … days after receiving the L/C.
我们承诺在收到信用证后……天发货。

(8) We feel you may be interested in some of our other products and enclose a descriptive booklet for your reference.
我们觉得贵方也许会对我公司其他产品感兴趣,遂附寄彩页产品宣传册以供参考。

(9) Much to our regret, the price you quoted is on the high side.
我们感到非常遗憾,贵方的报价实在是太高了。

(10) We suggest an allowance of ... on your quoted price.
我们建议贵方在报价基础上给予……的折扣。

(11) Should you be prepared to reduce your price by ..., we might come to terms.
若贵方能降价……,我们将考虑订货。

(12) Considering our long-standing mutual relationship, let's meet half way.
考虑到我们长久互惠的业务来往,我们再各让一半吧。

(13) The best we can do is to make a reduction of ... in our previous quotation.
我们能作出的最大让步就是在原报价基础上再降价……。

(14) We feel sorry to say that the price we quoted is our bottom price so we are unable to make a further reduction.
很遗憾,我们的报价已是最低,所以无法再降价。

5) Writing Practice

I. Translate the following expressions into English.

(1) 实盘　　(2) 虚盘　　(3) 反报价/还价　(4) 零售价　　(5) 批发价
(6) 船上交货价　(7) 成本加运费价　(8) 利润　　(9) 以……为准　(10) 确认

II. Translate the following sentences into Chinese.

(1) The prices quoted are for orders of invoice value below US$ 2,000. For larger orders we offer an extra 5% discount.

(2) We may entertain your order if you allow us a 3% discount.

(3) The offer is made subject to the goods being unsold.

(4) The shipment of the goods could be made immediately upon receipt of a firm order.

(5) We intend to send the goods in several equal lots.

(6) It seems that your price is on the high side, which prohibits us from placing an order with you.

(7) In view of your business amount, we would agree to meet you half way.

(8) It's a pity that we are unable to make a further reduction.

III. Compose a letter of offer by referring to the given notes.

商品:真皮手工制手套
报价(伦敦到岸价),按每款200副报价:
　　男式中号每副3美元;
　　男式小号每副2.8美元;

女式中号每副 2.6 美元；
女式小号每副 2.5 美元。

付款要求：即期信用证
装运时间：7 月份，以报盘方最后确认为准。

另外，询盘方要求报盘方邮寄一份目录及一套做手套用的各种皮革样品。

4. Placing Orders and Confirmation （订购并确认）

1) What are letters for placing orders and for confirmation?

订购函是买方接受卖方报价函后，向卖方发出的要求订购货物的商务信函。订购函可以采用一般商业书信的形式，但很多时候为了方便，也采用统一印刷格式的订货单。写订购函/单最重要的两点是要保证信息的精确、清楚。通常来说，买方需在订购函中标明商品目录编号或型号，准确无误地说明所需货物的品名（Name）、规格（Specification）、品质（Quality）、等级（Grade）、数量（Quantity）等细节，并交代清楚单价（Price）、包装（Packing）、装运方式（Shipping）、装运时间、交货（Delivery）时间和地点等各项交易条件。

当卖方在收到买方订购函后，一般应立即作出回复，表明是否接受对方订货。如接受，则要对买方提出货物数量、交货期、货款金额等订购条件进行确认。如卖方因供不应求等各种原因无法接受订单，也应及时回函，向买方说明情况并表示歉意。如有可能，卖方也可向买方推荐其他合适的替代货品。拒绝接受订单的信函要注意语气的委婉，要做到既坦诚又留有余地。

2) How to write a letter for placing orders and for confirmation?

As mentioned above, accuracy and clarity are especially important to an order letter. So when writing an order letter, you should include in it the following details:

- full details of the goods you order, such as the name, the item No., the specifications, the quantity, the unit price, etc.
- your requirements on packing and shipping, such as the date of shipment, the port of loading, destination, shipping marks, etc.
- your requirements on payment, such as terms and conditions, documents to be presented, bank details, etc.

An order letter usually concludes with a request for acknowledgement and speedy delivery.

When writing a letter for confirming an order, you should:

- express your pleasure and thanks for receiving the order;
- guarantee the quality of the goods the buyer ordered and ensure a prompt delivery of the goods;
- confirm the other important items such as the payment, etc.;
- express your wish for further orders in future.

【Sample 1】

这是一封订购函。开头买方先对卖方报价及附赠商品目录表示感谢，并表示对产品质量和价格都比较满意，进而提出订货要求。接着买方详细地列出所订购货物的名称、数量、货号、规格、单价等，并且对到货日期和付款方式提出了具体要求。

Dear Sirs,

Thank you for your quotation of March 10 and the illustrated catalogue. We find both the quality and the price satisfactory and take pleasure in enclosing our Order No. 287 for the following items:

Item	Quantity (dozen)	Size	Unit Price (per doz.)
Women's Nylon Garments	150	Small	USD 80.00
Ditto	150	Medium	USD 100.00
Ditto	150	Large	USD 120.00

We note that you can supply these items from current stock[①] and hope that they reach us no later than April 30.

For your reference, we wish to effect payment by[②] irrevocable L/C at sight. Please kindly let us have your confirmation.

Yours faithfully,

---

① supply these items from current stock：现货供应　　② effect payment by...：以……方式付款

敬启者：
　　感谢贵方 3 月 10 日发来的报盘及彩色产品目录。我们对产品质量和价格都很满意，很乐意向贵方订购下列产品，详见附件第 287 号订单：

项目	数量（打）	尺寸	单价（每打）
女士尼龙外套	150	小号	80.00 美元
同上	150	中号	100.00 美元
同上	150	大号	120.00 美元

　　我们注意到贵方有现货供应，还希望能在 4 月 30 日之前到货。
　　作为参考，我们希望能以不可撤销的即期信用证付款。请尽快回函确认。
敬上

【Sample 2】

这是一封订购确认函。卖方首先对买方的订货表示感谢，表示完全能按买方要求进行供货。进而确认了到货期及已和对方开户银行谈妥付款事宜。最后，卖方提醒买方填写随函附上的两份销售确认合同以供双方备案并表示今后继续发展交易的愿望。

Unit 10　Business Letters（商务书信）

Dear Sirs,

Thank you for your letter of August 16, 2016 and for the Order No. 8546 enclosed. We now have pleasure in confirming that we have all the items in stock and are now making up the order①. The goods can be shipped by the end of August and are due to arrive② in London on October 4, 2016.

We can also confirm that your banker, the Westminster Bank Ltd., have accepted our Draft for USD 10,310.80, payable within 60 days at sight and all the relevant documents have been successfully negotiated③.

Enclosed are two copies of our Sales Confirmation No. 97064 made out against your order mentioned above. Please kindly sign and return one copy for our file④.

It has been a pleasure doing business with you and we look forward to being of service to you again in the future.

Yours faithfully,
Longwear Shoes Ltd.

Encl.：two copies of Sales Confirmation No. 97064

①...making up the order：正在准备所订购货物　　②...are due to arrive：将于……到达
③...all the relevant documents have been successfully negotiated.：……所有相关单证都已商订备齐。　　negotiate：议付
④ for our file：以便我们存档

敬启者：
　　感谢贵方2016年8月16日来函并寄来第8546号订单。我们现在很高兴地向贵方确认，贵方订购的商品我们都能现货供应，并正在准备装船。我们将在8月底发货，货物将于2016年10月4日抵达伦敦。
　　我们同时向贵方确认，贵公司开户行——威斯敏斯特银行，已经接受我们开出的金额为10 310.80美元的汇票，将于见票后60天内付款，所有相关单证都已商订备齐。
　　兹附上我方第97064号销售确认书两份，以确认以上提到的贵公司第8546号订单。请签退一份，以备存档。
　　和贵公司进行贸易一直是我们的荣幸，盼望以后能更多地为贵公司提供服务。
Longwear 鞋业
敬上
附：第97064号销售确认书两份

［Sample 3］

　　这是一封订单拒绝函。买方欲向卖方订购真丝印花绸，但卖方由于库存短缺，无法满

足买方订购要求。但卖方建议买方尝试其新产品——"优莲"牌人造丝绸,卖方强调这款新品人造丝手感和质量都和真丝一样好,并且具有一定的价格优势。同时提出如订购数量够大的话,还将有特别折扣。

Dear Sirs,

We thank you for your order of April 15 for 15,000 yards of Printed Pure Silk Fabrics. But we regret to inform you that owing to shortage of stock, we are not in a position to supply you with the desired article①.

However, we would like to take this opportunity to recommend an excellent substitute②, our new "Youlian" Brand Rayon, which feels the same smooth as the pure silk and is not a little inferior in quality③, but 10% lower in price. The large number of repeat orders we have received from leading distributors④ and dress manufacturers is a good evidence of the popularity of this brand. So we are sure that it will also sell well in your country.

Furthermore, we usually allow a special discount of 5% on orders exceeding USD 100,000. The enclosed is a sample cutting⑤ for your reference. Please contact us ASAP if you are interested in it.

Yours faithfully,

---

① ... owing to shortage of stock, we are not in a position to supply you with the desired article.:由于库存短缺,我们暂时无法供应贵方所需要的货物。
② recommend an excellent substitute:推荐一款优良替代品　　③ not a little inferior in quality:质量一点也不逊色
④ leading distributors:主要分销商　　　　　　　　　　　⑤ a sample cutting:剪样

敬启者:
　　感谢贵公司4月15日向我们订购15 000码的真丝印花绸。但是很遗憾,由于库存短缺,我们暂时无法供应贵方所需要的货物。
　　然而,我们想利用此机会推荐一款优良的替代品,我们的新品牌——"优莲"牌人造丝绸,它有着和真丝一样光滑的手感,且质量也丝毫不逊色,但是价格却比真丝低10%。我们已从主要分销商及服装制造商处收到大量的重复订单,这充分证明了这一品牌的受欢迎程度。因此我们确信在你们国家也会销售得不错。
　　此外,我们通常对金额超过100 000美元的订单给予5%的特别折扣。附寄剪样供贵方参考。若贵方对这一产品感兴趣,请尽快联络我们。

敬上

---

3) Notes & Analysis

(1) 写订购函或订购确认函时,买方或卖方一般都会写上准确的订货单编号,如例1 "... enclosing our Order No. 287 ...",及例2 "Thank you for your letter of August 16,

2004 and for the Order No. 8546 enclosed."。这样做的目的，一方面是买卖双方为了方便自己公司备案，另一方面也是为了让对方更清楚地辨认。

(2) 在卖方向买方确认接受其订购要求时，有时会随函附上一式两份的销售合同或销售确认书，要求对方仔细核对后签字并返还其中的一份，如例2。经双方签字后的销售合同或销售确认书具有法律约束力，若其中的一方违反了合同规定或条款，另一方可要求相应的赔偿或提起诉讼。

(3) 当卖方因种种原因不能接受买方订货要求时，也要及时回函表达歉意，诚恳地说明不能接受的原因。如有可能，可向对方推荐相当的替代品，以显示与对方保持业务的诚意。如在例3中，卖方先诚恳且礼貌地解释了为什么不能供货"But we regret to inform you that owing to shortage of stock, we are not in a position to. ..."接着提出"However, we would like to take this opportunity to recommend an excellent substitute, ..."并对新产品做了一定介绍。这样一来，卖方的拒绝函便很可能成为下一笔业务的开始。

4）Useful Expressions

(1) an initial order 首次订货
(2) a repeat order 续订
(3) a standing order 长期订单
(4) ocean transport 海运
(5) rail transport 铁路运输
(6) air transport 空运
(7) container transport 集装箱运输
(8) international multimodal transport 国际多式联运
(9) place an order 下订单
(10) take/accept an order 接受订单
(11) confirm/acknowledge an order 确认订单
(12) decline an order 拒绝订单
(13) deliver an order 发货
(14) arrange shipment 安排船期
(15) Please find the enclosed order sheet for further details. 详细情况请查收附寄订单。
(16) Please find enclosed our Order No. ... for ...
   请查收附寄订单……号……（货物）
(17) Please accept our order as follows：... 请接受以下订购。
(18) Please acknowledge acceptance of our order, and confirm the conditions stated above.
   请告知订单收到，并确认其中各条款。
(19) Please note that delivery should be completed before ...
   请注意必须在……之前发货。
(20) Please note that the goods must reach us by ... at the latest.
   请注意最晚到货期为……
(21) Please kindly confirm the above order. 请确认上述订购要求。

(22) Thank you for ordering . . .　感谢贵方订购……

(23) We thank you for your Order No. . . .　感谢贵方发来第……号订货单。

(24) We are pleased to receive your Order No. . . . and confirm that we have all the items in stock.　很高兴收到贵方第……号订货单，我们向您确认贵方所订购的货物我们全部能现货供应。

(25) Upon/On receipt of your relevant credit, we shall not fail to effect shipment in time.
一俟收到对方有关信用证，我们会及时办理装船。

(26) We trust the consignment will prove to be satisfactory.
我们相信货物会使贵方满意的。

(27) We hope that you will place repeat orders with us in the near future.
我们希望贵方在不久的将来向我方续订货物。

(28) We regret to inform you that we are unable to entertain your order of . . . , owing to . . .
很遗憾，由于……，我们现无法接受贵方对……的订购要求。

5) Writing Practice

I. Fill in the blanks with the words or phrases given.

| Purchase Confirmation | the package | offer | dispatch |
| for our file | satisfactory | sample | the first order |

Dear Sirs,

Please _____ to us 12,000 pairs of sheep leather gloves as the terms stated in your _____ of March 25.

Would you please take special care of the quality and _____ of this order? The leather should be of the same quality as that used in the _____. We hope that you can pack each pair in an airtight polythene bag, a dozen pairs of gloves in a box and then 20 boxes to a strong seaworthy wooden case. We will order more if _____ with you proves to be _____.

We are enclosing our _____ No. 2003-398 in duplicate for your signature. Please sign and return one copy _____. Upon receipt of your confirmation, an L/C will be issued.

Sincerely yours,

II. Translate the following sentences into English.
(1) 我公司对贵公司各种型号的自行车感兴趣，决定试订一批。
(2) 我方客户急需这些货物，望早日发货装运为盼。
(3) 相关信用证已由中国银行上海分行开立。在收到信用证后，请安排装船，并以传真通知船名及起航日期。
(4) 接受订单后三周内交货，货款以不可撤销的信用证、凭即期汇票支付，海险由我方承保。

(5) 贵方9月20日第WG721/BP号订单已收阅,谢谢。

(6) 很抱歉,由于大量承约我们暂不能接受你方1 000台计算机的订单。

Ⅲ. Read carefully the order letter below and then write a confirmation letter to the buyer.

Dear Sirs,

We have received with thanks your letter of February 21 and all samples. We have now examined your samples and are satisfied with both quantity and prices. Please accept our order for the following items:

1,200 doz. silk handkerchiefs at $2.00 each, $2,400
2,000 pair tan pig skin leather shoes, size 6 at $4.00 each, $8,000
3,000 doz. assorted orlon socks at $1.50 each, $4,500
TOTAL $14,900
Delivery: By the end of March, 2001
Payment: Draft at sight under irrevocable L/C
Invoice: Commercial Invoices in triplicate

The order No. 16 must be stated on all invoices and correspondence. Final shipping instructions will be enclosed later. We request you to acknowledge acceptance of our order, and to confirm the condition stated above.

Faithfully yours,

---

5. Making Payments(付款)

1) What are letters for making payments?

国际贸易中最常见的付款方式是信用证,即 L/C(Letters of Credit)。

信用证是由买方银行开立的以卖方为受益人的保证付款的书面凭证。信用证上的条款包括信用证本身的说明、有关交易货物的详细信息(货物名称、数量、规格、单价、装运、包装等)、信用证付款所要求的各种单证等。因此,卖方在收到买方银行开出的信用证时,应仔细审核信用证上的各条款,审核无误后即可按销售协议发货。若卖方审核时发现信用证条款有误,如有些条款与销售协议不符,或无法按信用证规定装运日期交货,应及时提醒或要求买方对信用证作出修改,以保证交易的顺利完成。

因此,付款信函的撰写可能是为了不同的目的,如建议开立信用证、买方通知信用证已开立、卖方催开信用证、信用证条款的修改、要求延长信用证装运日期等。

2) How to write a letter for making payments?

When you as a buyer writes to tell the seller that an L/C has been opened, you should make clear the following details:

- what L/C has been opened(L/C No., credit amount)

- the name of the opening/issuing bank
- the validity of the L/C
- documents required (usu. documents related to goods, transport documents, insurance documents, etc.)

When you as a seller writes to ask for amendment to an L/C, you should first remind the buyer of what you both parties have originally agreed on, then state your reason clearly and sincerely why an amendment has to be made. For example, you may want to extend the date of delivery because you failed to book a ship, or you may point out a careless mistake made by the opening bank. Finally, you ask for the understanding of the buyer and express that their effort to amend the L/C would be appreciated.

[Sample 1]

在下面这封信函中，买方在向卖方订货时建议用信用证付款。

Dear Sirs,

We would like to place an order for 100 IBM ThinkPad R51 2887E5C computers at your price of US $1,300 each, CIF Guangzhou, for shipment during July/August.

We would like to pay for this order by a 30-day L/C. This is a big order involving① US $130,000 and, since we have only moderate cash serves, tying up funds for three or four months would cause problems for us②.

We much appreciate the support you have given us in the past and would be most grateful if you could extend this favor to us③. If you are agreeable, please send us your contract.

On receipt, we will establish the relevant L/C immediately.

Yours faithfully,

---

① a big order involving…: 一笔涉及……的大订单
② …since we have only moderate cash serves, tying up funds for three or four months would cause problems for us.: 我们只有适量现金储备，占用资金三四个月将造成麻烦。
③ …extend this favor to us.: 继续给予优惠

敬启者：
　　我们欲按贵公司报价条件，以每台1 300美元的价格，CIF广州价，订购100台IBM ThinkPad R512887 E5C计算机，于7至8月装船。
　　这项交易款额高达130 000美元，我们只有适量现金储备，占用资金三四个月将造成麻烦，故建议以30日有效期的信用证付款。

Unit 10　Business Letters（商务书信）

承蒙贵公司一向照顾，若能继续给予优惠，我们将感激不尽。如同意上述建议，烦请寄来合同，一俟收到，我们将立即开立信用证。

敬上

【Sample 2】

这是一封买方发出的通知卖方信用证已开立的信函。信中买方首先明确说明了信用证的开立行、金额及有效期。接着指出该信用证授权卖方在每次装运5箱货物后按其发票金额开立以旧金山商业银行为付款人的见票后60天付款的远期汇票。最后提醒卖方银行汇票承兑所要求的单据：提单一式三份、伦敦到岸价发票一份、保险凭证或保险单及原产地证。

Dear Sirs,

This is to inform you that we have now established an irrevocable letter of credit in your favor① for the amount of £6,000 with the Commercial Bank of San Francisco, valid until April 30.

The terms of the credit authorize you to draw at 60 days on the bank in San Francisco for the amount of your invoices after each shipment of five cases②. Before accepting the draft, which should include all charges to London, the bank will require you to produce the following documents③: bills of lading in triplicate④, one copy of the invoice covering CIF London⑤, a certificate or policy of insurance⑥ and certificate of origin⑦.

We will expect your first consignment about the middle of next month.

Yours faithfully,

① establish an irrevocable letter of credit in your favor：开立以你方为受益人的不可撤销信用证
② The terms of the credit authorize you to draw at 60 days on the bank in San Francisco for the amount of your invoices after each shipment of five cases.：该信用证授权贵方在每批5箱货物装运后，按发票金额开立以旧金山商业银行为付款人的见票后60天内付款的远期汇票。
③ Before accepting the draft, which should include all charges to London, the bank will require you to produce the following documents.：在承兑汇票前，银行将要求贵方出示以下单证；汇票款额包括货物装运至伦敦的所有费用。
④ bills of lading in triplicate：提单一式三份　　⑤ the invoice covering CIF London：伦敦到岸价发票
⑥ a certificate or policy of insurance：保险证明/单　　⑦ certificate of origin：原产地证

敬启者：
　　兹通知贵方我们已向旧金山商业银行开立以贵方为受益人的金额为6 000英镑的不可撤销信用证，该证有效期至4月30日。
　　该信用证授权贵方在每批5箱货物装运后，按发票金额开立以旧金山商业银行为付款人的见票后60天内付款的远期汇票。在承兑汇票前（汇票款额包括货物装运至伦敦的所有费用），银行将要求贵方出示以下单证：提单一式三份，伦敦到岸价发票一份，保险证明/单及原产地证。

我们期待着下月中旬收到贵方发来的第一批货物。

敬上

[Sample 3]

这是一封催开信用证函。由于没有在销售确认书规定的日期4月22日按时收到买方寄来的信用证，卖方无法按时发货，因此去函催促买方尽快开立信用证，以保证买卖的顺利进行。

Dear Sirs,

We are writing concerning our Sales Confirmation No. TE136 for Silk Shirts, which stipulates that L/C reach us by 22 April, 2017. However, up to the present we have not received your L/C. This caused us some inconvenience and has made it difficult for us to complete shipment before the scheduled date.

We are, therefore, requesting you to open the relevant L/C immediately. We should appreciate your immediate attention to this matter.

Yours sincerely,

敬启者：
我们第TE136号关于丝绸衬衫的销售确认书规定，贵方应于2017年的4月22日之前将信用证寄给我方。然而，迄今为止我们未收到贵方的信用证。这给我们造成了一些不便，使得我们很难在预定的日期前完成装运。
因此我们请求贵方立刻开立相关信用证。望即刻处理，不胜感激。

敬上

3) Notes & Analysis

当买方由于种种原因未能及时开出信用证时，卖方通常应及时去函提醒其尽快开立信用证，以免耽误发货期。写催促函时，要注意语气的适当。如例3中，卖方的信函语言既显示了适当的急切，但又不至于过于急躁粗鲁。

4) Useful Expressions

（1） irrevocable L/C   不可撤销信用证
（2） revocable L/C   可撤销信用证
（3） confirmed L/C   保兑信用证
（4） unconfirmed L/C   不保兑信用证
（5） documentary L/C   跟单信用证

（6）Please open an irrevocable L/C for ... in favor of ...
请开立以……为受益人的不可撤销信用证

（7）This L/C remains valid until ... inclusive. 此信用证有效期至……（包含……）

（8）For your information, we have instructed our bank, ... Bank, to open a confirmed L/C for ...
根据贵方要求，我方已要求我们的开户行——……银行开立……保兑信用证。

（9）We wish to remind you that the date of delivery is approaching, but we have not received the covering L/C.
我方欲提醒贵方注意，发货期将至，但我方至今尚未收到贵方开来的信用证。

（10）We have received your L/C No. ..., but we find it contains the following discrepancies:
... 我方已收到贵方开来的第……号信用证，但发现其中有一些与先前协议不符之处。

5) Writing Practice

I. Translate the following into English.

（1）开立以某人为受益人的信用证   （2）修改信用证
（3）催开信用证   （4）装运单据
（5）开证行   （6）议付行
（7）远期信用证   （8）即期信用证
（9）可转让信用证   （10）截止期

II. Translate the following into Chinese.

（1）Please be informed that a confirmed, irrevocable L/C bearing No. 36745 has been established in your favor through the Bank of China, Nanjing Branch on 21 June 2004 for US $ 32,000. The credit will remain valid until 21 July, 2004. Please make arrangements to effect shipment before 21 July.

（2）The payment is available for 100% of invoice value against your draft drawn on us at sight.

（3）Documents must be dispatched by courier services in one cover to the Hong Kong and Shanghai Banking Co., Ltd.

（4）Under such circumstances, we regret having to ask for a two-week extension of the L/C covering Order No. 3661.

III. Write a letter to ask for amendment to L/C according to the notes given below.

已收获你方通过利物浦标准渣打银行开立的、关于我方第1249号销售确认书项下的第4785号信用证。信用证规定货物装运不得迟于5月21日且不可转船。但尽管我方一直多方努力准时订舱，却仍被告知5月26日以前没有直达船开往你方港口。因此，请求你方将装运日期和信用证有效期分别延迟至5月31日和6月16日或允许转船。

6. Shipping（装运）

1) What are letters of shipping?

国际贸易中最常用的运输方式是海运（Ocean Transportation），海运可以是班轮或不定期货船。就装运方式而言，集装箱服务最受欢迎。货物的装运不一定总是整批装运，有时是分批装运（Partial Shipment）。在无法直运的情况下，就需要转运（Transshipment）。但这些装运条件都应在销售合同及信用证中标示清楚。

装运信函的主要目的有，卖方告知买方装运事宜、卖方通知买方货物已装运、买方催促卖方尽快装运等。

2) How to write a letter of shipping?

The most common letter of shipping is shipping advice, which is written by the seller to inform the buyer of the completion of shipment. A typical shipping advice contains three sections:

① informing that shipment has been completed and giving details concerning the order No., shipping date, means of shipping, destination, etc.

② reminding of the enclosed/attached shipping documents or other relevant documents such as packing list, insurance policy, etc.

③ assuring satisfaction or hoping for further services

[Sample 1]

这封信函的目的在于通知买方装运事宜。信函中卖方既详细又简洁地说明了装运货物的订单货号、承运船务公司的名称、船名、启程日期、抵达日期、抵达港口。并在最后承诺次日将空寄相关单据以供买方提货。

Dear Linda,

We are pleased to inform you that your Order No. 221 has now been shipped by M/S Ever Golden of the Evergreen Shipping Co., Ltd., sailing on 14 July from Guangzhou and is due to arrive at Liverpool sometime in early August.

As is our normal practice, we are sending you tomorrow by registered airmail the B/L, invoice and insurance certificate.

Sincerely yours,
Richard Jiang

亲爱的琳达：

我们很高兴通知你，你们第221号订单下的货物现已装上长荣海运"长富"号轮。轮船将于7月14日由广州起航，预期于8月上旬抵达利物浦。

根据惯例，我们将于明天空寄提单、发票及保险凭证给你。

理查德·江敬上

Unit 10　Business Letters（商务书信）

【Sample 2】

这是一封买方发给卖方，要求更改装运目的港的信函。信中买方解释因为原指定目的港的罢工事件，建议将货物先运至鹿特丹港口，再经铁路运输至目的地。买方承诺将承担额外运输费用并提醒卖方加固包装。

Dear Sirs,

Referring to our Order No. 956-S2, we are writing to you asking for an alteration[①] in port of destination as the strike going on at our port shows no sign of letting up[②] for at least another two weeks.

Please ship the goods in question[③] to us via Rotterdam within the original time of shipment. The extra expenses arising from transshipment will be borne with us[④]. Owing to the increased distance, the goods will have to be sent to us by rail after they arrive at Rotterdam. Please pay special attention to the packing and make sure that it is suitable for the long voyage and can withstand rough handling[⑤].

Your understanding and early reply will be greatly appreciated.

Yours faithfully,

---

① alteration：改变，更改　　② let up：停止　　③ in question：被谈论的
④ The extra expenses arising from transshipment will be borne with us.：由于转运造成的额外费用将由我方承担。
⑤ withstand rough handling：经得起粗重搬运

敬启者：
　　关于第956-S2号订单下货物，由于目的港工人罢工仍在持续，且迹象表明至少两周内不会停止，故致函贵方请求更改目的港。
　　请于原定时间将货物经由鹿特丹港口转运。因转运造成的额外费用将由我方承担。由于货物抵达鹿特丹后，仍须经火车运送，路途增加，故烦请贵方特别注意包装以确保货物能经受长途运输及任何粗重搬运。
　　若贵方能理解我方处境并早日回复，将不胜感激。

　　敬上

【Sample 3】

这是一封催促卖方尽快装运的信函。信中买方开门见山表明其迫切想知道其3271号订单下300打女式皮手套装运情况的心情，接着提醒对方其客户急需这些货物，敦促早日交货，因此希望卖方能尽快发货，否则将会给其带来不便甚至损失。最后买方提醒卖方信用证就要到期并且不能再次延期。

Dear Sirs,

We are very anxious to know about the shipment of our Order No. 3271 for 300 dozens of women's leather gloves. We sent you an irrevocable L/C for this order a month ago but up to the present we haven't received any news about the shipment.

As you have been informed, our buyers are in urgent need of① the goods and are in fact pressing us for assurance② of early delivery. Thus we hope you inform us of the delivery time and effect shipment as soon as possible since any delay would cause us inconvenience and financial loss③.

And finally we feel it our duty to remind you that the L/C expires④ on March 21, 2017 and it is impossible for us to extend it again.

We are looking forward to your reply ASAP.

Faithfully yours,

① in urgent need of：急需……　② assurance：承诺，保证　③ financial loss：经济损失　④ expire：终止，到期

敬启者：
　　我方迫切地想知道我方第3271号订单项下300打女式皮手套的装运情况。我方已于一个月前寄给贵方不可撤销信用证，但至今仍未收到任何装运通知。
　　我们曾告知贵方，我方客户急需该货，并一直在敦促我们确保尽早到货。因此我们希望贵方尽快告知我方交货时间并办理装船，因为任何耽搁都将会给我们带来不便和经济损失。
　　最后，我们必须提醒贵方，我们的信用证将于2017年3月21日到期，且不可能再延期。
　　早复为盼。

敬上

3) Notes & Analysis
(1) 当买卖双方是较为熟悉的交易伙伴时，装运通知函往往写得更为简洁。如例1中，卖方除了提供必要的装运信息外，并没有使用任何套话，如We hope the goods will be to your entire satisfaction and we look forward to . . . 。
(2) 有时因为一些不可预测的原因，买方或卖方需要更改原定装运条款。这时买方或卖方应及时去函向对方告知装运条款更改事宜，并请求对方的谅解和合作。这类信函的写法可参照例2。

4) Useful Expressions
(1) consignment　　装运的货物
(2) consignor　　发货人

(3) consignee 收货人

(4) shipping space 船/舱位

(5) shipping agents 装运代理人

(6) the carrier 承运人

(7) draw a draft 开具汇票

(8) seaworthy packing 适于海运的包装

(9) Please make sure that the packing is suitable for a long sea voyage.
请确保包装能经得住长途海运。

(10) Your order No. ... will be shipped by ... on ...
贵方第……号订单货物将于……月……日装运。

(11) The duplicate shipping documents including Bill of Lading, Invoice, Packing List, and Inspection Certificate will be sent to you today.
我方今天会将一式两份的装运单据包括提单、发票、包装单、检验证等寄送贵方。

(12) We are writing to inform you that we have dispatched your goods ... by ... on ...
现去函通知贵方货物已于……月……日通过……发出。

(13) In accordance with your instructions, the goods are packed in ... and we are sure that they will reach you in good order.
根据贵方要求,我方将货物以……包装,并确信它们将安全无损抵达。

(14) Much to our regret, we cannot ship the goods within the time limit of the L/C owing to ...
很遗憾,由于……,我方未能在信用证有效期内及时发货。

(15) Your delay in shipping has placed us in an awkward position, and if prompt delivery cannot be effected again, we will feel sorry to cancel the order because ...
贵方未及时发货使我方处境尴尬,若收函后仍不能进行装运,我们将不得不取消订货,因为……。

5) Writing Practice

I. Translate the following terms into Chinese.

(1) port of loading   (2) port of unloading   (3) shipping marks
(4) cargo vessels   (5) container vessels   (6) Bill of Lading
(7) Shipping by Chartering (8) Certificate of Origin   (9) Packing list
(10) Commercial Invoice

II. Fill in the blanks with a word or expression that fits best.

Dear Sirs,

We are sorry to receive your letter of 18 March, _____ about the delay in _____ . The _____ was _____ factors we could not have known about when we signed the _____ and accepted your _____ . Now we are doing everything in our power to guarantee the delivery _____ two days. We apologize once again for the _____ the delay has caused you.

III. Translate the following sentences into English.

（1）我们很高兴地通知贵方，你们的第1134号订单现已装运妥当，将乘"东风"轮明日起航。
（2）请查收并确认附件中有关运输单据。
（3）我们在第310号销售合同中同意贵方于2016年6月交货，但现在因客户急需，欲提前至4至5月交货。
（4）我们很抱歉地通知贵方，由于船位没有及时订妥，不得不延迟至下月发货。请尽快回函确认。
（5）该批货物将于10月8日由厦门乘"水手"号轮船起航，预计于10月23日运抵伦敦。
（6）为保证及时交货，请允许转船。

7. Complaints & Claims（投诉和理赔）

1) What are letters of Complaints & Claims?

国际贸易中争议的发生可能有很多原因，如货物装运延迟、货物损坏、货物质量不合格、货物与样品不符等。当争议发生时，遭受损失的一方往往会根据合同或法律向对方提出赔偿要求，也称索赔（Complaints/Claims），而对方对索赔要求的受理（同意或拒绝赔偿）则称为理赔（Reply to Complaints/Claims）。

索赔要求的提出有一定的期限规定，一般是在到货后30天内提出，逾期则无权索赔。索赔函应开门见山、清楚明白、有理有据。受理索赔方（卖方或承运人或保险公司等）在接到索赔要求后，也应及时妥善处理。如确实是自己的责任，应诚恳表示歉意并承诺赔偿；如不是，也应清楚说明原因并礼貌拒绝赔偿。

2) How to write a letter of Complaints & Claims?

To write a letter of complaints/claims, you should follow these steps：

- feel sorry to complain about or claim for ... and state exactly the details of damage, loss, etc.
- provide evidence of damage/loss and explain why you have the right to complain or claim
- suggest compensation or settlement

To write a reply to complaints/claims, you should follow these steps：

- feel sorry to receive the complaints/claims
- acknowledge the loss and assume responsibility for it or refuse to take responsibility and explain why
- apologize again and ensure the settlement/compensation or suggest claims with whoever should be responsible for the loss

【Sample 1】

这是一封索赔函。买方在收到货物后发现10箱瓷器中有两箱已完全破损，无法出售，故致函要求对方调换或再给20%的折扣。并附寄破损货物报告和发票。

Unit 10　Business Letters（商务书信）

Dear Sirs,

We duly received the 10 cases of porcelain you sent us on 26 June, but regret to find on examination that 2 cases have been wholly damaged in transit. As the damaged porcelain becomes unsuitable for selling and not of use to us, we have to request a replacement for them or a special allowance of 20%.

Please find attached a copy of Damaged Cargo Report and the Invoice and let us know how you propose to do as soon as possible.

Yours faithfully,

敬启者：
　　我方已于6月26日准时收到贵方发来的10箱瓷器，但是经过检查，非常遗憾地发现其中的2箱在运输过程中已完全破损。由于破损瓷器无法销售，对我们已没有用处，因此我们要求贵方予以调换或给20%的折扣。
　　请查核附件中破损货物报告及发票，并尽快告知我们贵方的处理建议。

敬上

[Sample 2]

　　这封索赔函中买方的索赔理由是货物质量不合格。原合同规定买方订购的液化氮纯度为99.99%，但经检验，实际收到的液化氮纯度为99.9%，因此买方要求卖方赔偿其质次损失及检验费共10 500美元。

Dear Sirs,

With reference to the consignment of Liquid Nitrogen which reached us on 4 July, we, on examination, regret to inform that the quality is not in conformity with[①] what we agreed in the contract[②].

What we ordered is Liquid Nitrogen with a purity[③] of 99.99%, but we just received the Survey Report from Qingdao Commodity Inspection Bureau evidencing the purity of 99.9%. We are now sending you the original copy of Inspection Certificate and we hereby formally lodge a claim against[④] you as follows:

Our claim on poor quality　　　US $ 10,000
Plus survey charge　　　　　　US $ 500

Total amount of claim   US $ 10,500

Your early settlement will be appreciated.

Yours faithfully,

① in conformity with：与……一致　　② contract：合同
③ purity：纯度　　④ lodge a claim against：对……提起索赔

敬启者：
　　关于7月4日收到的液化氮，通过检验，我们很遗憾地告知贵方其质量与我们在合同中约定的不符。
　　我们订购的是纯度为99.99%的液化氮，但是我们刚刚收到的来自青岛商检局的调查报告表明，该液化氮纯度仅为99.9%。我们现在将检验证书原件寄给贵方，并正式向贵方提起以下索赔条件：

　　　　　　　　质量损失　　　　　10 000 美元
　　　　　　　　检验费用　　　　　　 500 美元
　　　　　　　　总索赔额　　　　　10 500 美元

　　若贵方能尽早处理，将不胜感激。

敬上

【Sample 3】

这是一封理赔函。卖方由于装箱失误给对方带来了不便，真诚道歉并表示已及时作出补救措施，即于当天上午将9 000支圆珠笔及相关单据空寄给对方。最后卖方再次表示歉意并承诺以后不再发生类似失误。

Dear Ms. Leung,

Thank you for your fax of 17 January. We are extremely sorry to learn that an error was made in Carton 16 of the above order. The missing 9,000 ball pens were sent this morning by Virgin Airways and the documents have already been forwarded to you.

We greatly regret the inconvenience caused by the errors and offer our sincere apologies. We can assure you that every effort will be made to ensure that similar errors do not occur again.

Yours sincerely,
Robert Williams

Unit 10　Business Letters（商务书信）

亲爱的 Leung 女士：
　　感谢您 1 月 17 日发来的传真。我们非常抱歉将上次订单下货物发错。我们今天上午已经通过维珍航空将丢失的 9 000 支圆珠笔空运给贵公司，相关单证也已寄出。
　　对于我们的失误给贵方带来麻烦，深感抱歉。我们向您确保以后将尽力避免类似失误。

罗勃特·威廉斯敬上

【Sample 4】

　　这是一封理赔函。理赔方（卖方）首先对对方遭受的损失表示遗憾，接着解释这些瓷器在离港时仍处于完好状态，因此损失并非由自己所造成，对方应向船务公司索赔。

Dear Sirs,

We much regret to receive your complaint about the damage to the porcelain we sent you on 9 May, 2018 by SS Victory.

However, we would like to assure you that the goods were packed with great care strictly in accordance with your instructions and were in perfect condition when they left here, and the damage must have occurred by rough handling during transit. Thus we assume we are not responsible for① the damage and we suggest you lodge your claim with the shipping company.

At any rate, we are deeply sorry to learn from you about this unfortunate incident and we hope you will be able to find a satisfactory settlement② soon.

Yours faithfully,

① be responsible for：对……负有责任　　② settlement：解决

敬启者：
　　我们从贵方 5 月 9 日来函中遗憾地获悉，我方经由"胜利"号发运给贵方的瓷器已破损。
　　然而，我们向贵方保证，货物是严格遵照贵方的包装要求仔细包装的，在发运时完整无损。所以货物破损一定是由于运输过程中的粗重搬运引起的。因此我们认为此损失不应由我方负责，我们建议贵方向船务公司提出索赔。
　　无论如何，我们对这次不幸事故深感抱歉，并希望此事能尽快得到满意解决。

敬上

　　3）Notes & Analysis
（1）在写索赔函时，应注意信函的语气。应尽量客观、克制地表示不满，避免过于情绪化和粗鲁的语言。比如，在例 1 中，撰写者在陈述损失要求赔偿时，用了非常客观的语言 As the damaged porcelain becomes unsuitable for selling and not of use to us, ... 而不是带有愤怒情绪的 You have made us such a loss that...。又如在例 2 中，撰写者用了第一人称强调我方的损失，而不是贸然指责对方怎样。如 What we ordered is..., but we just received...。事实上，这样的长句表达本身也缓和了不满的语气，使索赔函不至于显得过于激愤，有利于问题的解决。

(2) 在受理索赔时，如受理方发现对方所遭受的损失并非自己的责任，也应礼貌拒绝索赔。做到有理有节。如例 4 中，卖方在解释为什么损失不是由自己方面造成时，用了较为正式的语体。如 However, we would like to assure you that... 以及 Thus we assume we are not responsible for the damage and we suggest...。最后，尽管损失并非由自己造成，卖方仍礼貌、耐心地再次表示遗憾并希望该问题能尽快得到满意解决。

4) Useful Expressions

(1) We duly received the goods of Order No. ... and we thank you for the prompt shipment. However, when opening the case, we found that...
我方已按时收到贵方发来的第……号订单下货物，对此深表感激。但开箱时我们发现……

(2) While appreciating your prompt shipment, however, we found ... cases were broken with the result that...
对于贵方及时发货我们深表感谢，但是，其中的……箱货物在到达时已破损，由此造成……

(3) Please find enclosed a Survey Report, ... etc. in support of our claim.
随函寄上的货物破损调查报告可以作为我方的索赔佐证。

(4) We guess it was a mistake, and we hope you can look into the matter and let us have your suggestions about the disposition of incorrect shipment very soon.
我们猜测这是个装运失误，希望贵方能认真查此事并尽快告知我方你们的处理建议。

(5) We will be obliged to have your explanation and know how you intend to settle the matter.
若贵方能作出解释并告知处理措施，我方将不胜感激。

(6) We are sorry to have your complaint about... 接到贵方索赔来函，我方深感歉意。
We regret to learn that you are not satisfied with... 我们遗憾地得知贵方对……不甚满意。

(7) To cover you loss, we agree to make you a special allowance of...
为了赔偿贵方损失，我方同意给予贵方……的特别折扣。

(8) We take the responsibility for the mistake and we will arrange for the replacement to be sent to you at once.
我方应对此失误承担责任并将立刻为贵方调换错运的货物。

(9) We are sorry to have your complaint but regret that we do not hold ourselves responsible for the loss because...
收到贵方的索赔函，我们深感遗憾，但责任并不在我方，因为……

5) Writing Practice

I. Put the following expressions into English.

(1) 索赔人　(2) 向……提出索赔　(3) 损害鉴定　(4) 同意理赔　(5) 拒赔
(6) 短/缺交　(7) 解决/清偿　(8) 对……有责任　(9) 检验证　(10) 赔偿

II. Write a letter of complaint according to the notes given below.

收到 8 月 12 日发运的 20 箱汽车部件，但开箱后发现货物与同日开具的发票不符。显然发货有误。通知此货物暂存仓库，留待处理。要求尽快告知何时发运所订货物。

III. Reply to the following Claim to justify it.

Dear Sirs,

With reference to our telephone of 15th May, in connection with the down quilt shipped per SS Patriot in execution of contract No. 3726-21-S3S, we provide the following information in detail. A thorough examination by commodity inspection organization concerned showed that the short weight was due to the improper packing, the inferior quality was due to the deficiency of down content. We now lodge claims with you as follows:

Claim Number	Claim for	Amount
PBC78	Short-weight	US $1,453.20
PBC79	Inferior quality	US $3,107.15
	Plus survey charges	US $68.25
	Total Amount	US $4,628.60

To support our claims, we enclose one copy of the Survey Report together with our Statement of Claim which amounts to US $4,628.60.

We feel sure that you will give our claims your most favorable consideration and let us have your settlement at an early date.

Sincerely yours,

Unit 11

Contracts & Agreements（合同与协议）

- General Introduction
- Sample Reading
- Useful Expressions
- Writing Practice

General Introduction & Sample Reading

What Are Foreign Economic Contracts and Agreements?

　　涉外经济合同是我国的企业或其他经济组织同外国的企业和其他经济组织或个人之间，在国际经济贸易关系方面为规定相互间权利和义务而订立的书面文件。

　　涉外经济合同依法签订，受国家法律管辖和保护，对签约各方均有法律约束力。

　　涉外经济合同，按其繁简程度的不同，可以采用正式合同（Contract）、协议书（Agreement）、确认书（Confirmation）、备忘录（Memorandum）、订单（Order）等书面形式。本章主要讨论比较复杂的正式合同及协议书的写作。

How Is a Contract or Agreement Laid out?

<pre>
                            CONTRACT
Contract No. _____   Date: _____   Signed at: _____
Party A: _____   Party B: _____
Address: _____   Address: _____
Email: _____   Email: _____

Fax: _____   Fax: _____
_____
_____
</pre>

Unit 11　Contracts & Agreements（合同与协议）

　　_____
　　_____
　　_____

　　Party A：_____　　　　　　Party B：_____

Rules for Writing Contracts and Agreements

1. General Requirements

签订涉外经济合同，应注意以下各点。

（1）合法性：合同是依法签订的法律性文件，一切条款都必须符合有关国家的法律、法令、条例的规定，如有抵触就可能引起违法事件，不但合同不能执行，而且还会带来不良的经济、法律后果。

（2）全面性：合同的内容要力求全面表达订约各方在洽谈过程中所达成一致的意见，防止遗漏或擅自增添条款，以免日后造成纠纷。

（3）明确性：合同的用词要力求准确、严密、清楚、易解，避免模棱两可、似是而非、含糊不清，否则则可能引起解释上的分歧。

（4）主动性：在不违反上述三点的情况下要争取主动，为自己留有回旋余地，要事前防范，尽量不留下漏洞，以免日后给人以可乘之机而使自己陷入被动。

2. Requirements to the Language of Contracts and Agreements

1）Diction

（1）多使用正式或法律用语。例如：

- At the request of Party B, Party A agrees to send technicians to assist Party B to install the equipment. 应乙方要求，甲方同意派遣技术人员帮助乙方安装设备。
- The Employer shall render correct technical guidance to the personnel. 雇主应对有关人员给予正确的技术指导。
- This Contract shall be governed by and construed in accordance with the laws of China. 本合同的签订与解释均根据中国法律。
- In case one party desires to sell or assign all or part of its investment subscribed, the other party shall have the preemptive right. 如一方想出售或转让其投资的全部或一部分，另一方应有购买优先权。
- The authorities approved (the) said application of 3rd November, 2004. "the said" 或 "said" 此处是公文体，意为"该""上述的"。

（2）多把"here""there""where"加后缀使用，例如：

- hereafter：after this time；in the future 此后，今后
- hereby：by means of；by reason of this 据此
- herein：in this 在此

- hereinafter: later in this contract, etc. 在下文中
- hereinbefore: in the preceding part of this contract 在上文中
- hereof: of this 于此
- hereto: to this 到此
- heretofore: until now 直到此时
- hereunder: under this 在下
- hereupon: at this point; in consequence of this 因此
- herewith: with this 同此，因此
- thereafter: afterwards 其后
- thereby: by that means; in that connection 因此，从而
- therefrom: from that 从此
- therein: in that; in that particular 在那里
- thereinafter: later in the same contract, etc. 以下
- thereinbefore: in a preceding part of the same contract, etc. 在上文
- thereon: on that 在其上
- thereof: of that; from that source 其中
- thereto: to that 另外，到那里
- thereunder: under that 依据
- thereupon: then; as a result of that 因此
- therewith: with that or it 与此
- whereas: considering that; but 尽管
- whereby: by what; by which 为何
- wherein: in what; in which 在何处
- whereof: of what; of which 关于
- whereon: on what; on which 在……上

（3）多用成双成对的同义词以限定或确定或强调其意义，例如：

- The parties may, through consultation, make amendments to any revisions of this Contract as and when the need arises. 双方可在必要时通过协商修改本合同。
- This Agreement is made and entered into by and between ABC Co. and DEF Co. ABC 公司和 DEF 公司双方签订本协议。
- Each party to this Agreement shall fulfill or perform any of the obligations under this Agreement. 本协议双方应履行协议规定的义务。
- This Agreement and any rights or obligations hereunder are not transferable or assignable by one party to this Agreement without the consent of the other party hereto. 本协议以及本协议规定的权利和义务，未经另一方同意不得擅自转让。
- The amendments to or alterations of this Contract become effective only after they are signed by both parties and approved by the original approving authorities. 本合同的修改只有在双方签字并在原审批主管机关批准后才能生效。

（4）多用"shall"代替"will"或"should"以加强语气和强制力。

- The persons employed by Party A shall be responsible to the Manager of Party A. 甲方雇用的所有人员都必须向甲方的经理负责。
- Party A shall, at most favorable prices, supply Party B with spare parts of the leased equipment. 甲方应以最优惠价格向乙方供应所租设备的备件。
- This Contract shall become effective upon and from the date on which it is signed. 本合同应于签字之日开始生效。

注意：在合同中，"shall"并非单纯的将来式，而是常常用来表示法律上可以强制执行的义务；它译成中文为"应""应该""必须"，以表示其具有的约束力。"will"在合同中虽也用作表示承担义务的声明，但语气比"shall"弱，强制力也比"shall"差；它译成中文应为"将""愿""要"。"should"在合同中通常只用来表示语气较强的假设"万一"，极少用来表示"应该"。这都是英语合同用词与基础英语用词的不同之处。

2）Expression

（1）用语要力求准确、明白、严密，举例说明如下。

- Payment shall be made by Party B in a week。这句话模棱两可，因为它既可理解为在一个星期之内，又可理解为在一个星期之后。因此，如果想说前者就应用 within a week；如果想说后者就应用 after a week。
- Party A shall send technicians to train Party B's personnel.

这句话含糊不清、不够具体，因为费用由谁负担和技术员何时派出均不明确。因此，必须明确而具体地规定：Party A shall send technicians at Party B's expense to train Party B's personnel within 30 days after signing the Contract. 甲方应于签约后30天内派遣技术人员培训乙方人员，有关费用，由乙方承担。

- The goods are to be shipped by a steamer at a port or ports on the West Coast as per bill or bills of lading dated or to be dated not later than April 30, 2000. 这句话的用语不够清楚，以致是否可以分批装运不明确。因为它既说由一艘船装运，又说可由一个港口或两个以上的港口以一个提单或两个以上的提单装运。因此不如明确地说：The goods are to be shipped by a steamer at a port on the West Coast as per bill of lading to be dated not later than April 30, 2000. 即明确地说"不准分批"。
- Shipment is to be effected bimonthly at 600 metric tons each. 这句话用语模棱两可，以致装船的时间和数量无法确定。因为"bimonthly"这个词，既可解作"两个月"，也可解作"半个月"。因此就难免产生歧义，究竟每两个月运出600公吨，还是每半个月运出600公吨。

（2）多用主动语态，少用被动语态，因为主动语态比较自然、明确、直接，有力。试比较：

- A: The rules and regulations of the worksite shall be observed by workers. 工地的规章应被工人遵守。

  B: Workers shall observe the rules and regulations of the worksite. 工人应遵守工地的规章。

- A: Party B is hereby appointed by Party A as its exclusive sales agent in Singapore. 乙方被甲方委托为在新加坡的独家销售代理。

B：Party A hereby appoints Party B as its exclusive sales agent in Singapore. 甲方委托乙方为在新加坡的独家销售代理。

（3）多用现在时态。尽管合同的条款是规定签约以后的事项，通常仍以使用现在时态为原则，例如：

Before completion of the project, Party A may at any time increase or decrease the amount of work of the project. 在工程竣工之前，甲方可以随时增加或减少工程数量。

上述条款是规定签约以后的事项，但是不用将来时态而用现在时态。

（4）多用直接表达方式，少用间接表达方式，例如：

A：This Article does not apply to bondholders who have not been paid in full. 本条款不适用于尚未全部偿付的债券持有者。

B：This Article applies only to bondholders who have been paid in full. 本条款只适用于已经全部偿付了债券的持有者。

相比较而言，合同中应使用 B 句。

（5）能以一个动词表达就用一个单独的动词，避免使用与其同义的动词短语。例如：

- Party A shall make an appointment of its representative within 30 days after signing the Contract. 甲方应于签约后30天内指派其授权代表。如果我们用"appoint"取代"make an appointment of"这句话将变得更为简洁、有力。

- Party A will give consideration to Party B's proposal of exclusive agency. 甲方愿意考虑乙方独家代理的建议。

应用"consider"取代第二句中的"give consideration to"。

（6）多用某些特殊用语，例如：

- WHEREAS 鉴于

它是在合同前文中用作引出签约背景和目的的连词。正式而重要的合同，尤其是英美法系的合同，多有此条款。

- WITNESS 证明

它在合同前文中常用作句首的谓语动词。

This Agreement, made by...
WITNESSES ...
WHEREAS ..., it is agreed as follows：

本协议由……签订……证明。鉴于……特此达成协议如下：

- IN WITNESS WHEREOF 作为所协议事项的证据

这个短语常在合同结尾条款中使用。

IN WITNESS WHEREOF, the parties have executed this Contract in duplicate by their duly authorized representatives on the date first above written.

作为所协议事项的证据，双方授权代表于上面首次写明的日期正式签署本协议一式两份。

- IN CONSIDERATION OF 以……为约因

In consideration of the premises and the covenants herein contained, the parties hereto agree as follows：

兹以上述各点和契约所载条款为约因，订约双方协议如下：

- NOW THESE PRESENTS WITNESS 兹特立约为据

用在 WHEREAS 条款之后以引出具体协议事项，PRESENTS：the present writings.

NOW THESE PRESENTS WITNESS that it is hereby agreed between the parties hereto as follows：

兹特立约为据，并由订约双方协议如下：

- IN THE PRESENCE OF 见证人

本短语只在有见证人时使用，即在定约双方当事人签名的下方由见证人签名作证。见证人一般是有关的律师（Attorney）或公证行（Notary Public）。

Sample Reading

【Sample 1】

以下是一份销售合同（Sales Contract）。此类合同在贸易实践中最为常见，所包含的条款也可视为多种合同的基本内核。本篇合同术语使用规范，条款明晰准确，记忆其中的一些规范表达将对合同写作大有裨益。大家对正式合同可能还很陌生，而我国签订的国际商务合同常常需要英、汉两个版本，因此对后附的汉语版本也应给予足够的重视。

CHINA NATIONAL
CHEMICALS IMPORT & EXPORT CORPORATION
NANJING BRANCH
SALES CONTRACT

ORIGINAL

Contract No. CE102　　Date：November 5, 2017　　Signed at：Nanjing

Sellers：China National Chemicals Import & Export Corporation, Nanjing Branch

Address：52, Ninghai Road, Nanjing, China

Cable：　　　　　Telex：　　　　　Fax：

Buyers：Smith & Sons Co., Ltd.

Address：No. 1368 Greek Road, Singapore

Cable：　　　　　Telex：　　　　　Fax：

This Sales Contract is made by and between the Sellers and the Buyers whereby the sellers agree to sell and the buyers agree to buy the under-mentioned goods according to the terms and conditions stipulated below：

1. Name of Commodity Specifications & Packing	Quantity	Unit Price	Total Value
Lithophone Zns content 28% min. Paper-lined glass-fibre bags	50 m/tons	RMB ¥982 per M/T CIFC 3% Singapore	RMB ¥49,000

The Sellers are allowed to load 5% more or less and **price shall be calculated according to the unit price.**

2. Shipping Mark:

To be designated by the Sellers: SINGAPORE
No. 1-up

3. Insurance: **To be covered by the Sellers for 110% of invoice value** against All Risks and War Risk as per the relevant Ocean Marine Cargo Clauses of the People's Insurance Company of China. If other coverage or an additional insurance amount is required, the Buyers must have the consent of the Sellers before shipment, and the additional premium is to be borne by the Buyers.

4. Port of Shipment: Tianjin

5. Port of Destination: Singapore

6. Time of Shipment: During December, 2017, allowing partial shipments and transhipment.

7. Terms of Payment: **The Buyers shall open with a bank acceptable to the Sellers an Irrevocable Sight Letter of Credit** to reach the Sellers 30 days before the month of shipment, valid for negotiation in China until the 15th day after the month of shipment.

8. Commodity Inspection: **It is mutually agreed that** the Certificate of Quality and Weight issued by the Chinese Import and Export Commodity Inspection Bureau at the port of shipment shall be taken as the basis of delivery.

9. Discrepancy and Claim: **Any claim by the Buyers on the goods shipped shall be filed within** 30 **days after the arrival**, of the goods at port of destination and supported by a survey report issued by a surveyor approved by the Sellers. Claims in respect of matters within the responsibility of the insurance company or of the shipping company will not be considered or entertained by the Sellers.

10. Force Majeure: If shipment of the contracted goods is prevented or delayed **in whole or in part due to Force Majeure**, the Sellers shall not be liable for non-shipment or late shipment of the goods under this Contract. However, the Sellers shall notify the Buyers by cable or telex and furnish the latter within 15 days by registered airmail with a certificate issued by the China Council for the Promotion of International Trade at testing such event or events.

11. Arbitration: **All disputes arising out of the performance of, or relating to this Contract, shall be settled amicably through negotiation.** In case no settlement can be reached through negotiation, the case shall then be submitted to the Foreign Economic and Trade Arbitration Commission of the China Council for the Promotion of International Trade, Beijing, China, for arbitration in accordance with its Provisional Rules of Procedure. The

Unit 11　Contracts & Agreements（合同与协议）

arbitral award is final and binding, upon both parties.

12. Other Terms:

　　　　THE SELLERS　　　　　　　　　　　　　　　THE BUYERS

中国化工进出口公司南京分公司
售货合同　（正本）

合同号码：CE102　　　　日期：2017 年 11 月 5 日　　　　签约地点：南京

卖方：中国化工进出口公司南京分公司

地址：中国南京宁海路 52 号

电报挂号：　　　　　电传：　　　　　传真：

买方：史密斯父子有限公司

地址：新加坡，希腊路 1368 号

电报挂号：　　　　　电传：　　　　　传真：

兹经买卖双方同意由卖方出售买方购进下列货物，并按下列条款签订本合同：

1. 商品名称、规格及包装	数量	单价	总值
Lithophone Zns content 28% min. Paper-lined glass-fibre bags	50 m/tons	RMB 982 per M/T CIFC 3% Singapore	RMB 49,000

　　卖方可多装或少装百分之五，价格仍按上述价格计算。

　2. 唛头：由卖方指定

　3. 保险：由卖方按中国人民保险公司条款依照发票总值110%投保综合险及战争险，如买方欲增加其他险别或超过上述保额时须于装船前征得卖方同意，所增加的保险费由买方负担。

　4. 装船口岸：天津

　5. 目的口岸：新加坡

　6. 装船期限：2017 年 12 月份装船，允许分批和转船。

　7. 付款条件：买方应由卖方可接受的银行于装船月份前30天开立并送达卖方不可撤销即期信用证，至装运月份后第 15 天在中国议付有效。

　8. 商品检验：买卖双方同意以装船口岸中国进出口商品检验局签发的品质和重量检验证书作为品质和数量的交货依据。

　9. 异议和索赔：买方对于装运货物的任何索赔，必须于货到目的港30天内提出，并须提供经卖方同意的公证机构出具的检验报告。属于保险公司或轮船公司责任范围内的索赔，卖方不予接受。

　10. 不可抗力：如由于不可抗力的原因，致使卖方不能全部或部分装运或延迟装运合同货物时，卖方对于这种不能装运或延迟装运不负有责任。但卖方须用电报或电传通知买方，并须在15天内以航空挂号信件向买方提交中国国际贸易促进委员会出具的证明此类事故的证明书。

　11. 仲裁：凡因执行本合同所发生的或与本合同有关的一切争议，双方应通过友好协商解决。如果协商不能解决时，应提交北京中国国际贸易促进委员会对外经济贸易仲裁委员会根据该会仲裁程序暂行规定进行仲裁。仲裁是终局性的，对双方都有约束力。

　12. 其他条款；

卖方：　　　　　　买方：

[Sample 2]

以下是一份包销代理协议书（Exclusive Sales Agreement），此类赋予销售方独家代理某货物或委托经销某货物的合同还包括独家代理协议（Sole Agency Agreement），独家经销协议（Sole Distributorship Agreement）等类似名称的商业合同。

Exclusive Sales Agreement

Through friendly negotiations, **this Agreement is entered into**[①] between China National Import and Export Corporation, Beijing, China (hereinafter called Party A), and ×××Company, Cairo, Egypt (hereinafter called Panty B) on the following terms and conditions:

1. Party A entrusts Party B with the exclusive sales in the territory of Egypt for "Tiantan" brand Men's Shirts. This Agreement is valid from May, 2017, to May, 2018.

2. Quantity: During the above-mentioned period, **Party B shall endeavor to push sales**[②] of not less than 2 million, of "Tiantan" brand Men's Shirts, **the quantity of which should be spread over quarterly periods in approximately equal proportions.**

3. **During the validity of this Agreement, Party A refrains from offering the above mentioned goods to other merchants with Egyptian ports as ports of destinations** while Party B undertakes to refrain from purchasing, pushing sales of or acting as agents for the commodity of other suppliers the same as or similar to that stated in Article 1 and guarantees not to transship in any way the said goods supplied by Party A to any area, where exclusivity or sales agency has been granted by Party A. If any violation[③] of the above is found, Party A has the right to cancel this Agreement.

4. **Should other buyers in the territory under exclusivity approach Party A for the purchase of the above-mentioned goods, Party A should refer them to Party B.** If such buyers insist on concluding business directly with Party A, Party A may do so. Party A may likewise conclude business with Egyptian buyers who come to visit China or attend the Chinese Export Commodity Fair at prices not lower than those quoted to party B. In the above events Party A agrees to reserve for Party B a commission of 1% on the basis of FOB value of the business thus concluded and send a copy of the relative contract to Party B.

5. During the period of this Agreement, **both parties should strictly abide by**[④] **the terms and conditions of this Agreement**. In the event of any breach of them by one party, the other party is entitled, when necessary, to claim the termination of this Agreement.

6. Party B should be responsible for the sending of reports every month to Party A for their reference, setting forth local market conditions of the said goods (including details of price level and demand for variety in articles).

7. **At its expiration**[⑤], the termination or renewal of this Agreement will be decided by both parties through negotiation.

Unit 11　Contracts & Agreements（合同与协议）

8. **This Agreement is made out in Chinese and English languages, both texts being equally binding**⑥**. One copy of each is kept by either party.**

　　Party A　　　　　　　　　　Party B

　　　　　　　　　　　　　　　　　　　　　　　　　　April 26, 2017.

① enter into: made 缔结　　② Push sales: 促销　　③ Violation: 违反
④ Abide by: 遵守　　　　　 ⑤ Expiration: 期满, 终止　⑥ Equally binding: 同等效力

包销协议书

　　经友好协商，中国，北京，中国国家进出口公司（以下称甲方）与埃及，开罗，×××公司（以下称乙方）就下列条款条件缔结协议：

　　1. 甲方委托乙方在埃及地区包销"天坛"牌男式衬衫。此协议有效期自2017年5月至2018年5月。

　　2. 数量：在上述时间内，乙方应努力促销，其"天坛"牌男式衬衫销售量不低于两百万件，每季度销售量应大致均等。

　　3. 在此协议有效期内，甲方不应以埃及各港口为终到港向其他厂商提供上述货物，同时乙方保证不购买、促销或代理任何其他厂商提供的与条款1所述货物相同或类似的产品。乙方保证不将上述货物转运至任何甲方已经授权包销或代销商的地区。一旦发现任何违反上述协议的行为，甲方有权终止本协议。

　　4. 如包销地区其他买家向甲方提出购买上述货物，甲方应介绍其向乙方购买。如对方坚持直接向甲方购买，甲方可以进行交易。同样，甲方可以不低于给乙方报价的价格与访问中国及参加中国出口商品展览会的埃及买主进行交易。在上述情况下，甲方同意付给乙方每单交易船上交货价的1%的佣金，并向乙方提供交易相关合同的副本。

　　5. 在此协议有效期间，双方应严格遵守协议各条款规定的条件。如任何一方违反协议，必要时另一方有权宣布终止本协议。

　　6. 乙方负责每月向甲方寄送报告以供参考。报告包括上述货物的当地市场情况（关于价格水平的细节以及对商品品种的需求）。

　　7. 本协议期满后，双方将通过协商决定终止或续签协议。

　　8. 本协议分别由中、英两种语言书写，两种文本具同等法律效力。双方均持有一份。

　　甲方：×××　　　　　　　　乙方：×××

　　　　　　　　　　　　　　　　　　　　　　　　　2017年4月26日

Analysis

　　（1）保险条款（Insurance）在商务合同中非常重要，例1中有此项条款。一般在合同中可能涉及的主要险种有：平安险（free from particular average，FPA）、水渍险（with particular average，WPA）、综合险（All Risks）。此外还有附加保险，分为一般保险和特别保险，比如战争险（War Risks）、罢工险（Strike Risks）等。

　　（2）一般的购销合同中都应包括支付条款（Payment），如例1。国际贸易中的有多种支付方式，主要有以下几种。

- Remittance（汇付）

根据付款方式，分为 Mail Transfer（M/T；M. T.）（信付）、Telegraphic Transfer（T/T；T. T.）（电付）、Demand Draft（D/D；D. D.）（票汇）、Check（支票）、International Postal Money Order（国际邮政汇票）。

根据支付时间，汇付可分为 Payment in Advance（预付）、Cash against Documents（现付）、Deferred Payment（延付）。

- Collection（托收）

可分为 Collection on Clean Bill（光票托收）、Collection on Document（跟单托收）、Documents against Acceptance（D/A 承兑交单）、Documents against Payment（D/P 付款交单）。

- Installment Payment（Progressive Payment 分期付款）
- Deferred Payment（延期付款）
- Letter of Credit（信用证）

可分为 Revocable Letter of Credit（可撤销信用证）、Irrevocable Letter of Credit（不可撤销信用证）、Confirmed Letter of Credit（保兑信用证）、Unconfirmed Letter of Credit（非保兑信用证）、Sight Letter of Credit（即期信用证）、Time Letter of Credit（远期信用证）、Revolving Letter of Credit（循环信用证）、Unrevolving Letter of Credit（非循环信用证）、Transferable Letter of Credit（可转让信用证）、Non-Transferable Letter of Credit（不可转让信用证）、Reciprocal Letter of Credit（对开信用证）、Back to Back Letter of Credit（对背信用证）、Anticipatory Letter of Credit（预支信用证）、Swift Letter of Credit（环银电协信用证）。

（3）在包销、代理合同中特别应注意协议所辖的范围和期限，如例2中相关的两个条款，如有遗漏将带来很多麻烦。

Useful Expressions

Trade Terms in Contracts and Agreements

贸易术语（Trade Terms），又称价格术语、价格条件等，是用一个简短词语或英文缩写字母来表达贸易中的价格结构及合同双方在贸易中应尽的义务。每一特定的术语都相应规定了贸易双方的责任、风险、应支付的费用及各自应办理的手续等，不仅反映商品价格，而且是一种成交条件。因此，在最终敲定合同之前，准确理解你所认同的贸易术语的含义是非常重要的。

以下首先对国际商会制定和颁布的《国际贸易术语解释通则2000》（*Incoterms 2000*）中归纳的13种贸易术语进行简要说明。

（1）EXW

　　Ex Work ... (named place) 工厂交货（指定地）

（2）FCA

　　Free Carrier ... (Named Place) 货交承运人（指定地）

(3) FAS

Free Alongside Ship… (named port of shipment) 装运港船边交货（指定装运港）

(4) FOB

Free on Board… (named port of shipment) 装运港船上交货（指定装运港）

(5) CFR（C&F）

Cost and Freight… (named port of destination) 成本加运费（指定目的港）

(6) CIF

Cost, Insurance and Freight… (named port of destination) 成本加保险和运费（指定目的港）

(7) CPT

Carriage (or freight) Paid to… (named place of destination) 运费付至（指定目的地）

(8) CIP

Carriage and Insurance Paid to… (named place of destination) 运费、保险费付至（指定目的地）

(9) DAF

Delivered at Frontier… (named place) 边境交货（指定地）

(10) DES

Delivered Ex Ship… (named port of destination) 目的港船上交货（指定目的港）

(11) DEQ

Delivered Ex Quay (Duty Paid)… (named place of destination) 目的港码头交货（关税已付）（指定目的港）

(12) DDU

Delivered Duty Unpaid… (named place of destination) 未完税交货（指定目的地）

(13) DDP

Delivered Duty Paid… (named place of destination) 完税后交货（指定目的地）

Useful Sentences

现选取一些合同中经常出现的句子根据合同内容不同分类罗列如下，以供参考。由于随经济发展商务合同涉及的内容日益广泛，合同语言也在不断发展变化中，想要提高合同写作水平，除熟悉本章所述内容外，还需要作者们在未来的工作和学习中，不断总结收集一些规范的常用表达。

1. Useful Sentences on Buying Import Commodities（购买进口商品）

(1) They are regularly interested in importation of oilseeds.
他们均有意进口油籽。

(2) We accept your order subject to payment in advance.
如能预付货款，我们将接受你方订单。

(3) All pending orders will be executed next month.
未交订货必须下月完成。

2. Useful Sentences on Agencies（机构）

(1) After careful consideration, we have decided to entrust you with the sole agency for... in the territory of...
经慎重考虑，我方决定授予你方在……地区的……的独家代理权。

(2) If your work turns out to be satisfactory, the agency agreement can be renewed on expiry. We shall consider a longer period at that time.
如你方的工作证实令人满意，代理协议期满可以续签。那时我方将考虑更长周期的代理权。

(3) We have already had agency arrangement with Messrs... for the sale of this product in your region.
在你区域我方已与……先生们签订此产品的销售代理协议。

3. Useful Sentences on Processing and Assembling Trade（三来一补贸易）

(1) We agree to pay for the equipment and technology by installments with the processing fees payable to us.
我方同意用可收取的加工费分期支付设备及技术费用。

(2) As the trademark and the labels to be used on the finished products will be designated by you, it shall be your responsibility in case any disputes should arise in regard to patent and other rights involved.
由于成品上使用的商标和标签将由你方指定，如出现任何关于专利权和其他相关权利的争端将由你方负责。

(3) The overall processing fee is US$... per unit, including charges for labour, packing, depreciation of machinery, storage and transport.
全部加工费为美国标准……每单位，包括劳务、包装、机器折旧、仓储及运输费用。

(4) The rate of substandard products should not exceed 5%.
等外品比例不超过5%。

4. Useful Sentences on Compensation Trade（补偿贸易）

(1) It is required that the equipment and technology to be provided by you should be up to advanced world standards, reasonable in price and suitable to our condition of production.
你方提供的技术、设备应达到国际先进水平，价格合理并适合我方的生产条件。

(2) We shall reimburse you the total value of the entire equipment by installments in 4 years, whereas you will undertake to buy back all the products turned out with the said equipment.
我方将4年内分期还清全部设备的总价，反之你方应购回所有上述设备生产的产品。

(3) An irrevocable Letter of Guarantee (L/G) will be issued in your favour by the Bank of China here, to guarantee timely payment of the installments with the interest due, provided that you have fulfilled your obligations under the contract.
此地的中国银行将开具不可撤销信用证，保证如你方完成合同中规定的任务我方将按时付给分期款项及应付利息。

Unit 11　Contracts & Agreements（合同与协议）

5. Useful Sentences on Leasing Trade（租赁贸易）

（1）The rental is to be calculated on the basis of the export price of the equipment plus charges for pre-lease consultation, after-lease maintenance service, interest, depreciation, handling charges, etc.
租金以设备的出口价格加租前咨询、租后技术维护、利息、折旧费、装卸费等为基础计算。

（2）In case of breakdown of any of the machines, repairs will be made on the spot free of charge because maintenance service charges are included in the rental. However, if the breakdown is due to negligence or misuse on your part, you will have to pay the expenses for repairs.
一旦任何机器损坏，应在现场免费维修，因为技术维护费用包含在租金内。如损坏是由你方疏忽或使用不当造成的，维修费用应由你方支付。

（3）In accordance with the terms of the lease, we have the option either to extend the lease on its expiration, or to purchase the equipment then at a price equal to 10% of its original value.
依据租约条款，我方有权在租约期满后选择延长租约或以相当于原价10%的价格购买此设备。

Writing Practice

I. Fill in the blanks with appropriate prepositions.

（1）Payment: The Buyers, upon receipt from the Sellers _____ the delivery advice specified in Article 14 hereof, shall, in 15-20 days prior _____ the date of delivery, open an irrevocable Letter of Credit with the Bank of China, _____ favor of the Sellers, for an amount equivalent _____ the total value of the shipment. The Credit shall be payable _____ presentation of draft drawn _____ the opening bank and the shipping documents specified in Article 13 hereof. The Letter of Credit shall be valid until the 15th day after the shipment is effected.

（2）Guarantee of Quality: The Sellers guarantee that the commodity hereof is made _____ the best materials with first class workmanship, brand new and unused, and complies in all respects _____ the quality and specifications stipulated in this Contract.

（3）Penalty: If the Sellers fail to effect the delivery at the contracted time _____ delivery, the Buyers shall have the option to cancel this Contract and demand _____ all losses resulted therefrom, or alternatively, the Sellers may postpone delivery _____ the Buyers' consent, _____ condition that the Sellers pay to the Buyers a penalty of 1.5% of the goods value _____ a delay within 30 days and further 0.5% _____ every 15 days thereafter. The penalty shall be deducted _____ the paying bank during the negotiation _____ payment.

(4) EXCLUSIVE SALES: Exclusive sales are established _____ a seller and an exclusive distributor by means _____ an exclusive sales agreement, _____ which the exclusive distributor is authorized by the seller _____ an exclusive right to buy, and then, sell the designated goods in the specified area within a specified period of time. With such an arrangement the seller should _____ no means make use _____ any other channels to market the designated goods to others in the area, and the exclusive distributor, reciprocally, should guarantee to buy a specified amount _____ the designated goods _____ the seller within a certain period.

II. Translate the following parts into English.

(1) 本合同由依～法律成立的 ABC（全称）公司，其登记注册地在～，法定地址为～（以下简称买方）和依～法律成立的 DEF（全称）公司，其登记注册地在～，法定地址为～（以下简称卖方）于 2018 年 10 月 15 日在中国南京订立，双方同意按下述条款买卖下述货物。

(2) ① 货物名称
　② 规格、数量和单价
　③ 总金额（按美元计）
　④ 生产国和制造商：
　⑤ 包装：包装必须适于海上运输、坚固、耐野蛮装运。紧压打包、外加紧箍，内层防水，外层为优质帆布。箱子或其他外包装体积要尽量小，并能确保货物安全。每件包装的两侧和一端须完整刷上标志和装运号码，采用优质印色，字大而清晰。每包均须标明"请勿用钩"。

(3) ① 本合同正文一式两份，分别以中文和英文书写，两种文本具同等效力。若对其解释产生异议，则以中文本为准。
　② 本合同第 20 章列出的附件为本合同不可分割的组成部分。
　③ 本合同的任何修改和/或补充，只有双方授权代表在书面文件上签字才能生效，并成为本合同不可分割的组成部分。
　④ 本合同将在双方授权代表签字后正式生效。

(4) 如果合同一方未能在合同规定的时限内履行合同义务，并在收到未违约方的通知后 15 天内未能消除违约或采取补救措施，而且在被允许推迟履行的期限内仍未履行合同，在此情形下，未违约的一方应书面通知违约方解除合同，同时有权要求违约方赔偿损失。

Unit 12

Bidding（招标）

- General Introduction
- Sample Reading
- Useful Expressions
- Writing Practice

General Introduction & Sample Reading

What Are Bids?

招标是指招标人或招标单位根据自己的需要，提出招标项目，拟购商品或发包工程等招标条件，公开或书面邀请投标人或投标单位在接受招标文件要求下前来投标，以便招标人从中择优选定的一种交易行为。

目前，国际上用的招标方式大体有三种：国际竞争性招标（International Competition Bid, ICB）、国际邀约性招标（Invitation For Bid, IFB）和限制性招标（Limited Bidding, LB）。

Types of Bid

国际竞争性招标（ICB）

国际竞争性招标是国际招标中最为常见的一种公开招标方式。其特点是：招标人或单位通过国内外主要报纸及其他新闻渠道公开发布招标通告，邀请有愿意参加投标的供应商或承包商参加投标。国际招标公告除了刊登在国内发行的主要中文报纸上之外，还要用英文刊登在《中国日报》(China Daily)上。世界银行、美洲开发银行、亚洲开发银行贷款的总采购通告首先发表在联合国发展论坛报商业版《一般采购通知》上。具体招标的商品内容和时间则刊登在受援国官方报刊上。

国际邀约性招标（IFB）

国际邀约性招标（也叫不公开招标）是指不公开刊登广告邀请合格者参加投标。招标人或单位根据招标内容确定若干具有招标能力的厂商或单位为邀请对象，将其招标的通告或招标邀请函直接送往这些厂商或单位。

限制性招标（LB）

限制性招标常见于国际金融机构资助的项目，虽然也属于世界范围内招标，但对投标人的范围有严格限制，只允许属于该资助机构的成员国参加投标，一般限制性招标在具体做法上与公开招标基本相同，但在评标时更强调资信。

投标

投标是指投标人或单位接到招标通知书后，在同意招标条件的前提下，对招标项目提出自己的报价和相应的条件，企图通过竞争成为中标人的一种交易方式。招标和投标活动是通过招标通告和呈交投标文件来进行的。

How Are Inviting Bids Laid Out?

招标邀请函一般由 4 或 5 部分组成。

第一部分：通常是以标题表示的。内容包括：招标人或招标单位名称、项目所在地国家及单位名称、地址、招标号、贷款号等。

例如：

招标公告

The People's Republic of China
International Tendering Company
China National Technical Import and Export Corporation
Invitation For Bid for
Forestry Development Project
（IDA CREDIT No. 1605-CHA） TCBW-903006

中国技术进出口总公司国际招标公司招标通告
林业发展项目
（国际开发协会贷款号 1605-CHA） TCBW-903006

第二部分：包括具体的招标项目，拟采购的设备、承包工程内容及资金来源。

例如：

The People's Republic of China has received a loan from Asian Development Bank（ADB）in US dollars toward the cost of Dalian Water Supply Project（the Southern Works）and it is intended that part of the proceeds of this loan will be applied to eligible payments under the contract for C2 Manufacture and Installation of Steel Pipeline. Bidding is open to all bidders from eligible source countries of ADB.

中华人民共和国已得到亚洲开发银行的一笔贷款。这笔贷款将用于大连供水项目（南段工程），部分贷款的资金将用于C2钢管线制造与安装合同项目下的合格支付。本次招标面向所有亚洲银行合格的成员国的投标人。

第三部分：开始购买招标文件的日期、地点及价格等。
例如：

Bid documents are available between 8:00 – 11:00 a.m. from May 25, 2020 (Sundays and holidays excepted) upon nonrefundable payment of RMB 240 (USD 50) for each set of the document.

投标者可根据以下地址于2020年5月25日起（星期日和节假日除外）上午8:30—11:00购买招标文件，每套售价为人民币240元（美元50元），售后不退。

第四部分：投标的截止日期、投标保证金金额、开标时间、地点。
例如：

The deadline for receipt of bids by ITC is June 25, 2020 at 9:00 a.m. Beijing Time. Bids received thereafter, or which are not accompanied by a Bid Bond furnished as provided for in the bidding conditions, will not be accepted. Bid will be opened on June 25, 2020 at 1:30 p.m. Beijing Time in Negotiation Building, Erligou, Xijiao, Beijing, China.

截标日期为2020年6月25日北京时间上午9:00，其后所到达的文件或未按标书规定提交投标保证金的投标文件恕不接受。兹定于2020年6月25日北京时间下午1:30在中国北京西郊二里沟谈判大楼公开招标。

第五部分：招标人或单位的具体地址、联系人、邮编、电报号、电传号、传真号、电话号。
例如：

Tianjin International Tendering Co. of Machinery and Electric Equipment
Mr. Zhang Xiaohu, Mr. Wang Dabiao
at the address：100 Machang Road, Hexi District, Tianjin 300204
Tel：021-3283145 ext. 47   Fax：021-3283146

天津机电设备国际招标公司
联系人：张小虎、王大标先生

地址：中国天津河西区马场路100号	邮编：300204
电话：021-3283145 分机：47	传真：021-3283146

 Sample Reading

【Sample 1】

下文是一篇完整的招标邀请函，分层叙述了上述5个方面的内容。

Invitation for Bids

Date：_____, 2020
Loan No. 1313-PRC
Bid No. CMCA 956105

(1) The People's Republic of China has received a loan from the Asian Development Bank (ADB) in US dollars towards the cost of Dalian Water Supply Project (Part II) and it is intended that part of the proceeds of this loan will be applied to eligible payments under the contract for C2 Manufacture and Installation of Steel Pipeline. Bidding is open to all bidders from eligible[①] source countries of ADB.

(2) China National Machinery Import/Export Corporation (a subsidiary of CMC) and China Shenyang Machinery & Electric Equipment Tendering Corporation (SYTC) (hereinafter called C&S) authorized by the Dalian Water Supply Company to be the tendering agent, invite sealed bids from prequalified eligible bidders for the construction and completion of C2 Manufacture and Installation of Steel Pipeline with the brief description stated as follows：

The Works includes the manufacture and installation of steel pipeline from Wanli to Dashagou Water Plant and the installation of its values and fittings as required by the bidding contracts. The total length of the said pipeline shall be 16.85 km, of which 2.35 km is D1820 pipes with the thickness of 14 mm and 14.5 km is D1620 pipes with the thickness of 12mm.

(3) Bidders may obtain further information from, and inspect and acquire the bidding documents at, the office of China Shenyang Machinery & Electric Equipment Tendering Corporation (SYTC), at the following address：

No. 1032 Nanjing Street, Shenhe District, Shenyang, PRC.
Zip Code：110014
Telephone：(024) 2717027 or 2826069   Fax：(024) 2826161
Person in Charge：Mr. Tian Yongshan and Mr. Zhu Haizhou

(4) A complete set[②] of bidding documents may be purchased by prequalified eligible bidders on submission of a written application to the above office, and upon payment of a

nonrefundable[3] fee of RMB 3,000. In this case, SYTC will promptly dispatch[4] the documents by express airmail, but under no circumstances can it be held responsible for late delivery or loss of the documents so mailed to the applicant.

(5) All bids must be accompanied by a security of the amount not less than 2% of the total bid price or an equivalent amount in a freely convertible currency, and must be delivered to C&S at the following stated address:

The Office of Dalian Water Supply Project
Southern Component Headquarter
Dalian Water Supply Company
No. 118 Shengli Road, Shahekou District, Dalian, PRC.
Zip Code: 116021
Tel: (0411) 4306946   Fax: (0411) 4306945

at or before 9:00 a.m. (Beijing Time) on _____, 2020. Bids will be opened immediately thereafter in the presence of bidder's representatives who choose to attend.

注：① eligible 合格的；② set 一份；③ nonrefundable 不可撤销的；④ dispatch 派遣（急件）。

日期：2020 年 月 日
贷款号：1313-PRC
合同号：CMCA 956105

（1）中华人民共和国已得到亚洲开发银行的一笔美元贷款。这笔贷款将用于大连供水项目（南段工程），部分贷款的资金将用于 C2 钢管线制造与安装合同项目下的合格支付。这次招标面向全部亚洲开发银行合格成员的投标人。

（2）中国机械进出口公司（中国机械进出口总公司的子公司）与中国沈阳机电设备招标公司（SYTC）（两公司以下简称 C&S）受大连自来水公司的委托，作为本项目招标代理，现在邀请资格预审合格的投标人对大连供水项目（南段工程）C2 钢管的制造与安装工程的承建和完成密封投标。其工程内容简述如下：

本工程范围包括本招标文件所要求的对于从湾里到大沙沟水厂的输水管线的制造与安装，以及附属阀门、管件的安装。其中直径 1 620mm，壁厚 12mm 的钢管长度为 14.5km，直径 1 820mm，壁厚 14mm 的钢管长度为 2.35km。本工程钢管的制造与安装总长度为 16.85km。

（3）投标人可以从中国沈阳机电设备招标公司即 SYTC 的办公室获得更详细的资料，并翻阅和获取招标文件。

公司地址：沈阳市沈河区南经街 1032 号
邮编：110014
电话：(024) 2717027 或 2826069   传真：(024) 2826261
联系人：田永山 朱海州

（4）资格预审合格的投标人向上述办公室递交一份书面申请，并支付不可撤销的费用 3 000 元人民币后可以购买一套完整的正式招标文件（中英文本）。SYTC 将尽快用航空快件邮寄给投标人，但 SYTC 不承担文件迟到和丢失的责任。

（5）所有投标都应附送一份不少于投标总报价2%的投标保证金，或者相当于前述数额的一种可以自由兑换的货币，并且必须在2020年____月____日北京时间上午9：00之前按下述地址递交到C&S：

大连引碧供水项目南段工程指挥部办公室（大连自来水公司下设机构）

大连市沙河口区胜利路118号，邮编：116021

电话：（0411）4306946　　　　　　传真：（0411）4306945

此后，一俟有愿意参加此次招标的投标人代表到场，将立即开始投标。

[Sample 2]

下例是针对上述招标邀请函发出的投标书。

Form of Bid

Name of Contract：Dalian Water Supply Project（the Southern Works）

_____（Contract Package No. ）

To：China National Machinery Import/Export Corporation（CMC）and China Shenyang Machinery & Electric Equipment Tendering Corporation（SYTC）

Gentlemen,

(1) Having examined the Conditions of Contract, Specification, Drawings, and Bill of Quantities and Addenda No. _____ for the execution of the above named Works, we, the undersigned, offer to execute the complete such Works and remedy any defects therein in conformity with the Conditions of Contract, Specification, Drawings, Bill of Quantities and Addenda for the sum(s) of _____
(_____)
as specified in the Appendix to Bid or such other sums as may be ascertained in accordance with the said[①] Conditions.

(2) We acknowledge that the Appendix forms part of our Bid.

(3) We undertake, if our Bid is accepted, to commence[②] the Works as soon as is reasonably possible after the receipt of the Engineer's notice to commence, and to complete the whole of the Works comprised in the Contract within the time stated in the Appendix to Bid.

(4) We agree to abide by this Bid for the period of 90 days from the date fixed for receiving the same, and it shall remain binding upon us and may be accepted at any time before the expiration[③] of that period.

(5) Unless and until a formal Agreement is prepared and executed, this Bid, together with your written acceptance thereof, shall constitute a binding contract between us.

(6) We understand that you are not bound to accept the lowest or any tenderer you may receive.

Dated this _____ day of _____ 20 _____

Signature _____ in the capacity of _____ duly authorized to sign bids for and on behalf of _____ [in block capitals or typed]

Address _____

Witness _____

Address _____

Occupation _____

①said 上述的；②commence 开始；③expiration 终止日期。

投标书正文

合同名称：大连供水项目（南段）

_____（合同包号）

致：中国机械进出口总公司（CMC）和
    中国沈阳机电设备招标公司（SYTC）

先生们：

(1) 在审核了关于承建上述工程的合同条件、技术规范、图纸、工程质量清单，以及补遗 _____（文件号）以后，我方即文末签字人，愿以在投标书附录写明的____元的总价，或经查实确与上述招标条件相一致，重新确定的另一份金额，实施和完成本工程，并依照合同条件、技术规范、图纸、工程量清单和补遗文件要求，修补其任何缺陷。

(2) 我方确认投标书附录是我方投标的组成部分。

(3) 如贵方接受我方投标，我方保证在收到工程师开工指令后，尽快在合理的时间内开工，并在投标书附录中规定的时间内完成合同规定的全部工程。

(4) 我方同意在从规定的递交标书截止日起 90 天内遵守本投标，在该期限期满之前，本投标对我方始终有约束力并随时有被接受的可能。

(5) 在正式合同协议制订和签署之前，本投标书连同贵方的中标通知书应成为约束我们双方的合同。

(6) 我方理解，贵方不一定必须接受标价最低的或任一可能收到的投标。

20_____年_____月_____日

签字：_____ 以 _____ 资格经授权并代表 _____ 签署标书

地址：_____

见证人：_____

见证人地址：_____

见证人职务：_____

Useful Expressions

(1) Entrusted by..., we are purchase, in near future, the following... by way of international competitive bidding.
受……委托,我们近期以国际竞争性招标方式采购下列……

(2) Authorized by... (name of unit), (name of tenderer) intend(s) to call for international tenderer for...
(招标单位名称)受(单位名称)委托,对……进行国际招标。

(3) The last date and time for receipt of bids by (name oftenderer) is (time)... Bids received after that date and time will not be accepted.
截标日期和时间为……(时间),其后收到的投标恕不接受。

(4) Documents which are received late will not be considered and returned unopened.
迟到的文件将不予考虑,并原封不动退回。

(5) All bids must be accompanied by a security of not less than...% of the total bid price.
所有投标都必须附有一份投标保证金不少于投标总报价的……%。

(6) Bids will be publicly opened at (time) at (address).
兹定于(时间)在(地址)公开招标。

(7) Tenders are invited for building materials and must be in on or before October 2007.
建筑材料将在2017年10月之前进行招标。

(8) Referring to your letter of September 2, we take the pleasure to advise you that the time period for bidding is set from October to the end of October.
根据你们9月2日的信,我们很乐意建议你们从10月到月底进行招标。
Tender-opening is done publicly this time and all the bidders shall be invited to join us to supervise the opening.
这次将进行公开招标,并且所有投标方都被邀请监督这次招标。

(9) Bid documents are available at the address below between... and... from and on (Month, Date, Year) to (Month, Date, Year) upon nonrefundable payment of RMB... or USD... for each set of the document.
(投标者)可以在以下地址(年、月、日)到(年、月、日)之间购买招标文件。每套售价为人民币……元或……美元,售后不退。

(10) Interested potentials bidders may obtain further information and pre-qualification documents from...
感兴趣的投标者可以从……得到进一步信息和资格预审文件。

(11) Tender documents can be obtained at... against payment of RMB 100.
招标文件在……领取,需要支付100元人民币。

(12) Tenders should have the needed technical knowledge, great experience and enough financial power.
投标方应具备所需的技术知识,丰富的经验和足够的经济实力。

（13） Bids will be opened in public at 2:00 p.m. on September 1, 2008 (local time) at this Corporation.
开标将定于本公司当地时间2018年9月1日下午2点。

（14） 3A Wanshousi, Suzhoujie Street, Haidian District, Beijing, China
中国北京海淀区苏州街万寿寺甲3号

Writing Practice

I. Translate the following phrases from English to Chinese or vice versa.

1. come to an arrangement
2. be subject to
3. bid quotation
4. sealed bid
5. advertised bid
6. 合资企业
7. 公开招标
8. 投标保证
9. 报价
10. 中标，得标

II. Translate the following English into Chinese.

1. This is to introduce ourselves as one of the leading exporters from the United States, of a wide range of chemicals. We have enjoyed an excellent reputation through fifty year's business experience. We are sure that you will be quite satisfied with our services and the excellent quality of our goods.

2. Enclosed please find our quotation sheet. If the quality and prices of these articles meet the requirements of the market at your end, will you please send us your order at an early date so enable us to make the necessary arrangements for you.

3. In reply, we are pleased to tell you that we have today established with the National Bank the confirmed irrevocable Letter of Credit No. 6783 in your favor for the amount of USD 63,000 payable by sight draft accompanied by a full set of the shipping documents.

4. According to the contract stipulations, the aforesaid goods should be shipped three lots: April, June, and August, but up to the present moment, even the first lot has been shipped. Our end-users are waiting for the goods and they are very much surprised that you should have been much behind with the delivery.

5. As you see in our survey report stating twenty sets of heaters severely damaged. Therefore, we would ask you to ship replacements for the broken goods as soon as possible while we will file our claim with the insurance company. We hope the matter will come to your best attention.
6. Their share of the trade in the Asian market has amounted to 60%.
7. According to international practice, bidders need to hand in cash deposit or letter of guarantee from the bank when bidding.
8. Many companies bid on the new bridge and only the one that bids the lowest price will win the contract.
9. A number of laws and regulations have been promulgated with respect to the establishment of joint venture.
10. What taxes does your government impose on royalties and initial payment?

III. Translate the following into Chinese.

Bid Bond

We, ABC Bank, hereby guarantee to pay the above-mentioned amount under this Letter of Guarantee subject to the following conditions:

The above-mentioned amount to be paid to the beneficiary through your bank in case of the accountee does not enter into contract with the beneficiary owing to reasons solely attributed to the accountee.

This Guatantee remains in force until..., 20... after which date this Guarantee becomes null and void automatically and should be returned to us.

This Guarantee shall be released in full immediately when the accountee fails the bid.

Unit 13

Advertisements (广告)

- General Introduction
- Sample Reading
- Useful Expressions
- Writing Practice

General Introduction & Sample Reading

What Are Advertisements?

广告是由特定的商品经营者或者服务提供者以承担费用的方式通过一定传播媒介对商品、服务或观念等信息的直接或间接的非人员介绍及推广。

Types of Advertisements

广告可以划分为两大基本类别：商业广告和非商业广告。商业广告以盈利为目的，通过宣传以促进销售；非商业广告即慈善机构、宗教、民间或政治团体等非营利性组织发布的公告及启事等。本书主要论述商务英语写作，因此着重商业广告，对于后者在此恕不涉及，下文所指广告（Advertisement）均为商业广告。

广告还可分为分类广告（Classified Advertisement）和醒目排印广告（Display Advertisement）。前者一般采用分行式广告（Line Advertisement），即所有信息按照同样的字体逐行排列，没有特殊的版面设计；该类广告通常位于报刊中缝或末尾处，文字简洁，常常只有几行，且多使用短句、缩略词；内容多为求职、招聘、求租、出租等。而后者是报纸杂志中较重要的一类，使用多种字体，字体也根据需要大小不同，而且可能配有插图或辅以各种色彩，本章重点在于醒目排印广告，但仅着重于广告构成本身，而非配图或色彩等。

按照广告的宣传对象，可以分为产品广告和服务广告。产品广告通常由产品生产厂家或销售商发布，并面向产品消费者或购买者。服务广告兼具产品广告的特点，但由于服务本身无形性的特点，服务广告往往更具想象力，而且措辞与产品广告也略有不同，多借助数字、文字等使无形的服务具体化，使受众能有身临其境享受高质量服务的感受。

另外，还有一些其他类型的特殊商业广告，如招聘广告（Recruiting Advertisement）、投标广告（Bid Advertisement）等。尤其值得一提的是招聘广告，它不同于产品及服务广告，其读者是主动阅读，因而一般不用竭力吸引读者的注意，其语言直接简练、层次分明。

How Is an Advertisement Laid out?

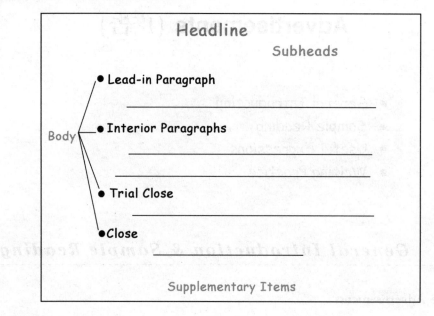

1. 标题（Headline）

标题是广告中最重要的组成部分之一，也最容易引起人们的注意。"好的标题，等于广告成功了一半"，广告标题的重要性可见一斑。清晰（clarity）和生动（force）是广告标题的主要特点。标题往往起着吸引注意、选择对象、连接正文、提出观点、体现新意、承诺清晰可见的利益的作用。

标题可分为直接性（direct）标题、间接性（indirect）标题、综合性（combined）标题。直接性标题将产品的主要情况直接告诉消费者，但仅使用直接性标题，往往不能引起消费者的足够重视，因而一般要用黑体字、大号字体等方法加以强调。间接性标题不介绍产品本身，而在于使读者感到好奇，从而继续往下看，但要避免使用生僻的文字而使人费解。综合性标题将前两者相结合，文义清晰。

2. 副标题（Subheads）

副标题的作用是通过简短的描述对广告的主题加以强化，进一步宣传新产品及服务的特点等。其位置一般处于标题之下，通过字体等加以突出。

3. 正文（Body）

正文是广告的主体部分，是对广告主题的详述，可以根据不同的宣传对象采用不同的叙述方式，如直陈式、叙述式、对话式、独白式等。

直陈式直接对宣传对象进行各方面的具体描述，尤其适用于工业产品，而较少运用于日常消费品。叙述式是以讲述故事的方式进行宣传。对话式采用让人物对话的方法来宣传对象，能够加强内容的可信度。独白式采用相近的方法，但是以广告人物自己的话来宣传。

不论采用何种方式，正文通常由如下 4 个部分构成。

1）引言（Lead-in Paragraph）

引言衔接正文主体与标题，使消费者对广告的兴趣转化为对宣传对象的兴趣。某些短小的广告也常常终止于引言部分。

2）内部段落（Interior Paragraphs）

内部段落是正文的中心部分，它要通过较为详尽的描述使宣传对象清晰明了，具有戏剧性、说明性，能够给消费者深刻印象，从而引起消费者的兴趣。

3）收尾（Trial Close）

收尾部分通常是宣传对象的订购信息，能够令消费者一目了然。

4）结束语（Close）

广告的结束语往往分为两种，一种直接建议消费者进一步咨询详细情况或者购买宣传对象，而另一种则以间接的方式暗示消费者购买宣传对象。

4. 附文（Supplementary Items）

在广告的最后，往往要加入一些附属部分，这些部分是对广告内容的进一步补充说明。附文部分包括公司商标（Trademark）、公司标识（Logotype）、权威机构的认证标记（Seals）、公司地址及电话等（Address, Telephone & Fax Number, Account Number, etc.），以增强广告所宣传对象的可信度，具有重要的推销作用。

Sample Reading

【Sample 1】

下面是一则对某品牌的传真机所做的直叙式广告，通过对该传真机的用途及使用方法的直接描述，显示出其特点。

CAN YOUR TELEPHONE READ AND WRITE?
OURS CAN!

Ordinary telephones can only talk.

Now there's a telephone that can read and write, too!

Qwip Systems Show'ntell Phone®—the educated telephone.

This incredible① telephone, in addition to② being used for incoming and outing calls, also sends and receives letters!

It can take almost anything you put on paper and send a copy of it —words, pictures and all cross-town or cross-country... in four minutes flat③. (Finally making it possible for you to deliver④ all those urgent things people wanted yesterday.)

Show'ntell is simple to install.

Just plug it into a telephone jack⑤ and an electrical outlet⑥ and it's ready to go. And anybody who can push a button can operate it. Why should your company be equipped with educated telephones? Because ordinary phones can only give you the message verbally, while a Show'ntell Phone puts it in writing. And anybody in business can tell you, that's quite a difference.

QWIP SYSTEMS SHOW'NTELL PHONE
(THE TELEPHONE THAT CAN READ AND WRITE)

① incredible：难以置信的 ② in addition to：除……之外 ③ flat：一律的
④ deliver：发送 ⑤ jack：插口 ⑥ electrical outlet：电源插座

您的电话会读写吗？
我们的会！

普通电话只能用来讲话。

现在已经有了能读也能写的电话了。

那就是 Qwip 系统公司的 Show'ntell® 电话——受过良好教育的电话。

这是一种令人难以置信的电话，除了可以打出、接入电话外，还可以发送、接收信件！

它可以记下你写在纸上的一切，并发出一份复印件——词语、图片，并且可以跨城、跨国传送……这些均只需 4 分钟。（最终，它还可能把人们昨天急需的一切都发送出去。）

Show'ntell 电话安装非常简便。

只需将其插入电话插孔及电源插座，就可以立即使用了。任何人只要会按按钮，就能操作使用。为什么您的公司需要装备这种受过良好教育的电话呢？因为普通电话只能传递口头信息，而 Show'ntell 电话能以文字形式将其表现出来。而且所有生意人都会告诉您，这一点是完全不一样的。

QWIP 系统公司 SHOW'NTELL 电话
（能读会写的电话）

[Sample 2]

下面是一则关于缝纫机的独白式广告，通过一位著名设计师口述自己的故事，说明了该缝纫机的优点所在，并大大增强了广告的可信度。

"My Sears Kenmore Sewing Machine has 9
different stretch stitches①—imagine！"

—says famous designer Bonnie Cashin

"My mother was a dressmaker and before I could write I could sew." says Bonnie Cashin, the lady who so greatly influenced American fashion with the poncho②—all those leathers and suedes③—the boot. All Bonnie Cashin — all firsts!

Unit 13　Advertisements（广告）

"I collect fabrics from all over the world. I'm always experimenting — with knits④—leathers —suedes. And my Kenmore handles anything I feed and so easily!"

"My new Kenmore not only zigzag⑤, it has 9 stretch stitches. Imagine, 9! Everything from a straight to an overcast⑥—what a help with knits and jerseys⑦! As for leather and thick layers of materials — wait till you see the control and power this Kenmore gives you at slow speed."

"Sewing relaxes me. But I do want a sewing machine to have as many automatic features as possible. My Kenmore has a truly automatic buttonhole stitcher, for example. Even an automatic monogrammer⑧."

"Now, tell me, why pay more for a sewing machine when you can get one like this Kenmore at Sears?"

Sears Kenmore Sewing Machine

For women who want the best even if it does cost less.

① stitch：针法　　　② poncho：穗饰披巾　　③ suede：小山羊皮　　④ knit：编织
⑤ zigzag：将……做成"之"字形　⑥ overcast：锁边　⑦ jersey：平针织物　⑧ monogrammer：织交织字母的工具

"我的 Sears Kenmore 缝纫机有9种弹织法 ——想想吧！"
　　　　　　　　　　　　　——著名设计师伯尼·卡茜如是说

"我母亲是位裁缝，在我会写字之前，我就已经会干缝纫活了。"伯尼·卡茜说。她制作的穗饰披巾对美国时尚产生了巨大影响——那些皮料和小山羊皮——还有靴子。这些都是伯尼·卡茜首先制作的！

"我从世界各地收集布料，经常用编织皮料、小山羊皮做试验。而且我的 Kenmore 缝纫机能够轻松自如地处理所有的活儿。"

"我的新 Kenmore 缝纫机不但能够成'之'字形编织，而且有9种编织法。想想看，9种！从直线到锁边，一切都可缝纫——这对编织和平针编织是多大的帮助啊！至于皮料和厚料子，只需等着看这种 Kenmore 以慢速能带给你什么。"

"缝纫令我放松。但我确实想要一种自动功能越多越好的缝纫机。比如我的 Kenmore 缝纫机就有一个全自动的锁眼机。甚至还有一个自动织交织字母的装置。"

"现在，告诉我既然在 Sears 您能买到像 Kenmore 这样的缝纫机，您为什么还要为一台别的缝纫机花更多钱呢？"

Sears Kenmore 缝纫机

专为想要最好的女性准备，
即使它的价格更低。

【Sample 3】

下面是一则招聘广告，招聘多部门的多个职位，要求简单明了，重点突出，一看即知。

Coats PRC Ltd.

Coats Lorileux of the Total Group in France is one of the largest ink producers in the world and to cope with the company's expansion① plan, we invite application for the following positions:

(1) PRODUCTION MANAGER

Male, aged 32-43;

At least 5 years production supervisory② and management experience in chemical manufacture field;

(2) LABORATORY TECHNICIANS

Diploma③ holder in Chemistry;

Some lab experience in printing ink or paint industry is preferred;

(3) ACCOUNTING MANAGER

At least 4 years experience in auditing, taxation, financial reporting and other accounting function;

Good computer skill and familiar with banking transactions;

(4) ADMINISTRATIVE ASSISTANT

At least 3 years working experience;

Possess a pleasant personality and positive work attitude and be willing and able to work diligently④ without supervision;

Ideally below 30 years of age and good character;

(5) PURCHASING CLERK

Male, aged 25-28;

2 or 3 years experience in purchasing chemical material or consumable material;

Initiative⑤;

Willing to work under pressure and travel;

Knowledge of Import and Export procedure;

An excellent employment package is offered.

Write, with full CV, send to Mr. J. Dive, Personnel Manager⑥, Box 3129 Paris.

---

① expansion：扩张，发展　　② supervisory：监督，管理　　③ diploma：文凭
④ diligently：勤勉地　　　　⑤ initiative：主动　　　　　　⑥ personnel manager：人事经理

Coats 中国有限公司

法国 Total 集团下属的 Coats Lorileux 公司是世界最大的墨水生产商之一。为与公司的发展计划相适应，我们希望招聘下列职位：

(1) 生产经理

男，32～43 岁；

在化工生产领域有至少 5 年生产监督管理经验；

> （2）实验室技术员
> 拥有化学专业学位；
> 在印刷墨水及印染工业方面有相关经验者优先；
> （3）会计经理
> 在审计、税收、财务报告及其他会计方面有至少4年工作经验；
> 良好的计算机运用能力，熟悉处理银行往来业务；
> （4）执行助理
> 拥有至少3年工作经验；
> 品性优良，工作态度积极，愿意并能在无监督情况下努力工作；
> 30岁以下及性格好者尤佳；
> （5）采购员
> 男，25～28岁；
> 有2～3年的化学品及消费品采购经验；
> 积极主动；
> 愿意在压力下工作及出差；
> 拥有进出口程序的相关知识；
> 应提供完整的应聘信息。
> 来信请提供完整个人简历，寄往人事部 J. Dive 先生，3129 信箱，巴黎。

【Sample 4】

下面是一家快递公司的广告，通过一系列的重复，使得主题鲜明，令人对该公司过目难忘。

> *From Andorra to Aruba.*
> *From Cameroon to Costa Rica.*
> *From Hong Kong to Holland. From Kenya to Kuwait.*
> *From Malaysia to Martinique. From Turkey to Thailand.*
> *One By One.*
>
> To earn your trust, not just your business. This has always been the aim of UPS.
>
> It takes a commitment to service. But more, it means giving you the practical worldwide network your business needs and being a partner who does business where you do business, which is why UPS now offers express delivery of parcels and documents to cover 180 countries and territories. Worldwide.
>
> The task may be as simple as getting your shipment from A to B, but at UPS we never forget that trust is earned by doing it right.
>
> Every single time. To every single place.
>
> **United Parcel Service**
> **As sure as taking it there yourself**

从安道尔到阿鲁巴。

从喀麦隆到哥斯达黎加。

从香港到荷兰。从肯尼亚到科威特。

从马来西亚到马提尼克。从土耳其到泰国。

一个接一个。

赢得您的依赖，而不仅仅是生意。这就是UPS永远追求的目标。

我们对我们的服务作出承诺。但更重要的，是为您提供您所需要的世界范围的实用网络，能够在任何您做生意的地方成为您可以依赖的伙伴。这就是UPS目前提供的可在180个国家和地区内进行包裹及邮件快递的业务。全世界均可投送。

这项工作也许和将您的货物从甲地运到乙地一样简单。但是对于我们UPS而言，我们永远铭记信任是通过完美地完成任务而取得的。

任何时间，送往任何地点。

联合货运服务公司

就如同您亲自送达目的地

Analysis

（1）由于受到时间、空间、资金等方面的影响，必然要求广告的简练，讲求"Keep It Sweet and Simple"（KISS）。这就要求在广告英语中，多用简单句、省略句、分离句、缩略词。

（2）广告英语应尽量通俗易懂，应多使用口语甚至俚语，以及小词汇（small words），才能更加贴近消费者。但同样也要使用高雅的语言，以烘托产品的品质特性。

（3）广告要努力营造出一种体贴消费者的氛围，要达到这一效果，在广告英语中就要多用现在时。

（4）广告英语中大量使用动词，尤其是单音节的动词，如 buy, get, give, like, love, make, need, use 等。

（5）广告英语中形容词使用非常广，同时比较级和最高级的使用也很多，但在使用最高级时，应避免夸大其词。

（6）复合词的灵活多变，在广告英语中几乎随处可见，用连字符连接的复合词尤为常见。

（7）广告英语中的句子必须大众化。清晰有力、口语化的简单句易为消费者所接受，冗长的句子会使人厌烦而失去兴趣。

（8）分离句是广告英语中特有的句法，通常利用句号、破折号、分号、连字符等，将句子分割成更多的信息单位，被分割出的部分往往是所宣传对象的重要信息。

Unit 13 Advertisements (广告)

Useful Expressions

Common Expressions

a complete range of specifications	规格齐全
a great variety of styles	款式多样
a wide selection of colors & styles	花色繁多
adopt advanced technology	采用先进工艺
aesthetic appearance	式样美观
agreeable to taste	味道适口
aromatic flavor	香味浓郁
as effectively as a fairy does	功效神奇
attractive and durable	美观耐用
available in various designs and specifications for your selection	备有各种款式现货，任您挑选
be awarded a gold medal	荣获金奖
be awarded super-quality certificate	荣获优质产品证书
be distinguished for	以……著称
be highly praised and appreciated by consuming public	深受广大消费者好评
be specially designed for	专为……而设计
can be repeatedly remoulded	可多次翻新
Catalogues will be sent upon request.	备有详细目录，惠索即寄。
comfortable feel	手感舒适
complete in specifications	规格齐全
convenient in use	使用方便
courteous service	服务周到
crease-resistance	防皱
delicacies loved by all	众所喜爱品尝之佳品
dependable performance	性能可靠
distinctive for its traditional properties	具有传统风味特色
dramatic results	效果卓著
durable in use	经久耐用
easy to handle	操作简便
easy to maintain and repair	维修简易
elegant and graceful	典雅大方
enjoy high reputation at home and abroad	誉满中外
famous throughout the world	全球闻名
firm in structure	结构坚固

guaranteed quality and quantity	保质保量
have a long historical standing	历史悠久
highly polished	光洁度高
ideal gift for occasions	节日送礼之佳品
Inquiries are welcome.	欢迎洽谈订购
latest technology	最新工艺
long and rich experience	历史悠久，经验丰富
moderate cost	价格适中
New varieties are introduced one after another	新品迭出
non-ironing	免烫
offer you best convenience	为您提供最大的方便
Orders are welcome.	欢迎惠订
outstanding features	特点突出
possessing Chinese flavors	具有中国风味
professional design	专业设计
rank first among similar products	居同类产品之冠
rapid heat dissipation	散热迅速
reliable performance	性能可靠
repeatedly admired	备受称赞
reputable all over the world	享誉全球
rich in poetic and pictorial splendor	富于诗情画意
selected materials	用料上乘
selling well all over the world	畅销全球
Stocks are always available in large quantities for prompt delivery.	备有现货，交货迅速
sufficient supplies	货源充足
suitable for the old and young	老少皆宜
unmatched in performance	性能超群
unique style	风格独特
up-to-date style	款式新颖
waterproof, shock-resistant and antimagnetic	防水、防震、防磁
win warm praises from customers	深受顾客欢迎

Frequently Used Adjectives

big, bright, clean, crisp, delicious, easy, extra, fine, free, fresh, full, good/better/best, great, new, real, rich, safe, special, sure.

Writing Practice

I. Look at the advertisements below and decide how they can be improved. Then REWRITE them in your own words.

(1) A new way to buy a new ESCORT car built in a new way. It still has four tires and the steering wheel in on the left. Other than that, everything else has changed for the 90's.

(2) You can have stronger, thicker hair in just 7 days. This is guaranteed. While healthier, shinier hair doesn't happen overnight, and it could take as long as 14 days.

II. Decide types of products (in the brackets) the following advertisements are for. If necessary, one can be used more than once.

(beauty, camera, car, cigarette, dress, drink, food, jewelry, medicine, mobile phone, PC, shoes, TV, vacuum, water, wine)

(1) Over 200 Years of Careful Breeding Produced This Champion

(2) Refreshment 16 Million times a Day

(3) Your Kid Just Spent 9 Months Totally Naked. Isn't It About Time You Got Him Something Fun To Wear?

(4) The Taste of Success

(5) To feel more beautiful, slip into something smoother.

(6) It's tracer, the new small sedan from mercury.

(7) VOLVIC from the Clairvic spring

(8) Choose Your Glasses Carefully

(9) When you see Dirt, see Red.

(10) The power of purity

(11) You've tried just about everything for your hay fever ... Now try your doctor.

(12) Do it the hard way, or do it the Sharp way.

(13) If your feet could dream! This is what they'd dream about!

(14) As easy to look at as it is to use.

(15) Tradition has a new taste.

(16) Proof that we don't cut corners

(17) It handles the road as easily as it handles Mother Nature.

(18) Dry scalp? It needs moisture more than medicine.

(19) Workout without wearout

(20) Spreadsome, Tastesome, Snacksome

(21) Safety, Security and Simplicity, All Wrapped Up In One.

(22) Yesterday's look, tomorrow's heirloom

(23) A price as thin as the monitor: $99.
(24) Feel & Look Young Again with Born Again DHEA Crème
(25) A Better School System for Your Kids.

III. Draft advertisements according to the notes given.

(1) 以分类广告的形式写一则招聘广告。招聘对象：① 两名具有文秘及组织才能的职员，主要工作是向经理汇报情况，负责办公室的日常运作；② 涉外营销人员三名，男性，精通英语，有5年以上营销经验，需经常出差。

(2) 以醒目排印广告的形式写一则招聘广告。Intertek Testing Services 公司要招聘多个职位：① 注册项目工程师，大学本科毕业以上，专业为电子、电气、机械、冷藏，三年以上电子及相关工作经验，有在国际检测机构工作经验者优先，良好的人际交流能力及团队精神，成熟自立；② 客户部职员，学士学位以上，英语或外贸专业，精通英语听、说、读、写，三年以上相关经验；③ 助理注册工程师，电子、电气或机械专业大学毕业，良好人际关系及团队精神，诚实好学，责任感强。所有三个职位均需良好的英语及计算机水平，并随附上中英文简介、学业证明、相关证明、身份证复印件，以及近照一张。来信寄往：上海浦东新区山西路201号 ETL SEMKO 人力资源部，邮编200120。

IV. Translate the following advertisements from Chinese into English or from English into Chinese.

(1)
珠江大酒店
精美日本菜肴
舒适的氛围　优美的音乐

如您想在本市寻觅日式精制菜肴，为何不到珠江大酒店这个既使人赏心悦目，又可以品尝可口菜肴的地方来聚一聚呢？

遵义南路888号
电话：7364621

(2)
To Rent
No. 768 East Nanking Road, Downtown Street

Formerly occupied by Li Hua Bedclothes Co. :

A five-storey brick building covering about 20 acres. Ground floor with a large clothing store. Large two-storied godown with vault and a garage at the back.

Dwelling house consists of ten large rooms with bath-rooms, etc., which may be rent separately in whole or in part. Water, electricity and gas laid on. Also very suitable for offices.

Apply to

Shanghai Garments Imp. /Exp. Corp.

Add. : East Zhongshan Road 1
Post Code: 200001

(3)   Chrysler Setting the Standard
Wherever We Go

Since 1925, the Chrysler Corporation has been setting the standard for automotive excellence in the United States. Today, we are doing the same in over 100 countries worldwide.

The home for all-new product development is the Chrysler Technology Center, one of the world's most technologically advanced vehicle research centers. It is here that platform teams of experienced designers, engineers, and manufacturing experts work together to create vehicles with some of the industry's most revolutionary designs.

Chrysler is committed to designing and manufacturing world-class automobiles that not only compete with the world's best, but surpass them as well. We invite you to see for yourself.

(4)   People with high standards value ours. Seiko

Far beyond the ordinary in styling and performance. Brilliant new timepieces with a solid emphasis on perfection, and the unequaled accuracy of a quartz movement. Handsomely refined. Meticulously detailed. Elegantly slender. To keep you looking your best every moment. From Seiko.

Unit 14

Introduction of Company (公司及产品介绍)

- General Introduction
- Sample Reading
- Useful Expressions
- Writing Practice

 General Introduction & Sample Reading

What Are Introduction of Company?

在商务活动中，常常需要对公司和产品的概况进行介绍。对公司和产品进行有效的介绍可以达到宣传公司，让更多的消费者、客户了解自己的公司，进而提高公司知名度和信誉度的目的。

公司介绍的篇幅根据需要可长可短，短至几行，长至好几页甚至一册。公司介绍应结合具体目的，有选择性地进行介绍，尽可能展示公司的良好形象，但也务必追求实事求是，以利于公司的声誉。

The Thinking of Writing Company's Introduction

在考虑比较详细的公司介绍的思路时，以下几个方面可作参考。

1. 概述

一般而言，在进行详细的公司介绍之前，往往先大致叙述一下公司的情况，如公司性质、组成、业务领域、主要产品等，让读者对该公司先有个大概的了解。例如：

Bausch & Lomb is the eye health company, dedicated to perfecting vision and enhancing life for consumers around the world. Its core business include soft and rigid gas permeable contact lenses and lens care products, and ophthalmic surgical and pharmaceutical products. The Bausch & Lomb name is one of the best known and most respected healthcare brands in the world.

2. 公司的历史简介

如果该公司享有悠久的历史，那么对这一部分进行介绍是十分必要的，因为这能大大增加读者对公司的信任感。从某种意义上讲，悠久的历史意味着产品或服务质量的保证和良好的信誉。因此，很多公司在介绍中会突出介绍这一部分。例如：

Panasonic Mobile Communication Co., Ltd., started out in January of 1958 as Matsushita Communication Industrial Co., Ltd., an offshoot of Matsushita Electric Industrial Co., Ltd., formed to specialize in industrial electronics equipment, including telecommunication devices, professional audio products, measurement equipment and more.

In the forty-four years since the company's inception, our history has been marked with an impressive track record or results. The following is a list of our major product developments and chievements:

1958

Installed stereophonic audio system for the Mainichi Osaka Center's Mainichi Hall.

1961

Installed Japan's first all-transistor audio system for the Tokyo Broadcasting System, Inc.

1967

Installed broadcast microphones for the annual NHK Red & White Song Contest: New Year's Eve Grand Song Festival.

1968

Began introducing pocket pagers for use by Nippon Telegraph & Telephone (NTT).

1975

Installed satellite gauges for the Institute of Space and Aeronautical Science, University of Tokyo.

1980

First awarded an Emmy for our digital video equipment. We received the same award in 1991 and 1993 as well.

1984

Installed Astrovision large-screen video system and RAMSA audio system at the Olympic Stadium for the Los Angeles Olympics.

1988

Received an Award of the Director-General of the Science and Technology Agency for the development of a device to train speech-impaired individuals to speak with greater ease.

1992

Introduced the first navigation system for the Toyota Mark II.

1996

Introduced the world's smallest, lightest cell phone for NTT Docomo, Inc.

1998

Installed car audio systems for General Motors vehicles.

1998

Installed emergency contact systems, E-call System, for Daimler Chrysler vehicles.

2001

Built the world's first W-CDMA base and introduced cell phones using that technology for NTT Docomo, Inc.

The above represent just some of the reasons behind Matsushita Communication Industrial's drive to exceed one trillion yen in consolidated sales for FY2000.

Effective January 2003, Matsushita Group has completed reorganization into 14 business domains in order to advance to the ever-expanding environment of 21 century. With the new name, Panasonic Mobile Communications Co., Ltd., the company is engaged in providing both infrastructure services of mobile communications and manufacturing of (advanced) mobile terminal handset. We make possible the seamless integration of telecommunication services and products as a whole.

上例对松下移动公司的历史进行了详细的介绍。它以列表方式讲述，使内容一目了然，条理清晰。

历史介绍部分可繁可简。对于成立时间不长的公司来说，这一部分可以稍加提及即可，重点可以放在其他更值得一提的内容上，如重大业绩等。

3. 公司现状介绍

毫无疑问，任何公司介绍的重点都应该放在公司现状的描述上。公司现状的介绍所包括的内容有的可能已在公司概述部分提及，但此部分会作更加详细的阐述。常见的内容包括：公司规模、公司管理机构及组成部门、经营范围、经营业绩、企业文化等。

（1）公司规模：可以从生产能力、资产数目、人员数目、下属机构等方面着手。例如：

Founded in 1853, the company is headquartered in Rochester, New York. Bausch & Lomb's revenues were $2.2 billion; it employs approximately 12,400 people worldwide and its products are available in more than 100 countries.

（2）公司管理机构及组成部门：公司部门的介绍应重点突出占据优势或对本公司具有重要意义的部门。例如，以下是对某公司研发部门的介绍。

AAA Corp. retains a strong commitment to innovation. The wealth of knowledge that AAA researchers have gain provides the basis for long-term, sustained growth. Research is essential capital for the future. In 2004, AAA spent $2bn on research and development and nearly 23,000 employees are engaged in research and development worldwide.

（3）经营范围：说明公司所从事的业务领域，所提供的产品或服务的种类，是必须介绍的内容。公司的行业地位也往往从中体现出来。例如：

We are best known to the public for our service stations and for exploring and producing oil and gas on land and at sea. But we deliver a much wider range of energy solutions and petrochemicals to customers. These in clude transporting and trading oil and gas, marketing natural gas, producing and selling fuel for ships and planes, generating electricity and providing energy efficiency advice.（Shell）

（4）经营业绩：公司的业绩可以充分反映公司的经营实力。它往往体现于销售额、产量和客户数量等有关方面。例如：

2014 fiscal year, in million：
- Net sales：29,758
- EBITDA：4,130
- Operating result（EBIT）：1,808
- Income before income taxes：985
- Net income：603
- Gross cash flow：3,210
- Net cash flow：2,450
- Stockholder's equity：12,268

（5）企业文化：企业文化（Corporation Culture）体现了企业的人文精神。良好的企业文化不仅能创造良好的企业氛围，提高员工的凝聚力和积极性，也有助于树立企业良好的社会形象。例如：

(**P&G**)

Core Values
- The values by which we live：
- Leadership
- Ownership
- Integrity
- Passion for Winning
- Trust

Principles

These are the principles and supporting behaviors which flow from our Purpose and Values：
- We Show Respect for All Individuals
- The Interests of the Company and the Individual Are Inseparable
- We Are Strategically Focused on Our Work
- Innovation Is the Cornerstone of Our Success
- We Are Externally Focused
- We Value Personal Mastery
- We Seek to Be the Best
- Mutual Interdependency Is a Way of Life

4. 公司前景展望

在此部分可以比较具体地描述一下公司近期的发展规划，也可以比较抽象地描述一下未来的发展趋势。例如：

Global Investments of Our Company

We are investing in the future by preparing for the market introduction of our recently-developed products.

To support this growth, we are expanding our production lines in Singen, Oranienburg and in the USA. In 2005, ALTANA Pharma laid the foundation for the ALTANA Research Institute in Waltham, near Boston. And a few tablet production plant is under construction in the vicinity of Cork, Ireland and in 2006, we will begin to build a research institute in Mumbai, India.

【Sample 1】

下面是关于美国汽车公司的片语式介绍,除了介绍厂商的联系方式和经营范围外,还用三言两语概括性地对公司进行了简介。

American Motors Corp. Address: American Center, 36 Franklin Rd. Southfield, MI 48034 USA Telephone: (007) 123456-5555 Brief Introduction: The corporation is mainly engaged in the manufacture, assembly and distribution of different models of automobiles and auto parts and components in the USA and Canada. Major products: Passenger cars, buses, leisure cars and their spare and auxiliary parts, and government special cars.	美国汽车公司 地址:美国密歇根州绍斯菲尔德市富兰克林路36号,美国中心,48034 电话:(007)123456-5555 简介:该公司主要在美国及加拿大制造、装配和销售各种汽车及汽车部件。 主要产品:客车,公共汽车,娱乐车及其备件、附件,政府专用汽车。

【Sample 2】

下面是关于福特汽车公司的篇章式介绍。详细具体地介绍了福特公司的规模、生产能力、经营范围等,使用户对福特公司有了比较全面的了解。在结束语以后注有厂商或公司的地址、电话等。

Ford Motor Company

Ford Motor Company is a multinational enterprises with active manufacturing, assembly[①] and sales affiliates in 29 countries, employing an average of 427,000 people worldwide. Ford products are now sold in nearly 200 countries and territories by a global network of some 14,000 dealers.

For 16 consecutive years, Ford has sold more cars and trucks outside North America than any other US-based vehicle manufactures in sales outside its own country. Ford is the second largest vehicles manufacture in the world. It has taken US truck market leadership in 10 of the past 13 years.

Unit 14 Introduction of Company (公司及产品介绍)

In addition to producing passenger cars and light, medium, heavy and extra heavy trucks, farm and industrial tractors, industrial engines, construction machinery, steel, glass and plastics, Ford Companies are established in finance, insurance, automotive replacement parts[②], electronics, communications, space technology, military weaponry and land development.

Ford's worldwide automotive manufacturing and marketing business is grouped into five principal regions; that is North America, Europe, Latin America, Asia-Pacific, and Mid-East and Africa. It's another organization—trade development operations—is largely engaged in development new business.

Address: The American Road Dearborn, MI 48121 USA
Telephone: (01) 313322-3000

①assembly 装配　②parts 部件

福特汽车公司

福特汽车公司是一个跨国企业，它在29个国家设有制造、装配和销售的子公司，在全世界范围内雇用的职工人数平均为427 000人。福特的产品通过一个由14 000家代理商组成的全球性销售网，向近200个国家和地区经销。

连续16年，福特的轿车和卡车在国外的销售额超过任何一家美国的同行企业。在世界各国的汽车制造业中，它的国外销售额也是最高的。福特是世界第二大车辆制造企业。在过去13年里，它有10年在全美国卡车市场中占据领先地位。福特汽车除了生产客车和各种轻型、中型、重型和特重型卡车，农用和工业用拖拉机，工业用发动机，建筑机械，钢材，玻璃与塑料外，还经营金融业、保险、汽车零件、电子技术、通信、空间技术、武器和土地开发工程。

福特的全球性汽车制造业和市场经营集中在5个主要地区，它们是：北美、欧洲、拉丁美洲、亚太地区和中东及非洲。该公司的另一个机构——贸易与发展处则主要从事新业务的开发。

地址：The American Road, Dearborn, MI48121, USA
电话：(01) 313322-3000

Useful Expressions

joint-venture enterprise	合资企业
backbone enterprise	骨干企业
star enterprise	明星企业
subsidiary	子公司
division	分公司
technical force/ capacity	技术力量
modern equipment	现代化设备
production line	生产线
assembly line	流水线
capacity	生产能力
storage	存储能力

registered capital	注册资金
annual turnover	年销售额
wholesale	批发
retail	零售
annual tax & profits	年利税
mature capacity	工艺成熟
flexibility	灵活性
market-prone	面向市场的
standardized	标准化的

Established in 1950, the company...
本公司创建于1950年,……

Taking advantage of the excellent geographical location, the factory...
本厂地理环境优越……

The Company is a technology-intensive enterprise for integrating mechanical and electrical engineering.
本公司是机电一体化的技术密集型企业。

The plant was authorized as the Grade A factory under the Quality Control Program in June 2008.
2008年6月,该厂被评为质量管理A级企业。

...with products of best quality in various dimensions and with perfect testing means as well as testing instruments.
……产品规格齐全,工艺设备精良,检测手段齐备。

Its capacity is 60,000 tons yearly.
年生产能力6万吨。

...with an annual sales value of 300 million yuan and a profit of 3 million yuan.
……年销售额3亿元,利润300万元。

The main products of the mill are...
本厂主要产品有……

Its products feature high durability and good appearance.
产品经久耐用,外观精美。

Overseas friends and associates are most welcome to make inquiries and business negotiations.
欢迎海外各界朋友前来垂询和前来洽谈业务。

I. Translating the following expressions into Chinese.

(1) backbone enterprise　　　　　(2) foreign exchange
(3) foreign currency earned　　　(4) supplier
(5) production line　　　　　　　(6) wear-resisting
(7) specification　　　　　　　　(8) durability

(9) cost-efficient   (10) future-oriented

II. Translating the following sentences into English.

(1) 产品获科技成果奖。
(2) 本公司制造的机器质量精良、可靠性高、品种广泛，为本公司在世界上赢得了重要地位。
(3) 该厂技术力量雄厚，生产工艺和设备先进。
(4) 公司连续多年产量、出口量、创汇量居全国同行业之首。
(5) 真诚欢迎世界各国朋友来我厂发展贸易关系，进行经济技术合作。
(6) 本产品便于操作，易于维修。
(7) 本产品深受用户好评。
(8) 毯面弯曲明显，水纹坚牢，光泽油亮，强力好，手感丰富，有弹性，保暖性强，图案新颖。
(9) 通用电气公司是主要的工业配电盘生产商。

III. Fill in the blanks to outline the corporation culture.

(1) _____

We work hard to exceed the expectations of our employees, customers, and associates.

(2) _____

We take pride in our work and our company.

(3) _____

We conduct business with integrity and trust.

(4) _____

We respond quickly to customer needs.

(5) _____

We *respect* each other and recognize excellent performance.

(6) _____

We believe in the *development* and *recognition* of our employees and associates.

(7) _____

We believe inconstant improvement—*a passion to be better*

(8) _____

We believe in *tensity* and *competition* fuel success.

(9) _____

We believe in being *a good corporate neighbor*.

(10) _____

And, we believe quality *growth* and increasing profit are the result.

Unit 15

Brochures, Instructions & Manuals
(指南、说明书及手册)

- General Introduction
- Sample Reading
- Useful Expressions
- Writing Practice

General Introduction & Sample Reading

What Are Brochure, Instruction and Manual?

Brochure 是指包括推销材料或产品信息的小册子，即说明书、背景资料、简介等。Brochure 与广告有相近之处，都是一种宣传手段，但也有很大的区别。广告是对产品和服务的宣传，而 Brochure 不仅如此，还可以是对会议、公司等的介绍与宣传，同时，内容也更加详尽，格式也不相同。

Instruction 是关于操作、实施步骤的详尽的指导，即操作指南、指导方法意见、书刊介绍等。

Manual 则是指能够提供如何进行操作、遵守规章制度的指南的手册、小参考书。

Types of Brochure, Instruction & Manual

Brochure 的种类主要是根据其宣传对象的内容而分的，其宣传对象主要为公司、会议、协会、城市、旅游景点等。公司宣传手册是对公司或企事业单位的职能、产品或服务、特点等方面进行的简单介绍。会议、论坛、展览会等的宣传推广手册主要是关于其主题内容的简要介绍，并对潜在的参与者发出邀请，还可以列出将出席或发表演说的重要人物。协会介绍是对该协会的历史、宗旨、发展情况、入会方式等的说明。旅游景点简介是用尽量简短的语言，对其最突出的特点进行描述，并说明其中相对著名的景点。

Instruction 同样按其说明的内容划分，大致可以分为产品说明、操作说明等。产品说明是用来说明产品的性能特点、功能、使用与保管方法。不同的产品，说明的方法也有出入，但基本的特点是相似的。操作说明主要是关于器具，尤其是电器一类产品的操作步骤及注意事项等。

Manual 同 Instruction 的内容有重叠之处，也包括了产品的使用手册、用户手册、操作手册等，另外，它还包括诸如员工手册、学生手册，等等。员工手册等主要是对所管辖人员设定的规章制度等。

Styles of Brochure, Instruction & Manual

由于这三种文件的内容多样，其格式并不完全固定，因而此部分所说的格式问题，只是通常所见的情况。

Brochure 一般包括标题、正文、附加信息三大部分。Instruction 则包括标题、使用前说明、目录、正文、索引等。Manual 中的产品说明与 Instruction 相类似，员工手册等则一般只分为标题、正文、结尾部分。

Sample Reading

【Sample 1】

下面是著名风景区嵩山的一则简短的旅游指南。

Scenic Spots on Songshan

- **Fantastic Rocks**
- **Ancient Trees**
- **Charming Water**

Songshan has 20 spectacular scenic spots featuring either peaks, ravines, caves, waterfalls, springs or woods, all equally majestic and charming. Tumbling waterfalls and mist curling around the peaks add much to the beauty of the mountain. Junji Peak is thick with pines, which rustle like a murmuring stream in a gentle wind but roar like angry waves when the wind blows hard. The mountain is particularly exquisite in autumn, when most of its trees turn golden and red.

Shaoshishan, the highest peak of Songshan, is a spot not to be missed. To scale Shaoshishan one must run the risk of negotiating a one-meter-wide passage hewn between precipitous cliffs, and clinging to iron chains as one goes. The summit provides a panoramic view of the surrounding peaks, wave-like forest-covered hills and other beautiful sights such as Miraculous Mist Gorge, Immortals' Gorge, Resounding Pool Ravine, Ice Cliffs, Water Curtain Cave and the Echo Pavilion.

嵩山——奇石、古树、冰瀑

中岳嵩山，翠峰挺拔，气势磅礴，景象万千。由峰、谷、洞、瀑、泉、林等自然景观构成的中岳二十景，嵩门待月、秀逸诱人，或飞瀑腾空、层峦叠嶂，多姿多彩。嵩山林木葱郁，一年四季迎送风雪雨霜，生机盎然。峻极峰上松林苍翠，山风吹来，呼啸作响，轻如流水潺潺，猛似波涛怒吼，韵味无穷。嵩山秋色，少室红叶更是迷人。金秋季节，群峰盈金，树叶流丹，峡谷山峰，丛丛、簇簇、似火、似霞、娇艳夺目。

少室山是嵩山森林公园的重点区域，山势陡峭险峻，奇峰异观，比比皆是。登少室须沿着绝壁上一米多宽的石缝，攀铁环、拽钢丝上下，断崖悬古道，人在空中行，其险峻使游人赞叹称绝。登上山顶环顾四周，群山碧绿，林海荡漾，云雾缥缈如临仙境。灵霄峡、大仙峡、响潭沟、持冰崖、水帘洞、回音楼、景物天成，引人入胜。

【Sample 2】

以下是名著《飘》的一则简单介绍，寥寥数笔，说明了其突出之处。

"Gone with the Wind" — written by Margaret Mitchell
- One of the greatest American novels of all time.
- A magnificent historical romance set against the panorama of the Civil War.
- Over 10 million copies sold.

《飘》——玛格丽特·米歇尔著
- 一部美国小说史上最伟大的著作。
- 一个基于美国内战全貌、壮观的历史爱情故事。
- 销售量超过1 000万本。

【Sample 3】

下面是极为常见的西药说明书，基本各项均已列全，但仍可加上保质期等信息。

ANTISTINE: DIRECTIONS FOR USE

Antihistamine for the Treatment of Allergic Affections

[**Properties**]:

Antistine either attenuates or suppresses the effects of histamine, which plays a major role in provoking allergic disorders. It is upon this experimentally confirmed ability to antagonize histamine that the indications for Antistine are based.

[**Indications**]:

Urticaria; food allergies; hay fever; vasomotor rhinitis; itching due to skin diseases, including eczema; pruritus; and serum sickness.

[**Administration and dosage**]:

Tablets

Adults: 1 tablet, 3 – 4 times daily.

Small children: 1/2 tablet, once daily.

Children of school age: 1/2 tablet, 2 – 3 times daily.

The tablets should be taken during meals and swallowed whole with a little fluid.

Ampoules

1 ampoule is given each time by intramuscular or slow intravenous injection, 2 – 3 times daily. For children the doses should be correspondingly reduced.

[Note]:

Since Antistine may cause temporary drowsiness, caution is indicated when it is employed, for example, to treat drivers of vehicles. Like other antihistamines, Antistine, too, may give rise to allergic reactions. In such cases the preparation should be withdrawn.

[Composition and forms of issue]:

2 – (phenyl-benzyl-aminomethyl) – imidazoline (= antazolin): tablets of 100 mg and ampoules of 2 ml containing 100 mg.

Made in Switzerland

安替司丁使用说明书

治疗过敏性病症的抗组胺剂

[性质]:

安替司丁可减弱或抑制组胺作用,组胺在激发过敏性病症中起重要作用。本品的适应症正是根据这种实验证明的抗组胺作用来确定的。

[适应症]:

荨麻疹、食物过敏、花粉症、血管舒缩性鼻炎;由皮肤病症引起的瘙痒(包括湿疹);瘙痒病和血清病。

[服法与剂量]:

片剂

成人:每次1片,1日3～4次。

小儿:每次1/2片,1日1次。

学龄儿童:每次1/2片,1日2～3次。

本片剂应在用餐时服用,用少量的水吞服。

针剂

每次1瓶,1日2～3次,肌注或缓慢静注。儿童剂量应相应减少。

[注意事项]:

本品可引起暂时性倦怠,使用时要严加注意。例如,对司机的服用就要慎重。正如其他抗组胺药物一样,本品也可能引起过敏性反应。如遇这种情况,应停止使用。

[成分和包装]:

2 – (苯基-苄基-氨甲基) -咪唑啉(= 安他唑啉);每片含100 mg;2 ml 装的安瓿含100 mg。

瑞士制造

I. Try to make tables of contents according to the requirement.

(1) A table of contents of a HOTEL
(2) A table of contents of a STEREO
(3) A table of contents of a brochure of a service COMPANY

II. Write a brochure of Xiamen.

要求：厦门的地理位置；作为经济特区发展迅速；厦门港的重要性；发达的金融业；外贸与投资情况等。

III. Translate the following brochure into English.

AFP

The Asia Forest Partnership（亚洲森林伙伴关系）

携手共建亚洲可持续森林经营

亚洲森林伙伴关系简介

亚洲森林伙伴关系（AFP）旨在促进亚洲地区的森林可持续经营，是由各国政府、国际组织、民间团体等多样的相关利益群体自愿参加的合作形式。

亚洲森林伙伴关系成立背景（从里约到AFP）

AFP成立于2002年约翰内斯堡召开的可持续发展世界首脑会议。它是在联合国可持续发展处登记的200多个伙伴关系之一。这些伙伴关系的共同目标是，以1992年里约地球首脑会议宣言和联合国千年发展目标为基础，促进可持续发展，补充而不取代政府间义务。AFP第一个阶段计划持续到2007年。

AFP重点领域

AFP以下面3个课题为重点，促进亚洲地区森林可持续经营

- 防止非法砍伐
- 控制森林火灾
- 恢复退化林地和造林

为了促进高效的森林经营，AFP还开展能力建设、良政建设和加强森林执法等工作。开展这些深层次和交叉主题的工作将有助于在上述三个领域取得更好的成果。

AFP——独特的工作方式

AFP工作方式是协调现有的计划和行动，减少重复。AFP通过建立起一个正式的共享信息和经验框架，强化现有项目的合作，开展新的活动，促进在各国内部、双边、多边及地区行动的合作。伙伴关系平等、自愿、开放的特征促进立场、观点不同的合作方加强

Unit 15　Brochures, Instructions & Manuals（指南、说明书及手册）

合作。
民间团体
- 大自然保护协会（TNC）（发起成员）
- 世界资源研究所（WRI）
- 全球环境战略研究所（IGES）
- 全球环境论坛（GEF）

各国政府
- 澳大利亚
- 柬埔寨
- 中国
- 欧盟
- 芬兰
- 法国
- 印度尼西亚（发起成员）
- 日本（发起成员）
- 韩国
- 马来西亚
- 菲律宾
- 俄罗斯
- 瑞士
- 泰国
- 英国
- 美国
- 越南

国际组织
- 亚洲生产力组织（APO）
- 亚洲开发银行（ADB）
- 国际林业研究中心（CIFOR）（发起成员）
- 联合国粮农组织（FAO）
- 国际热带木材组织（ITTO）
- 联合国森林论坛秘书处（UNFF）
- 联合国亚太经社会（ESCAP）
- 联合国大学（UNU）

AFP 欢迎新成员自愿加入

联络方式

AFP 信息共享秘书处

国际林业研究中心（CIFOR）

Jl. Cifor, Situ Gede, Sindangbarang
Bogor Barat 16680
Indonesia
电话：+62-251-622 622
传真：+62-251-622 100
E-mail：afp@cgiar.org
主页：www.asiaforests.org

Unit 16

Invitations（邀请函）

- General Introduction
- Sample Reading
- Useful Expressions
- Writing Practice

General Introduction & Sample Reading

What Are Invitations?

邀请函（Invitation）是书信的一种形式，常常是告知别人某事并邀请别人参加某项活动的文件。它的内容可长可短，格式可分为请帖式（Formal Invitation）和书信式（Invitation Letter）。

请帖式的邀请函又称请帖，有一定格式。企业、政府、机关、团体或个人如有什么隆重的活动需邀请对方参加，可以将要传达的意思简短地写成请帖的形式发给对方，如大型宴会邀请、官方会议及舞会邀请、盛大婚礼邀请、展览会邀请等。邀请面较广的内容往往还要登在报纸、杂志、电视、网络等大众媒体上。

书信式的邀请函除用于机关、单位、学校、团体等相互邀请，也可用于熟悉的人如朋友、亲戚之间的一般性邀请，如一般的婚礼邀请、就餐邀请、聚会邀请、出游邀请等。它一般书写在纸条上，书写形式没有书信那么严格，通常不用写开头语、写信人地址、收信人地址、结尾语等项目。但如果要求对方回复，而对方又不知你的地址，就有必要留下地址了。

邀请函要求用词简洁恰当，内容清晰有条理。

How Is an Invitation Laid out?

1. 请帖式的邀请函（请帖）（Formal Invitation）

```
                    INVITATION
              ××（who）and ××（who）
         request the pleasure of ××（who）
                  at dinner（purpose）
                ××（day），××（date）
                   at ×o'clock（time）
                     ××××（place）
```

正式的请帖。一般来说，请帖的上方往往有 INVITATION 或 INVITATION CARD 的字样，来引起对方注意。正式请帖一般都是印刷于卡片之上，偶尔也有手写的。它不像一般书信那样一行接一行地书写，而是以一种不规则地向内缩排形式来编排文字。

正文一般居于整张卡片的正中位置，常常以艺术字体呈现。设计、字体和卡片背景要美观大方。请帖上需写明邀请人姓名（name of the person who invites）、被请人姓名（name of the person who is invited）（姓名要写全名，不可缩写）、邀请事项（purpose）、时间（time）、地点（place）。如需回音，还应加上电话号码或邮政地址。正文要求简短精要，将内容讲清楚就可以，以便让对方一眼就能明了。正式请帖没有开头称呼和结尾署名，因为这两项已包括在正文中。

正式请帖的行文不使用第一人称（I would like . . .），而使用第三人称（Mr. and Mrs. ×× request the pleasure of Mr. ××）。

对此类请帖的回复也同样使用第三人称和同样的文字编排方式。通常应先表示感谢，再表示接受或拒绝。如接受，则在感谢后写明应邀出席的时间和地点。如拒绝，则在歉意后婉转注明不能出席的原因。

【Sample 1】

A. Chaney 夫妇将于 5 月 18 日（星期六）下午 3 时整在圣路易斯教堂为他们的小女儿 Jane 与 Anderson 先生举行结婚典礼，邀请亲友光临。邀请函采用了卡片的形式，突出了邀请人和被邀请人，给人以正式的感觉。

```
                 Mr. and Mrs. Dan Chaney
              request the honor of your presence
               at the marriage of their daughter
                           Jane
                            to
                  Mr. Lou Josef Anderson
              on Saturday, the eighteenth of May
```

Unit 16 Invitations（邀请函）

at three o'clock p. m.
Saint Louis Church
and afterwards at No. 312, the Olive Tree Avenue for the dinner
R. S. V. P. ①

① R. S. V. P. : 敬请赐复

　　兹定于5月18日（星期六）下午3时整在圣路易斯教堂为小女简与罗·约瑟夫·安德森先生举行结婚典礼，之后在橄榄树大街312号举行晚宴。
　　敬请
光临
　　　　　　　　　　　　　　　　　　　　　　　　　　　　丹·查利先生和夫人

敬请赐复

B. 接到 Chaney 夫妇请帖的 Deleon 先生应邀参加，并给予答复。

Mr. Joe Deleon
accepts with pleasure the kind invitation
of
Mr. and Mrs. Dan Chaney
at the wedding ceremony of their daughter with
Mr. Lou Josef Anderson
on Saturday, the eighteenth of May
and to the dinner which will follow at No. 312, the Oliver Tree Avenue.

　　乔·迪李奥先生愉快地接受丹·查利先生和夫人盛情邀请，将出席5月18日（星期六）下午3时整在圣路易斯教堂为他们女儿简与罗·约瑟夫·安德森先生举行的结婚典礼以及之后在橄榄树大街312号的晚宴。

[Sample 2]

下面是两则有关宴会邀请的请帖（Invitation to a Dinner）。

A. Roberts 医生夫妇定于6月3日（星期二）晚七时在喜来登饭店举行宴会，发出邀请。

Dr. and Mrs. Lea Roberts
request the pleasure of your company
at dinner
on Tuesday, the third of June
at seven o'clock p. m.
Sheraton Hotel

兹定于6月3日（星期二）晚七时在喜来登饭店举行宴会，敬请光临。

李·罗伯茨医生和太太

B．接到 Roberts 医生夫妇邀请的 Thomson 夫妇因故不能应邀而给予答复。

Mr. and Mrs. Danny Thomson

regret that a previous engagement

prevents their acceptance of

Dr. and Mrs. Lea Roberts'

kind invitation

to dinner

on Tuesday, the third of June

at seven o'clock p. m.

Sheraton Hotel

由于有约会在先，丹尼·汤姆森夫妇不能出席李·罗伯茨医生和太太于6月3日（星期二）晚七时在喜来登饭店举行的晚宴，对此深表遗憾。

丹尼·汤姆森夫妇

Analysis

（1）请帖的排版格式非常重要，以居中的方式排版，注意要美观大方。以上几例都采用了这种编排方式。婚礼请帖的版面色彩、形式可以设计得喜庆些，宴会、舞会请帖的设计也可根据需要采用不同的色彩和方式。

（2）请帖中的时间和地点一定要明确写出，不能模糊不定。一般来说，仅仅写出星期几是不够明确的，被邀请者很可能不清楚是哪个星期，所以需要加上具体日期，而且日期也大多用完整的字母来表示。如例1中的"on Saturday, the eighteenth of May"和例2中的"on Tuesday, the third of June"。

（3）不论接受还是拒绝，对请帖的回信也应按照请帖的格式书写。一般来说，时间、日期和地点都应重复。如例1（B）中的"on Saturday, the eighteenth of May and to the dinner which will follow"是对（A）中内容的重复。例2（B）中的"to dinner on Tuesday, the third of June at seven o'clock p. m. Sheraton Hotel"是对（A）中时间、地点的重复。

（4）欧美的正式邀请一般是一对夫妻共同做出邀请，所以夫妻双方的名字都应出现在请帖开头。此外，如果被邀请方也是一对夫妇，则他们的名字也应一同出现，回信也应当如此。如例1（A）中的"Mr. and Mrs. Dan Chaney request the honor..."和例2（B）中的"Mr. and Mrs. Danny Thomson regret that a previous engagement prevents their acceptance of Dr. and Mrs. Lea Roberts' kind invitation"。

（5）如期望对方回复，可以在请帖的末尾加上电话号码或地址，有时加上"R. S. V. P."

提醒对方回复，如例1（A）中的"R. S. V. P."。

2. 书信式邀请函（Invitation Letter）

Dear ××,
　　Will you _____
_____
_____.

　　　　　　　　　　　　　　　　　　　　　　　Sincerely yours,
　　　　　　　　　　　　　　　　　　　　　　　　　　××

　　根据需要邀请函也可以写成普通书信的形式，可手写也可打印。它的格式与普通书信一样，有开头称呼语（一般写全名）和结尾署名，具体格式如上所示。
　　一般邀请函采用第一人称，对它的回复也同样。回复的内容与正式请帖一样，分为接受与拒绝。

【Sample 1】

　　下面是两则有关婚礼邀请的邀请信（Invitation to a Marriage）。
　　A. Amanda 与 Andrew 定于1月20日（星期五）下午两时在家里举行婚礼，向她的叔叔 Paul 发出邀请。由于通信双方为熟悉的亲友，用词无须太过正式，让人读来觉得亲切万分。

Dear Uncle Paul,
　　I am pleased to tell you that Andrew and I have decided to be married at home on Friday, the twentieth of January, at two o'clock in the afternoon. **We hope** you and Aunt Sophia will be present and join the dinner afterwards.

　　　　　　　　　　　　　　　　　　　　　　　Affectionately,
　　　　　　　　　　　　　　　　　　　　　　　　　Amanda

亲爱的鲍尔叔叔：
　　我很高兴地告诉您，安德鲁和我决定于1月20日（周五）下午两点整在家里举行婚礼。我们希望您和索菲亚婶婶能来参加婚礼以及之后的喜宴。

　　　　　　　　　　　　　　　　　　　　　　　您亲爱的
　　　　　　　　　　　　　　　　　　　　　　　　阿曼达

　　B. Amanda 的叔叔 Paul 接到邀请后给予回复，表示参加。

Dear Amanda,
　　Please accept our hearty thanks for your kind invitation to your marriage on Friday, the twentieth of January, at two o'clock in the afternoon.

> **I am thrilled with** the news that you will be married. I remember you were a pretty little girl when I saw you last time. **You may be sure that** we will join you on that day to celebrate your wedding.
>
> Affectionately Yours
Uncle Paul

> 亲爱的阿曼达：
>   我们对你盛情邀请我们参加你1月20日（周五）下午两点整举行的婚礼表示衷心感谢。
>   听到你即将举行婚礼，我感到万分激动。我记得上次见到你时，你还是个可爱的小姑娘。我们一定会去参加并庆祝你的婚礼的。
>
> 鲍尔叔叔

【Sample 2】

下面是一则学术访问的邀请信（Invitation to an Academic Visit）。波士顿国家实验室的 Darter 主席向张华发出邀请，请他去实验室进行学术访问。

> Dear Mr. Zhang Hua,
>   **We would like to invite you to** visit Boston National Laboratory for a period of six months, beginning on about 15th July, 2014. This visit will provide an opportunity for you to contribute your expertise① to the biological DNA study.
>   **We will provide you with** workspace and other work-related support as needed. If you have any questions about the visit, please contact us at (510) 246-5677 or by E-mail (BNL @ lbl. gov).
>
> Sincerely
Bill Darter, Chairman
Boston National Laboratory

① expertise：专门技术

> 亲爱的张华先生：
>   我们想邀请您来波士顿国家实验室进行为期六个月的访问，访问大约开始于2014年7月15日。这次访问将为您提供机会，使您得以在生物DNA研究领域应用自己的技术。
>   我们将向您提供工作场所及其他与工作有关的必要条件。如您对于这次访问有任何疑问，请拨打电话 (510) 246-5677 和我们联系，也可以向我们电子邮箱（BNL@ lbl. gov）发信。
>
> 此致
主席，比尔·达特
波士顿国家实验室

【Sample 3】

下面是一则有关生物学大型展览会的邀请函（Invitation to an Exhibition）。北京的生

Unit 16 Invitations（邀请函）

物研究组织 CBA 定于 2003 年 5 月 14 日至 17 日召开大型的展览会，主席王城刚先生特此向 Hayes 教授发出邀请，请他到北京参加。

Dear Pro. Regent Hayes,

I am sincerely inviting you, **on behalf of** the Chinese Biological Association（CBA）, **to participate in** Tech China 2003 to be held in Beijing, China, from 14 to 17 May, 2003. Tech China achieved a great success in 2002. Since its beginning in 1995, it has been the best one in history. Compared with last year, the conference participants, exhibitors and visitors increased by one third in 2002. I am confident that Tech China will be much better in 2003.

Beijing, a cosmopolitan① city with a large population, is the business, economic and trade center of China. We warmly invite you to participate in Tech China 2003 in Beijing.

I am looking forward to seeing you in Beijing.

Sincerely Yours,
Wang Chenggang
President, CBA
Co-Chairman of Tech China

① cosmopolitan：世界性的

尊敬的雷吉特·海斯教授：

我代表中国生物协会，真挚地邀请您于 2003 年 5 月 14 日至 17 日来中国北京参加 2003 中国技术展会。中国技术展会在 2002 年取得了极大成功。从 1995 年第一届开始，中国技术展一直备受关注。与去年相比，2002 年的会议参与者、展出者和来访者增加了 1/3。我相信 2003 年的展会将更成功。

北京是一个人口众多的国际性大都市，是中国的商业、金融、贸易中心。我们热烈欢迎您来参加北京的 2003 中国技术展会。

我们期盼您的到来。

此致
王城刚
中国生物协会会长
大会联合主席

Useful Expressions

(1) request the honor of your presence at...　荣幸地邀请您参加……
(2) and afterwards at...　之后在……
(3) and to the dinner which will follow　和之后的晚宴
(4) I am pleased to tell you that...　很高兴地告诉您……

(5) hope ... will be present and join the dinner afterwards 希望……能出席并参加之后的晚宴

(6) We are planning to have ... 我们打算召开……

(7) We should be very pleased if you could honor us with your company. 如您能来，我们将不胜荣幸。

(8) We do hope you will find it possible to join us. 我们真的希望您能来。

(9) We invite you to participate in ... 我们邀请您参加……

(10) I am sincerely inviting you, on behalf of ..., to participate in ... 我代表……真挚地邀请您来参加……

(11) We will provide you with ... 我们将提供您……

(12) Having you with us for this special opportunity would ... 值此特殊时刻，您的参与将……

(13) I am looking forward to seeing you. 盼望见到您。

(14) We are honored to have ... 我们荣幸地请来了……

(15) We would appreciate your assistance with ... 我们将感谢您对……的帮助

(16) Please accept our hearty thanks for your kind invitation to ... 请接受我们对您盛情邀请的衷心感谢。

(17) I am thrilled with the news that ... 听到……的消息，我万分激动。

(18) You may be sure that we will join you ... 我们一定来参加……

(19) We are very obliged to your kind invitation to ... 对您的盛情邀请，我们十分感谢。

(20) will be delighted to dine with ... 很高兴与你们一起用餐……

(21) regret that a previous engagement prevents their acceptance of ... 很遗憾，先前与别人的订约使他们不能来参加……

(22) Please accept my sincere regrets for not being able to join ... 不能来参加……，我们感到非常的遗憾。

(23) I shall have to say sorry to you because ... 因为……，我不得不向你说声抱歉。

(24) R. S. V. P. 敬请赐复

Writing Practice

I. Look at the invitation below and rewrite it in an informal style.

Mr. and Mrs. Rod Robert
request the honor of
Mr. and Mrs. Ellis Chambers'
presence at dinner

on Saturday, November the fifth at six o'clock p. m. Scarlet Club R. S. V. P.   Telephone：   37-7836

II. Look at the invitation below and write a refusal.

Dear Mr. and Mrs. Daniel Becker,

    Will you join John and me in a party with several intimate friends on Sunday, March 9th, from three to five p. m. at the Country Musical Bar?

    We should be very pleased if you could honor us with your company.

Affectionately Yours
Joanna Thomas

III. Draft invitations according to the hints given.

（1）Charles M. Durham 先生和 Christine 小姐定于 2017 年 8 月 18 日星期五下午三时在 Maple 教堂举行婚礼，请以女方父母 David Bird 夫妇的名义帮他们向 Dustin Harman 医生夫妇写一封请柬，并留下电话号码 687 – 5452，以便回复。

（2）下面请写一份朋友间的邀请信。Joan 与她的丈夫 Joe 买到了四张下周五（4 月 12 日）晚八点"泰坦尼克号"的电影票，他们邀请 Betty 和她的丈夫 Dave 在六点半前来共进晚餐，然后同去看电影。

（3）Betty 和她的丈夫 Dave 欣然接受 Joan 与 Joe 的邀请（Draft 2），在感谢的同时答应来赴约。请帮他们写一封表示接受的回信。

（4）Betty 的丈夫 Dave 将去北京出差，下周内不能回来，因此 Betty 对 Joan 与 Joe 的邀请进行了委婉拒绝，在表示歉意的同时建议他们另行邀请一对夫妇。请帮他们写一封表示拒绝的回信。

（5）下星期六（12 月 24 日）是圣诞夜，数学与科学学院的学生想邀请外国语学院的学生来参加舞会。舞会从七点开始，十一点结束。请帮他们写一封邀请函。

Unit 17

Social Letters (社交信函)

- General Introduction
- Sample Reading
- Useful Expressions
- Writing Practice

General Introduction & Sample Reading

What are Social Letters?

　　虽然现代科技一日千里，通信手段也越来越先进，信函这一古老而普通的通信方式，始终为人们使用着，因为信函具有精确、长久、正式的特点。信函的种类繁多，但就其内容而言，大致可分为社交信函、事务信函和商业信函三大类。本章主要介绍前面两种。

　　无论哪一类书信，语言明了、简洁、准确乃是英语信函的首要要求。明了（Clearness）要求一封信一般说明一两件事，段落分明，层次清楚，主题突出，使对方一目了然。简洁（Conciseness）指言简意赅，必要的事项皆说清楚，不提无关之事。准确（Correctness）主要指语言准确达意，避免使用过多的修饰词。此外，还应注意礼貌（Courtesy），应文雅而有礼貌，掌握分寸，既不迎合恭维，也不吹嘘浮夸。

Components of an English Letter

　　(1) 信头（Heading），即寄信人的地址和日期，写在信笺的右上角。
　　(2) 信内地址（Inside Address），即写信人的姓名和地址，写在左上角。
　　(3) 称呼（Salutation），即对收信人的敬称或称谓，其位置在信内地址的下两行处，并与之平头。
　　(4) 正文（Body），即信函的内容。
　　(5) 结束语（Complimentary），即写信人表示自己对收信人的一种谦称。
　　(6) 签名（Signature），即写信人的姓名。
　　(7) 附件（Enclosure），缩写成 Encl。
　　(8) 再启或又及（Postscript），缩写成 P. S.，用于补叙信的正文中遗漏的话。

以上8项内容中,第1项至第6项是英语信函的主要组成部分,一般不可缺少。第7项和第8项是否需要,则视具体情况而定。

下面举一例以便更清楚地展示英语信函的结构及以上各项在信内的排列位置。

(1)信端(Heading)

Physics Department

Zhejiang University

Hangzhou, China

September 20, 1990

(2)信内地址(Inside Address)

Chairman

Department of Physics and Astronomy

Northwestern University

Evanston, Illinois

U. S. A.

(3)称呼(Salutation)

Dear Chairman,

(4)正文(Body)

I repeatedly tried to telephone you yesterday, but your line was busy all the time and I was unable to make contact with you, and therefore, I am writing this letter, to which I wish you would give me a prompt reply.

(5)结束语(Complimentary Close)

Sincerely yours,

(6)签名(Signature)

Liu Dawei

(7)附件(Enclosure)

(8)又及(Postscript)

P. S. Please send allmaterial by mail

Sample Reading

【Sample 1】

下文是一封祝贺信,表达了写信者对对方升职的热烈祝贺和进一步发展双方合作的诚挚期待。

Dear Mr. Minister,

　　Allow me to convey my congratulations on your promotion to Minister of Trade. I am delighted that the many years service you have given to your country should have been recognized and appreciated.

We wish you success in your new post and look forward to closer cooperation with you in the development of trade between our two countries.

Yours faithfully,
Bob Adams

尊敬的部长先生：

请允许我向您升任贸易部长表示祝贺。多年来你对国家的贡献被认可、欣赏，我非常高兴。我们祝愿您在新的职位取得成功，期待我们两国在贸易发展上进一步合作。

您诚挚的
鲍勃·亚当斯

下文是对上文的回复。

Dear Mr. Adams,

Thank you for your letter conveying congratulations on my appointment. I wish also to thank you for the assistance you have given me in my work and look forward to better cooperation in the future.

Sincerely Yours,
Alden Ade

尊敬的亚当斯先生：

感谢您来信对我的任命表达的祝贺。我也感谢您对我的工作给予的支持，并期望未来能有更好的合作。

您诚挚的
奥尔登·艾德

【Sample 2】

下文是一封抱歉信，简洁明了地陈述了道歉缘由，并许诺了补救措施。

Dear Mr. / Ms.,

We are sorry we cannot send you immediately the catalogue and price list[①] for which you asked in your letter of March 10. Supplies are expected from the printers in two weeks and as soon as we receive them, we will send you a copy.

Yours faithfully,
Charlotte Trent

---

① catlogue and price list 目录和价格单

尊敬的先生/小姐：

对3月10日来信所要目录和价格单，很抱歉不能马上寄去。印刷商两周后供货，一旦收到，我们将给您寄去一份。

您诚挚的
夏洛特·特伦特

【Sample 3】

下文是一篇解释信。针对来信的质疑，写信者解释了出错原因并承担责任，给予了道歉和说明了补救措施。

Dear Mr. / Ms.,

I was very concerned when I received your letter of yesterday complaining that the central heating system in your new house had not been completed by the date promised.

On referring to our earlier correspondence, I find that I had mistaken the date for completion. The fault is entirely mine and I deeply regret that it should have occurred.

I realize the inconvenience our oversight must be causing you and will do everything possible to avoid any further delay. I have already given instructions for the work to have priority and the engineers working on the job to be placed on overtime. These arrangements should see the installation completed by next weekend.

Yours faithfully,
Maria

尊敬的先生/小姐：

昨天收到你的来信，抱怨你新家的中央加热系统未按规定时间装好，对此我非常关心。参考较早的通信，我发现我搞错了完成日期。错误完全是我的，对此我非常抱歉。

认识到我们的疏忽给你造成的不便，我们将竭尽全力避免再耽搁。我已指示这项工作优先做并让工程人员加班。这样安排会于下周完成安装。

你诚挚的
玛利亚

【Sample 4】

下文是一篇抱怨信，信中写明了产品出现的问题，并表达了希望得到积极补救的态度，将重心放在补救措施而没有放在抱怨上，可谓恰如其分，有礼有节。

Dear Sir,

On 5th October I bought one of your expensive "Apollo" fountain pens from Julian's, a big department store of this town. Unfortunately I have been unable to use the pen because it leaks and fails to write without making blots[①]. I am very disappointed with my purchase.

On the advice of Julian's manager I am returning the pen to you and enclose② it with this letter for correction of the fault.

Please arrange for the pen to be fixed or replace it with a new one and send it to me as soon as possible.

Yours faithfully,
Allen

① blots 污点 ② enclose 附上

敬启者：
　　本人于10月5日在本市的朱利安大百货公司购买了你们出产的名贵"阿波罗"型号钢笔一支。但遗憾的是，我一直未能使用这支笔，因为它漏墨水，一写字就漏出一滴滴墨水污渍。我对所购买的产品非常失望。
　　现按照朱利安百货公司经理的意见，我随信把这支笔退还给你们，以便你们设法补救。
　　请你们安排修理此笔，或换一支新的给我，并望早日寄来为盼。

你诚挚的
安伦

【Sample 5】

下文是一封提示信，简洁说明了来信缘由，反映对方的疏忽，并再三提示对方应尽快重视起来。

Dear Mr. / Ms.,

On 14th November I submitted a bill for services rendered to your office at the Lille International Exposition①. More than a month has now elapsed② without payment or acknowledgment of my bill. Please check this oversight and remit③ payment at your earliest convenience. I look forward to future services to your corporation.

Thank you for your prompt attention to this matter.

Yours faithfully,
Jane

① exposition 博览会 ② elapse 时间过去 ③ remit 汇款

尊敬的先生/小姐：
　　11月14日我向你办公室在Lille国际博览会上提供的服务提交了账单。一个月过去了，你既没有付款也没有认可账单。请检查这一疏忽并在最方便的时候付款。期望以后还为你公司服务。
　　谢谢你能对此事尽快重视起来。

你诚挚的
简

Unit 17　Social Letters（社交信函）

【Sample 6】

下文是一封咨询信，开头表明了询问的事实，之后说明了来信者了解的状况和不解之处，就此在最后向对方提出咨询。

Dear Mr. / Ms. ,

　　We are much concerned that your sales in recent months have fallen considerably. At first, we thought this might be due to a slack market①, but on looking into the matter more closely, we find that the general trend of trade during this period has been upwards. It is possible that you are facing difficulties of which we are not aware. If so, we would like to know what we can do to help. We, therefore, look forward to receiving from you a detailed report on the situation and suggestions as to how we may help in restoring② our sales to their former lever.

　　　　　　　　　　　　　　　　　　　　　　　　　　　　　　　Yours faithfully,
　　　　　　　　　　　　　　　　　　　　　　　　　　　　　　　　　　Barbara

---

① a slack market 市场不景气　② restore 恢复

尊敬的先生/小姐：

　　我们非常关心你方销售近几个月大幅度下降的问题。开始我们以为是市场疲软，但仔细研究，我们发现过去这段时间贸易的总趋势是上升的。有可能你方面临我方还不知道的困难，如是这样，我方想知道是否能帮助什么。我们期望收到关于问题的详细报告，及建议我们怎样帮助才能把销售恢复到原来的水平。

　　　　　　　　　　　　　　　　　　　　　　　　　　　　　　　　　你诚挚的
　　　　　　　　　　　　　　　　　　　　　　　　　　　　　　　　　　巴巴拉

【Sample 7】

下文是一篇约见信，写明了来访者、来访缘由和预定的时间安排，最后征求了对方意见。

Dear Mr. / Ms. ,

　　Mr. John Green, our General Manager, will be in Paris from June 2 to 7 and would like to come and see you, say, on June 3 at 2∶00 p. m. about the opening of a sample room there.

　　Please let us know if the time is convenient for you. If not, what time you would suggest.

　　　　　　　　　　　　　　　　　　　　　　　　　　　　　　　Yours faithfully,
　　　　　　　　　　　　　　　　　　　　　　　　　　　　　　　Barack Obama

尊敬的先生/小姐：

　　我们的总经理约翰·格林将于6月2日到7日在巴黎开放有关样品房的事宜，他会于6月3日下午2:00拜访您。

请告知这个时间对您是否方便。如不方便,请建议具体时间。

您诚挚的

巴拉克·奥巴马

Any Assistance you may render to him will be highly appreciated.

您对他的任何协助,我将感激不尽。

We are pleased to advise you that Ms. Wang, the vice president of our company, is planning to visit your country in early July.

我们很高兴通知您我公司副总裁王女士计划七月初访问贵国。

If it is not convenient to you, please suggest another time.

如果此时间不合适,请您提议其他时间。

Would you be free (available) to meet me at 10:00 am on May 20?

请问我们可以在5月20日上午10点见面吗?

We have great pleasure in introducing to you, by this letter, Mr. Wu Di.

非常高兴通过此信向您介绍吴迪先生。

I'd be most grateful if you could…

如果您能……我将不胜感激。

I would like to provide you more information upon your request.

如有要求,我愿向您提供更多信息。

We are planning to send a purchasing group of four people to visit your country in October of this year.

我们计划派遣一个四人采购小组在今年10月访问贵国。

We are looking forward to your visit.

我们热切期待您的来访。

Mr. Liu plans to stay in Paris for a week to inspect your plant and discuss with you the details of compensation trade agreement.

刘先生计划在巴黎停留一周,考察你们的工厂并与你讨论补偿贸易协议的细节。

We should be grateful if you could send us an invitation to the Exhibition.

如果您能发给我们参加展览会的邀请函,我们将不胜感激。

Please reply whether this visit is convenient to you.

此次拜访是否方便,敬请回复。

Writing Practice

I. Please translate the following Chinese into English.

王女士：

　　您好！关于今天我们通过电话讨论的次品集装箱问题，您建议我只需要把顾客每月退回的次品集装箱的数量写个报告给你，而不是直接退集装箱。我计划立即付诸实际。但我想确认我是否理解正确，到下周为止，如我不能收到你的书面答复，我即认为你没有异议。

II. Write a letter in English according to the information given below.

　　给 Jack Smith 先生写一封短信，内容：已收到他 5 月 14 日的来信，请他于本月 25 日来你公司，讨论合作细节。

　　请注意：必须包括对收信人的称谓、写信日期、发信人的签名等基本格式。

III. Write a letter of congratulation according to the information given below.

亲爱的布尔先生：

　　值此 2022 年即将到来之际，我谨向你致以最良好的问候和祝愿。

　　我希望，在新的一年里我们双方公司的交流有进一步的增加，并希望我们与你们之间的友好关系继续下去。

Unit 18

Public Speeches (致辞与演讲)

- General Introduction & Sample Reading
- Useful Expressions
- Writing Practice

General Introduction & Sample Reading

What Are Public Speeches?

随着时代的发展,当代社会人们的交流机会日益增多,致辞与演讲的使用频率也越来越高。在各种正式和非正式场合中,与会者根据自己的身份发表各种演讲,有些是即兴的,有些是事先准备好的。对于正式场合的致辞或演讲常用于大型会议、仪式等场合,这类致辞或演讲要求结构严谨、语言规范。小型的仪式或个人举行的活动等非正式场合中的讲话,经常为即兴致辞,语言较为随和、轻松。但多数演讲都需要事先起草书面文书,在语言上具有用词准确、言简意赅、深入浅出、通俗易懂、扣人心弦等特点。

Public Speeches for Different Purposes

开头已经提到,场合不同,演讲和致辞的内容与风格也会有差异。常见的演讲或致辞有欢迎和欢送词、答谢词和告别词、开幕词和闭幕词,以及祝酒词等。接下来,本章将逐一介绍最为常见的4种演讲或致辞。

1. 欢迎词和欢送词(Welcoming Speeches & Send-off Speeches)

(1) What Are Welcoming Speeches and Send-off Speeches?

欢迎词指行政机关、社会团体、企事业单位或个人在公共场合欢迎友好团体或个人来访时致辞的讲话稿。欢迎词是社交礼仪演讲词的一种,使用较多,言辞热情,旨在对来宾表示欢迎和尊重,表达友好往来,增强交流与合作的心愿,营造和强化友好和谐的社交气氛。

欢送词是领导在欢送仪式或宴会上向来宾发表的表示热烈欢送的讲话稿，其主要功用与欢迎词除使用的时间、场合上的不同外，并无实质性的区别。欢送词在感情上表达对宾客的依依惜别之情。除内容外，写法上也与欢迎词大致相同。

（2）Formats of Welcoming Speeches & Send-off Speeches

欢迎词一般由标题、称谓、正文、结语和落款等部分构成。欢送词的格式大致上和欢迎词相同。

①标题。欢迎词的标题有三种：一是只写"欢迎词"；二是在"欢迎词"前加欢迎仪式或庆典的名称；三是欢迎仪式或庆典名称前再加致辞者的职务和姓名。当然，标题只限于书面刊登，致辞时就不必宣读了。

②称谓和问候语。称谓前要用敬语，并且要写全称，如"Dear President Obama"等。如果来宾来自不同的方面，要一一顾及，应使所有来宾都能感受到欢迎仪式的亲切、庄重和热烈。称谓之后通常加问候语。

③正文。正文的写法灵活多样，一般包括如下内容：

● 欢迎。首先表明自己的身份和代表谁（个体或团体或二者兼有）致辞，接着对来宾的到来表示欢迎。

● 致谢。回顾交往历史，畅叙合作经历，表达真挚热忱。

● 祝愿。展望合作前景，表达美好祝愿。

④结语。再次向客人致谢。

⑤落款。欢迎词的落款要署上致词单位名称、致辞者的身份、姓名，并署上日期。

[Sample 1]

下文是一篇欢迎词，对来访者表示了诚挚的欢迎和衷心的祝愿。

Ladies and Gentlemen,

We are proud and honored to have such a distinguished group of guests coming all the way from the United States to visit our company.

Our staff and employees will do their best to make your visit comfortable and worthwhile. Today, they will introduce you to our newly-built plant and R&D department[①]. Please do not hesitate to ask any questions you may have.

I take great pleasure in bidding you all a hearty welcome to our company and sincerely hope that your visit here will be pleasant and meaningful.

---

① R&D department 研发部

女士们、先生们：

各位贵宾从美国远道而来参观本公司，我们感到非常荣幸。

本公司员工一定会尽力使各位在访问期间既舒适又充实。今天，他们会带领各位去参观我们新建的工厂及研发部。各位如果有什么问题，请别客气，尽量提出来。

我向来本公司的各位致上最诚挚的欢迎，并衷心希望各位在此的访问愉快又有意义。

【Sample 2】

下文是一篇欢送词，对离任者过去的工作给予了肯定，对他的离开感到遗憾，表达了不舍之情。最后仍以积极乐观的言语表达了对升迁者的由衷祝福。

Ladies and Gentlemen,

 We are gathered here today to send off one of our managers, Mr. Allen, who has been appointed to his new post in the headquarter of New York.

 I am very happy that he has been promoted. For the four years Mr. Allen has been with us, his ability and dedication have always been a source of pride to us. We enjoyed every minute that we worked with. His absence from this office will be a great loss.

 However, it will definitely be a great gain for the New York office, Mr. Allen, we are going to miss you very much, and instead of concluding my speech with the customary "Good-bye", allow me to say "Good luck and much happiness!"

女士们、先生们：

 今天我们聚在这里替我们一位经理艾伦先生送行，他被指派到纽约总部就任新职。

 对于他的升迁，我感到很高兴。艾伦先生跟我们在一起的四年中，他的才能及尽职精神一直是我们的骄傲。我们和他一起工作的每时每刻都是高兴的。他离开这里将是我们的一大损失。

 不过，这对纽约公司来说，绝对是一大收获。艾伦先生，我们会非常想念你的。我不想用惯用的"再见"来结束我的讲话，允许我说："祝你好运和快乐。"

---

2. 答谢词和告别词（Thank-you Speeches & Farewell Speeches）

（1）What Are Thank-you Speeches and Farewell Speeches?

答谢词，是指在特定的公共礼仪场合，主人致欢迎词或欢送词之后，客人所发表的对主人的热情接待和给予的关照表示谢意的讲话。答谢词也指客人在举行必要的答谢活动中所发表的感谢主人盛情款待的讲话。

告别词，是指在特定的公共礼仪场合，为向公众宣布退出某个领域、工作或岗位而发表的讲话。告别词的写作重点在于说明退出的原因，并感谢大家的支持。

（2）Formats of Thank-you Speeches and Farewell Speeches

答谢词一般包括标题、称谓和正文三部分。

①标题。标题分为完全性标题和省略性标题。完全性标题由致辞人＋事由＋文种构成，如"××在××会上的答谢词"；省略性标题由事由＋文种构成，如"在××会上的答谢词"；也有的只写文种，以"答谢词"作为标题。

②称谓。它是对答谢对象的称呼，一般由"Ladies and Gentlemen"等开始，也有时候前面加上"Dear××"，"Respected××"，"Distinguished××"等。

③正文。正文要叙述双方之间的交往和友谊，强调对方所给予的支持和帮助，并表明对巩固和发展友谊与合作的打算和愿望等。结尾则再次表示感谢，并且表示良好的祝愿。

告别词的结构由标题、称呼、开头、正文、结语五部分构成。

①告别词的开头，应先宣布退出。

②告别词的主体，再进一步阐明自己退出的原因，要说得具体而且得体。其间也可回顾自己在这个具体的领域或岗位上所取得的成就、获得的支持和理解，并表达依依不舍之情。

③告别词的结尾，主要是再次表示感谢，感谢公众对自己一直以来的支持，并表明心迹。

[Sample 1]

下文是一篇感谢信，表达了对招待方热情款待的感谢和双方进一步友好交流的期待。

Ladies and Gentlemen,

Your hospitality① is extraordinary.

For myself and for our entire delegation, I thank you for your warm welcome.

I don't know how I can thank you sufficiently for holding this welcome party for us. It has been a long cherished② hope of ours to visit Netherlands some day. We are fortunate to have had this rare chance today. We feel specially honored to be given this opportunity to meet such a nice group of distinguished people like you. We are sure our stay here will be an enjoyable and fruitful one. We do hope to see more of you while we are here.

① hospitality 好客，殷勤 ② cherished 怀有的

女士们，先生们：

你们的款待是非同寻常的。

我以我个人及整个代表团的名义感谢你们的热烈欢迎。我们一直想来荷兰访问。幸运的是今天我们终于能如愿以偿。特别使我们感到荣幸的是我们能有机会遇到你们各位知名人士。我们深信这次的访问一定会既愉快又有收获。希望在访问期间能多多向各位请教。

[Sample 2]

下文是一篇告别词，对送行者表达了由衷的谢意，感激他们过去的帮助，并在最后表示不会辜负送行者的期望。

Dear Friends,

In the first place, I wish to say a word of thanks for holding this send-off party for me. Actually I did not expect at all that you would hold one for me. I owe a great deal to all of you.

It has been five years already since I came to work at this company. Doesn't time fly? I am leaving in just a few days and, for better or for worse, this will be our last meeting.

During the past years, if I have done anything useful here it's because of your help, for which I am so grateful. I will miss all of you while I'm away. Let's keep in touch at any rate①.

What's more, I am thankful to the company for giving me such a chance to work in New York, and earnestly hope that I will live up to② everyone's expectation.

① at any rate 无论如何 ② live up to 不辜负

> 亲爱的朋友们：
> 　　首先我想说句感激的话，感谢各位为我举办这个欢送会。实际上，我一点也没想到你们会为我举办这样的欢送会。我真是非常感谢你们。
> 　　我在这个公司工作已有5年之久了，时间过得真快啊！再过几天我就要走了。不管怎样，这是我们最后一次聚会了。
> 　　在过去的几年中，如果我曾做过什么有益的事，那是因为有你们的帮助。对此，我充满感激。离开的这段时间里，我会想念大家的。不管发生什么，让我们保持联系。
> 　　还有，我要感谢公司给予我去纽约公司工作的机会。我真诚地希望我不会辜负你们的期望。

3. 开幕词和闭幕词（Opening Speeches & Closing Speeches）

（1）What Are Opening Speeches and Closing Speeches?

开幕词是党政机关、社会团体、企事业单位的领导人，在会议开幕时所作的讲话。开幕词通常以简洁、明快、热情的语言阐明大会的宗旨、性质、目的、任务、议程、要求等，对会议起着重要的指导作用。

闭幕词是会议结束时，致词人代表组织所发表的热情友好、感谢的言辞。闭幕词是一些大型会议结束时由主要负责人或德高望重者向会议所作的讲话。具有总结性、评估性和号召性。它是大会的结束语，主要内容是概述大会的议程、基本精神、主要成果和意义，说明大会提出的号召、要求等。闭幕词是会议成功结束的标志。闭幕词和开幕词一样，具有简明性和口语化两个特点，其种类与开幕词相同。

（2）Formats of Opening Speeches and Closing Speeches

一则得体精妙的开幕词，可以给会议带来一个良好的开端。开幕词一般由标题、称谓、正文三部分组成。

标题。标题有两种写法：一种是会议全称加"开幕词"，标题下面注明开会的时间，外加括号，在下面写上宣读人的姓名；另一种是把宣读人的姓名写进标题中去。

称谓。标题下第一行顶格写称谓，通常加敬语。

正文。正文包括开头、主体、结尾三部分。

同开幕词一样，闭幕词也由标题、称呼和正文三部分组成。

【Sample 1】

下面是一篇闭幕词。用语要简短有力，热情洋溢。

> Ladies and Gentlemen,
> 　　Our symposium① has lasted three days. It has achieved tremendous② results. Twenty linguists and scholars have spoken at the symposium. Many more aired their views freely at

the group discussions, which proceeded in a friendly and lively atmosphere. I benefited greatly by attending this symposium.

English is a very important tool in communication, especially on the day when the economy and trade in the world is developing rapidly. At this symposium, many linguists and teachers gave their good suggestions on English-teaching methodology③, which will be helpful to the study of the language. Let's join our hands and do more work to make more people have a good command of English.

Ladies and Gentlemen, you have my best whishes for your still greater achievement in your career in the future.

Now, I declare this symposium closed.

Thank you.

① symposium 研讨会 ② tremendous 巨大的 ③ methodology 方法

女士们，先生们：
　　我们的研讨会开了三天，取得了巨大的成绩。有20位语言学家和学者在大会上发了言。更多的人在小组讨论会上自由地谈了自己的观点。讨论会开的生动活泼、气氛友好。我出席这次会议，感到受益匪浅。
　　英语是十分重要的交际工具，特别是在世界经济高速发展的今天更是如此。在这次研讨会上，许多语言学家和教师就英语教学法发表了许多好意见，这将有助于这门语言的学习。让我们携起手来，为更多的人好好掌握英语做更多的工作。
　　女士们，先生们，祝你们在未来的事业中取得更大的成就。
　　现在，我宣布大会闭幕。
　　谢谢诸位。

[Sample 2]

下面是一篇开幕致辞。致辞者首先表达了对与会者的感谢，之后简单介绍了下一个发言者的内容，以使与会者对接下来的会议内容有个先期的了解，并且期待会议能够在一个热烈的氛围中进行。最后，说明了会议后的晚餐安排。整篇致辞既表达了对与会者的感谢和尊重，也介绍了会议的进程和安排，详略得当，言辞昂扬。

Ladies and Gentlemen,

I want to welcome you all here for the third annual meeting① of our Southeastern Asian sales staff. I know you are all busy, so I appreciate your making time in your schedules to attend today.

There are 18 participants heretoday. First, Mr. Carl Allen, our sales manager, will make a few remarks. He will speak about the sales projection for the coming year and the problems that some of us have had in the past year. After Mr. Allen's remarks, the meeting will be opened for comments and discussion from the rest of you.

We hope that you will all earnestly take part in this meeting. You are all skilled and successful salesmen as shown by your records in the field. This company is growing by leaps and bounds[②], and the way to keep growing, and to stay ahead of the competition is to openly and freely exchange our opinions and our successful techniques, and to speak about our failures.

After the meeting, we will all adjourn to[③] the Lotus Room of this hotel for a buffet dinner[④]. Now shall we begin?

[①] annual meeting 年会 [②] leaps and bounds 跳跃式（增长、前进） [③] adjourn to 换至（某地） [④] buffet dinner 自助晚餐

女士们，先生们：
　　欢迎你们来此参加东南亚业务部员工第三次年会，我知道你们都很忙，所以非常感谢你们今天抽空参加。
　　今天有18位与会者，首先卡尔·艾伦先生，我们的销售经理，将发表谈话，他将谈谈未来一年的销售计划，以及过去一年里，有些人所遇到的问题。在艾伦先生的讲话之后，将由你们进行评述和讨论。
　　希望大家都踊跃参与此会。正如每一个人这方面的记录所显示，你们都训练有素且是成功的推销员。公司业务迅速增长，而保持增长及处于竞争领先地位的方法，就是开放自由地交换意见，交换成功的技巧，还有谈论自己的失败之处。
　　在会议之后，我们将移往饭店的芙蓉厅，享用自助晚餐。现在我们开始好吗？

4. 祝酒词（Toast Speeches）

（1）What Are Toast Speeches?

祝酒词是在酒席宴会的开始，主人表示热烈的欢迎、亲切的问候、诚挚的感谢、衷心的祝愿等内容的应酬之词。祝词的结构形式有简约型和书面型两种：简约型多用一两句精粹的话语，把自己最美好的祝愿表示出来，有时也可以引用诗句名言来表达自己的心意。另一种是文章式，全文由标题、称呼、正文和祝愿语等几部分构成。书面型标题可以直接写"祝词"，"祝酒词"等，也可以由讲话者姓名、会议名称和文种构成，如"××在××会上的祝酒词"等。

（2）Formats of Toast Speeches

正式的祝酒词一般有四个部分：标题、称呼、正文、结尾。

标题。可以只写祝酒词即可，也可以在前面加上什么场合什么人致辞等文字。

称呼。祝酒词的称呼往往要尽可能的全面，显得亲切。若为单独向某人敬酒，应根据双方的地位等因素选择恰当的称呼。

正文。正文可分三部分写。第一部分表示欢迎、欢送、问候、感谢等。第二部分是主体部分，要写实质性内容。如双方的合作、友谊，会谈、会见的历程、成果、发展、意义或对对方态度的称赞、感谢等。还可以对对方的成就和一贯的友好态度等给以肯定和赞誉。第三部分写祝愿、希望。最后提议为某某人或者某某事干杯。

写祝酒词，要根据对象、场合、双方关系的融洽程度，以及此前相关事务进展等情况

考虑措辞。一般都应当显示出热情诚恳、感情充沛、随和轻松的态度，如果能恰当地使用幽默的语言，宴会气氛会更加轻松、活跃。但要注意对方的习俗、禁忌。祝酒词虽然可以随和自由，不那么严肃、刻板，但轻松谈笑中，仍要避免失礼、失态。

【Sample 1】

下例是一篇祝酒词。致辞者首先对访问团的到来表达了热烈的欢迎。之后表达了对双方合作的信心和私人友谊的良好祝愿，言辞诚恳。

Ladies and Gentlemen,

　　It gives me great pleasure on behalf of this company to extend a warm welcome to the members of the Chinese delegation who have been invited to this country by this company. I understand that arrangements are being made for a comprehensive programm and I need not say more about this now.

　　I have, however, just heard that agreement has been signed by our two ministers in Brussel① for the increase of mutual trade. We are confident that this will surely help further the development of the two companies' cooperation. I should, therefore, like to propose a toast to② the broad prospects of extensive cooperation and exchange between us, to our growing personal as well as commercial ties③!

---

① Brussel 布鲁塞尔　② propose a toast to 提议为……干杯/为……祝酒　③ commercial ties 商业往来

女士们，先生们：

　　我很高兴代表本公司向应公司邀请来到我国的中国代表团成员表示热烈欢迎。我们知道，一个大的项目正在拟议中，对此我现在不必多说。

　　不过，我刚刚得到消息说我们两国部长已在布鲁塞尔签署增进双方贸易的协议。我深信这将有助于进一步发展我们之间的合作和交流。因此，我提议为我们之间的广泛合作和交流的广阔前景干杯，为日益增长的私人和商业往来干杯！

 Useful Expressions

　　I take great pleasure in bidding you all a hearty welcome to our company.
我由衷地欢迎各位来公司。
　　It is an honor and priviliege to receive a visit from such a distinguished group.
能够接待各位贵宾来访，真是我们的荣幸。（这是非常正式的说法）
　　Thank you for coming all the way to China.
感谢各位远道来中国进行访问。
　　I had long been looking forward to visiting Philips, a company of world fame.
我一直很希望参观享有世界声誉的飞利浦公司。

Allow me once again to express my sincere thanks to you all for your kindness and hospitality.

让我再一次感谢各位的好意和热情。

We are sure our stay here will be a worthwhile and meaningful one.

我相信我们在此地的访问将会充实而有意义。

We are now here to bid him farewell. How time flies!

现在我们再次热情欢送他。时间过得真快啊!

We are gathered here today to send off one of our collegeues, Mr. Miller, who has been appointed to his new post in New York.

今天我们聚在这里替我们的一位同事米勒先生送行,他被指派到纽约就任新职。

We want to take this opportunity to beg him to convey our profound friendship and best regards to his people.

我想借此机会请他转达我们深厚的友谊,并表达对他同胞良好的祝愿。

We are very happy to be here tonight when we can have the opportunity to express our thanks and to bid farewell to our Chinese friends.

很高兴今晚在此聚会,借此机会,我向中国朋友表示感谢并说声再见。

In the first place, I wish to say a word of thanks for holding this send-off party for me.

首先,我想说句感谢的话,感谢各位为我举办这个欢送会。

Let's propose a toast to our friendship!

让我们为友谊干一杯!

Now please raise your glasses and drink a toast, to the success of your visit!

现在请举起酒杯,为你们此次访问成功干杯。

Wish them a long life of happiness together.

祝他们白头偕老。

Congratulations on your twenty-fifth wedding anniversary. I am very excited to be a part of this celebration.

恭喜你们结婚25周年。我能参加这项活动感到非常高兴。

Thank you all for coming tonight to celebrate this happy and joyous occasion.

谢谢你们大家今晚来庆祝这个快乐的日子。

I wish you the best of luck in the new year.

我祝各位新年好运。

The Award committee has reached unanimous decision to give this award to Mr. Wu.

颁奖委员会已经达成一致决定,把这个奖颁给吴先生。

I am pleased to announce the recipients of this year's Award for Excellence.

我很高兴能宣布今年最佳表现奖的受奖人。

The honor you have presented me with this evening will always remain very special.

今晚诸位给我的荣誉我将终生难忘。

I want to thank all of you whose diligence and dedication made this possible.

我要感谢各位的勤奋和全心投入,你们使我获得了这次荣誉。

Writing Practice

Write public speeches according to the information given below.

1. 假如你是一家外贸公司的职员,加拿大的投资商即将来访,公司派你接待并致欢迎词。你需向他们介绍新建立的经济发展区和研究中心,并对外宾的到来表示热烈欢迎。
2. 两个月前史密斯夫妇来到中国,你们为他举行了欢迎仪式,时间匆匆过去,两个月前的事情还历历在目,却到了他们返回美国的时刻了。在中国的这两个月里,史密斯夫妇对中国的教育系统、政治、经济和文化都进行了相关的研究和了解。现在大家再次相聚,为他们举行欢送仪式,请你代表大家致欢送词并表达对他们的美好祝愿。
3. 你来自美国,和你同行的代表团一直期望到中国访问,现在终于如愿以偿,并受到了中国接待者的热烈欢迎。在接待者致欢迎词后,请代表美国代表团对中国的热烈欢迎做感谢致辞发言。
4. 你结束了在中国的访问,访问期间中国的一切给你留下了深刻的印象,你参观了公司、学校以及文化团体,同中国人民交谈并结交了朋友。借欢送会的机会,请你致告别词表达你的感受。
5. 你们公司和中国一个公司进行合作,在你们公司欢迎中国代表团的宴会上,你作为公司代表发言,提议为你们之间的广泛合作和交流的广阔前景干杯,为日益增长的私人和商业往来干杯。

Keys (练习答案)

Unit 1 Résumés

I. Rewrite

(1)
- Write periodical reports
- Update and distribute company address lists
- Draft correspondences
- Make travel arrangements
- Complete special projects as assigned

(2) Promoted as a result of my efficient discharge of duties.

(3) Seven-year business administrative background.

(4) Ranked second in class of thirty-two.

(5) Analyzed opportunity to invest in operations of national fast food chain.

(6)
- Directed MIS for headquarter
- Provided advice on computer to branches

(7) Career Objective: Position in Mechanical Design

II. 略。

III. Résumé writing

(1)

ZHANG DONG

Class 97081

Computer Science and Engineering College

Southeast University

Nanjing, Jiangsu, 210002

(025) 3847-9238

EDUCATION

Southeast University	Nanjing, Jiangsu
Bachelor of Science in Computer	2017-2021

- GPA: 91/100
  - Vice President of the Southeast University Student Council responsible for academic research
  - Active member of the University Society of Electronics

- Director of the University Association of Computer Science
- Winner of the University Scholarship in every academic year
- Winner of the Panda Prize for Excellent Students in 2018
- MCSE Certificate in 2019
- Author of two research papers on the programming in the *Southeast University Journal*

EXPERIENCE

ZHONGJI DEVELOPMENT COMPANY   Nanjing, Jiangsu
Intern Engineer   1/2021-Present

- Installed hardware and software for customers
- Wrote programs in the Traffic Computerization Project of Nanjing
- Received the Internship Award from the Southeast University

JINDIAN COMPANY   Nanjing, Jiangsu
Part-time Salesperson and Engineer   Summer, 2018

- Sold computers
- Repaired computers

ENGLISH PROFICIENCY

- Scored 630 on TOEFL in January 2019
- Good at English listening, speaking, reading, and writing
- Excellent technical communication skills in English

REFERENCES

Prof. Yang Huan, Computer Science and Engineering College, Southeast University, Nanjing, Jiangsu 210042 (025) 8736-2673

President Kong Lin, Zhongji Development Company, 12 South Section, Ring Road One, Nanjing, Jiangsu, 210005 (025) 3364-2564

Mr. Han Fei, CEO, Jindian Company, 73 People's Road, Nanjing, Jiangsu 210013 (025) 5574-7364

                                                                      Zhang Dong

(2) GAO XIN

P. O. Box 211, Nanjing University
25 Hankou Road, Nanjing 210093
Tel: (025) 4473-8475 Email: gaoxin@ online. sh. cn

Job Objective	Seeking a position as an architectural designer for office building in a small-to-middle sized architectural firm
Education	B. S. in architecture, June 2017
	Nanjing University, Nanjing, Jiangsu
	Completed four-year courses of architectural design.
	Coursework included Urban Design, Architectural Planning, Structural Engineering, Interior Decoration, Office Facilities Management, Computer-

	aided Architectural Design.
Special Skills	• Familiar with MS Word, MS Excel, AutoCAD, Photoshop
	• Knowledge of building codes and standards
	• Ability to work independently
	• Proficiency in English, TOEFL 632, Jan. 2016
Summer Work	Worked at construction projects of RHD Company for past three summers
Other Interests	Sketching, painting, photography, developing film in dark room
References	On request

Unit 2   Certificates

I. Translation

(1)

CERTIFICATE

This is to certify that Mr. Cai Minghui
has passed the Business English Test (Intermediate Level).

Shanghai Business English Test Center
Issuing Date: September, 2016

(2)

CERTIFICATE

This is to certify that Miss Song Jiawei has been awarded the title of
Model Student
in the Social Work of College Students sponsored by the Jiangsu Institute of Foreign Trade (JIFT).

JIFT Youth League Committee
December, 2019

(3)

**TRAINING CERTIFICATE
OF INTERMEDIATE COMPUTER**

This is to certify that Tang Fanghui, female, aged 27, has completed the four-month training in intermediate computer at the Suzhou Yi Jin College of Continuing Education and passed the qualifying examination.

STAMP
Suzhou Yi Jin College
of Continuing Education
Date: May 20, 2016

II. Translation

(1)　　　　　　　　San Francisco State University
　　　　　　Overseas Training and Orientation Program
　　Takes pleasure in awarding this certificate indicating successful completion of the Chinese-American Cross-Cultural Training Program to Visiting Manager from Shanghai with the San Francisco-Shanghai Sister City Committee business Management Program.

　　　　　　　　　　　　Wang Xiaofeng

　　　　　　　　　　　　　　　　　　　Jo Ann Craig
　　　　　　　　　　　　　　　　　　　　Director
　　　　　　　　　　　　　　Overseas Training and Orientation Program
　　　　　　　　　　　　　　Date：October 23，2017

(2)　　　　　　　　　　　CERTIFICATE

To Whom It May Concern：

　　This is to certify that the bearer, Mr. Wang Yingjing is an acquaintance of mine, a man whom I know to be thoroughly trustworthy.

　　　　　　　　　　　　　　　　　　General Manager of C. T. U. Co.

(3)　　　　　　　　　　　CERTIFICATE

Gentlemen：

　　I beg to certify that Mr. David Brown has been a salesman in this firm for four years and has shown diligence and ability in the discharge of his duties. He has gained the esteem of his colleagues and superiors alike.

　　　　　　　　　　　　　　　　　　　　　　　　Very truly,
　　　　　　　　　　　　　　　　　　　　　　　　　×××

Unit 3　Application Letters

I. Find out unsuitable parts

(1) 无经验、无学历，求职信就无法写了　　(2) 过于谦卑
(3) 提出不合理要求　　　　　　　　　　　(4) 不宜提以前被解雇的原因
(5) 履历过期仍不修正，说明不认真　　　　(6) 连"错误"都拼写错误，可见极不认真
(7) 拼写错误　　　　　　　　　　　　　　(8) 年代写错
(9) clerk 写错　　　　　　　　　　　　　　(10) 语气极为不恭、自大
(11) 不宜在这样的正式文书中使用俚称
(12) 不宜在这样的正式文书中使用俚语及口语化词汇

II. Translation

(1) In addition to the usual assistant work, I am responsible for receiving telephone calls and

visitors, scheduling all of the appointments, and organizing the paperwork and correspondence.

(2) Besides my seven years of designing experience at the present institution where I have been working, you will also find it to your satisfaction that my years at college has grounded me in the necessary skills and knowledge in the field where I can safely say that I can now do well.

(3) My work experience, together with my educational preparation, as shown in the enclosed résumé, would qualify me for the position.

(4) Should you wish to have more information? I would be happy to go and see you at a mutually convenient time.

(5) I think you will agree that I am, at least, a strong candidate for the position you are offering.

(6) I feel that I am competent to meet the requirements which you have specified.

III. Application letters writing

(1) Human Resource Division Director
Shanghai Office
R&H China Inc.
488 Wuning Road(s), Shanghai

Dear Mr. Director,

I have learned from the newspaper that you are employing an administrative secretary. I am very much interested in this position.

I have worked as an administrative secretary for a chemical company in Shanghai for three years, so I have some understanding of the chemical industry. I graduated from the East China University of Technology, holding a bachelor's degree. Having obtained certificates of CET4 and CET6. I find myself fluent in both spoken and written English. In addition, I am also quite familiar with computer skills.

Enclosed please find my résumé.
Looking forward to your early reply

Yours sincerely,
(signature)
Qian Xiaolu

(2) General Manager
E-Cubix Co., Ltd.
317 Xianxia Road, Shanghai

Dear Mr. General Manager,

  I graduated from Shanghai Jiaotong University in 2017 and I am currently working for a computer company. With five years of work experience, I have familiarized myself with computer skills, especially with COM +, DHTML and Java.

  It is to my delight to learn that your company has an opening for the technical manager. I think my academic and work experience will qualify me for the position.

  It is not that I seek for higher remuneration, but that I want to further develop my talent in the field of web development. E-Cubix is just where I can hope to realize my ideal and ambition.

  I should be most grateful to you if you would give me favorable consideration.

Yours sincerely,
(signature)
Wang Weifeng

(3) Dear Sirs,

  I am graduating from the Jiangsu Institute of Foreign Trade this summer. As a student of English for Business, I hope to work for a foreign company after graduation.

  In the past three academic years, I have proved myself to be a straight a student, awarded a succession of scholarships. My English is particularly good and German happens to be my second foreign language, which will live up to the requirements set by a wholly-owned foreign company like yours.

  I apply for the position of assistant to your marketing project manager. You will find me a good team player, self-motivated and eager to learn. I believe I can be of value to your company.

  I should be very happy if you would arrange an interview with me.

Yours sincerely,

(signature)
Yu Lihong

(4) Director of Consulting Center
Jiangsu Foreign Service Co., Ltd.
406 Maoming Mansion, 580 Maoming Road
Baixia District, Nanjing 210096

Dear Mr. Director,

I am currently working on Master's Degree in International Commercial Law at Nanjing University. My supervisor Mr. Liu Mingyu, a well-known professor of law, tells me that JFSC specializes in recommending qualified personnel to multi-national companies and suggests that I contact you for recommendation.

During the two years of studies at Nanjing University, I have not only acquired a lot of knowledge of international commercial law, but learned two foreign languages as well — English and Japanese. Moreover, I have published two papers in the university journal on problems that may arise after China's entry to the WTO. And they have been favorably accepted.

I am enclosing a résumé, copies of my published papers, and Professor Liu's letter of recommendation.

I sincerely hope you will introduce me to a famous multi-national company, to which I will dedicate myself.

Truly yours,
(signature)
Fu Jialin

Unit 4　Memorandums

I. Read the following memos and give appropriate subject headings

(1) Meeting on the Education Leave Request
(2) Request for Update on Stock Option Participation
(3) Training New Receptionists

II. Suggested rewritten version

MEMORANDUM
To: All member of staff, Northern Branch
From: K. L. J.
Date: 3 December, 2017
Subject: PERSONAL COMPUTERS

The board urgently requires feedback on our experience with PCs in Northern Branch. I need to know, for my report:

① What you personally use your PC for and your reasons for doing this. If you are doing work that was formally done by other staff, please justify this.
② What software you use. Please name the programs.
③ How many hours per day you spend actually using it.
④ How your PC has not come up to your expectations.
⑤ What unanticipated uses you have found for your PC, which others may want to share.

Please FAX this information directly to me by 5 p.m. on WEDNESDAY, 5 December.

If you have any queries, please contact my assistant, Jane David, who will be visiting you on Tuesday, 4 December. Thank you for your help.

III. Draft memos according to the notes given

(1)

Memo

To: All Department Heads
From: Wang Lin (Office Director)
Date: 3 Sept., 2017
Ref: Arrangements during Managing Director's Absence Abroad

The Managing Director Mr. Xu Daliang is leaving for Europe on 10 Sept. on a business trip. The progress meeting this week (12 Sept.) will be cancelled accordingly. Any important matters should be brought to his attention by 9 Sept.

During the absence of the Managing Director, Mr. Zhao Xing, the associate manager, will be in charge of routine business and will act as chairman for the next progress meeting, which is to be held on 19 Sept., at 8:00 a.m. in the usual place, the company conference room.

(2)

Memo

To: All workers, Dispatch Department
From: Mr. Augustus Foley, Managing Director
Subject: Dispatching Books
Date: 12 June, 2017

Several complaints have been received from customers who have been sent the correct orders with the wrong invoices and the wrong orders with the correct invoices. Please take extra care to ensure that both orders and invoices are correct.

I am aware that we have several new members of staff in this department and I am not putting the blame onto them. However, if anyone has a problem they should speak to Harry Hawke who will be able to assist them.

I am concerned as this problem has never happened before.

Unit 5 Notes

I. Suggested subjects

(1) Note of Thanks   (2) Asking for Sick Leave
(3) Asking a Friend to Call (4) Presenting a Gift
(5) Booking a Ticket   (6) Requesting an Introduction

II. Suggested rewritten version

3:00 p.m., 5 Feb

Dear Fei Ming,
　　I am conducting an experiment on computer and in badly need of the software you borrowed from me last month. I shall appreciate very much if you will return it at once to me.

Li

III. Suggested version

(1)

Wednesday

Zhou Yan,

    Our physical director has just told me that Thursday's football match between Japanese Ⅲ and English Ⅱ will be postponed till sometime next week as a result of the long wet spell. Please notify your classmates.

Yang Yu

(2)

Thursday

Dear Zhang Wei,

    I am in urgent need of 200 yuan. I wonder if you can lend me with this amount, which I am sure to return to you next Friday.

    Please favor me with an early reply.

Xu Ziqiang

(3)

Friday

Dear Xu Ziqiang,

    I am glad to meet your request and send you by Yang Hong the 200 yuan you are greatly in need of.

    Please rest assured that you are welcome to return it at your convenience.

Zhang Wei

(4)

November 24

Dear Sir,

    Please excuse Alice's absence from school today. She had a bad cold yesterday evening and could not fall asleep until well into the night. I felt it would disturb the other children if I allow her to attend school. So I am writing to ask you for one day's sick leave and will let her resume her study if she feels better tomorrow.

Alice's mother

Encl: Doctor's Certificate of Advice

(5)

> Tuesday
>
> Dear Xiao Ni,
>
> I'm afraid I have to rush to Fujian tomorrow morning on urgent business. Could I postpone our meeting on Friday till next Wednesday?
>
> Sorry for the inconvenience I've caused.
>
> Charles

(6)

> March 5
>
> Dear Zhang,
>
> Thank you for the guidance you gave me. It is your valuable guidance that has enabled me to go about the city without losing myself.
>
> I am going back to Australia by plane tomorrow morning. I'll contact you when I am back. Remember me to your family.
>
> John Smith

Unit 6　Notices & Announcements

I. Suggested subjects

(1) Broadcast notice　　(2) Business notice　　(3) Engagement notice
(4) Birth notice　　　　(5) Obituary

II. Suggested version

(1)

> Miss Xie Xuan
> and
> Mr. Dong Fei
> announce their marriage
> on Friday, the eighth of June
> Two thousand and fifteen
> Hilton Hotel
> Hong Kong

(2)

> NOTICE
>
> The Art Activities Group takes pleasure to announce that its New Year Evening is to be held in the concert hall on Friday, Dec. 28, at 6 p.m. The program includes songs, recitations, story-telling, skits and plays. Admission tickets may be obtained on application to Miss Li, Room 304, Office Building.
>
> Dec. 25, 2018

(3)

> Birth Notice
>
> A daughter, Evelyn, was born at 10:00 a.m. Monday, Feb. 23, to Mr. and Mrs. Bill Black, 87 Belgium Street, at Municipal Hospital.

(4)

> Notice
>
> Your attention, please. A visit is arranged for June 16, Saturday, to the Yangtze River Bridge and other places of interests in Nanjing.
>
> Those who wish to go will please gather at the front gate of Nanjing University at 7:00 a.m. that day. The coach will leave at 7:20 a.m.
>
> Reception Office
>
> June 6, 2014

Unit 7 Meeting Minutes

I. Suggested rewritten version

> Minutes of the Annual General Meeting of Education and Training Committee
>
> Minutes of the Annual General Meeting held at 2:40 p.m. on Tuesday, 22 May, 2007 at 21 Century's Hotel, Bukstock.
>
> PRESENT: R. P. Norman, Chairperson
>   W. M. Noel Chalmers
>   W. Robin Watson
>   H. R. Waller
>   T. K. White
>   C. Nigel Rye

A. E. Belly

M. Hunt Joes

Miss H. Newduck

E. P. Arnold, Secretary

Miss J. Crown, Secretariat

1) CORRESPONDENCE

Apologies for absence were received from two Committee members: H. Y. West and J. N. Nigel.

2) REVISION

The minutes of the meeting held on 20 April, 2007 had been circulated; they were taken as read and signed as correct.

3) MATTERS ARISING

There were no matters arising.

4) CHAIRPERSON'S REPORT

The Chairperson reported as follows:

The Committee had met five times during the year. Principal matters dealt with had included liaison with the local education authority. Both the Chairperson and the Secretary served on the Joint Committee to establish closer contact between schools and industry.

The Business/Teacher Liaison Scheme had continued, and ten visits for teachers had been arranged.

In March the Committee had assisted with the Careers Week Exhibition during which a panel from the Committee held advice sessions on careers for school leavers.

5) FINANCE

The Secretary reported on the financial statement on 25 October, 2006 in respect of the fund held for the payment of medals and prizes.

The accounts recorded a donation from Mr. M. Hunt Joes of £10 for prizes at the Bukstock College of Commerce.

The capital sum now stood at £199.28.

The report was accepted.

6) ELECTION OF OFFICE BEARERS

The Chairperson reported that he had served his term of office and that the Vice Convener, Mr. W. Dania, was unable to accept the position because of illness. It was agreed to invite Mr. W. Robin Watson, Principal of the Scotland College of Technology, to resume Chairperson of the Committee.

7) JOINT LIAISON COMMITTEE

    a) The Chairperson reported that ten teacher visits had been organized during the year. Head teachers had written to the secretary commenting on the success of these team visits.

b) The scheme for work experience for pupils had been started. The first response from firms and industry was encouraging.

c) Difficulty was being found in placing teachers for work experience. An ad hoc committee was appointed to examine the reason for this.

Mr. T. K. White (Youth Employment Service) and Mr. W. Robin Watson (Scotland College of Technology) spoke of encouraging results achieved by the Liaison Committee.

8) NEXT MEETING

This was left to the Chairperson and the Secretary to arrange.

9) ANY OTHER BUSINESS

There was none.

Meeting terminated at 4:20 p.m.

E. P. Arnold,
Secretary

II. Suggested rewritten version

Minutes of Progress Meeting

The meeting was held on Friday, 18 May, 2007, at 4:00 p.m.

Present: Mr. Robert Debbie, the chairperson
        Mrs. Bess Ivy
        Mr. Max Smith,
        Mr. Peter Madson
        Miss Jane Black, the secretary

MINUTES OF THE PREVIOUS MEETING

The previous minutes were taken as read and approved. Mr. Robert Debbie requested the secretary to send copies of minutes to all previous members of the association. After brief discussion it was resolved that Mr Debbie's request serve as a motion at the next general meeting.

MATTERS ARISING FROM THE MINUTES

Mr. Max Smith reported that the European Association had been approached on the matter of affiliation. This was noted. A letter would be written to the association to express gratitude for its consideration.

CHAIRPERSON'S REPORT

The chairperson's report was read and accepted with thanks.

ELECTION OF NEW COMMITTEE MEMBERS

The following members were elected to the new committee:
Mrs. D. Maxine and Mr. L. Hady

PURCHASE OF NEW SITES

On a motion by Mr. Max Smith, seconded by Mrs. Bess Ivy, it was resolved that two stands, numbers 12 and 14, would be purchased as new building sites on which three boathouses could be erected. It was further resolved that the building contractors would be approached for a quotation.

ACCOUNTS NEXT TERM

The treasurer informed the meeting that the accounts for the coming term would be discussed much sooner than the proposed date. This was unanimously accepted.

CORRESPONDENCE

The following correspondence was noted:

1) Municipality: water pollution

2) Farmers' Association: Gala

OTHER MATTERS

Mr. Peter Madson moved that a new siren be bought. Mr. Robert Debbie seconded the motion. After deliberation it was resolved that a new model would be bought during the next financial year.

CLOSING

The meeting closed at 6:00 p.m. with a vote of thanks to the chairperson.

Prepared by: Jane Black (secretary)

Robert Debbie

(chairperson)

III. Suggested version

(1)

Minutes of Progress Meeting held on Wednesday, 14 Feb., 2017

PRESIDING: Mr. Wu Qiang (Chairman)

PRESENT: Mr. Zheng Jian   Mr. Luo Wen   Mr. Ma Ke

Mr. J. K. Roberts

APOLOGIES FOR ABSENCE WERE RECEIVED FROM:

Mr. Zhang Jin

SUMMARY OF THE MEETING:

The Chairman called the meeting to be held at 4:00 p.m. As the first item on the agenda, he asked for approval of the report of the meeting held on 15 November, 2016, which was agreed on and signed, subject to the following amendments:

i. Para 3, Line 2 "marketing" should read "advertising".

ii. In Mr. Zhang Jin's report, Line 2 "all" should be revised to "most".

The Chairman first asked Mr. Zheng, the Personnel Manager, to inform the meeting of staff changes. Mr. Zheng said that the Company Accountant Jiang Shan had retired at the end of last December and Mr. Luo Wen had been appointed to replace her. He also mentioned that the Treasurer had resigned his position and would leave the Company at the end of March. A succeeding Treasurer post should be soon advised. Recommendations from Department leaders are welcome.

Mr. Luo Wen, the newly appointed Company Accountant, then presented the Accounting Plan for the next three months of the year (attached). After discussion the plan was agreed on unanimously and signed.

The Sales Manager Mr. Ma Ke made a brief report on the market development. He said that the Company was facing strong competition from a Japanese electronic manufacturer, the "Dawoo Electronics", which has been recently established in Tianjin. He outlines how action can be taken to compete with Dawoo's marketing strategies.

Other business raised at the meeting included:
1) Mr. Roberts, the Managing Director, called attention to high-quality job training for new employees.
2) Mr. Roberts explained the Bonus Scheme. He emphasized that bonus should be awarded on the basis of merit rather than on the length of service.

The next meeting scheduled for 20 March will be postponed because of the coming Spring Trading Conference. The staff would be notified in due course of the new date.

The meeting ended at 6:00 p. m.

Prepared by: Morphy Cai (Secretary)

Unit 8   Itineraries & Agendas

I. Suggested version

Mr. Black's Itinerary in Japan
Tokyo—Nagoya—Beijing

Tuesday, April 3 (Tokyo Head office)
 9:20 a. m. All the Branch Managers' meeting
 2:00 p. m. All the Sales Managers' meeting
 5:30 p. m. Company dinner at Hilton Hotel
Wednesday, April 4 (Tokyo to Nagoya)
 9:30 a. m. Bill, Manager at Tokyo, will pick you up at Hilton Hotel and drive to Haneda Airport.
 12:00 a. m. Leave Haneda Airport on Japan Airline Flight No. 95 (First class, Lunch)
 1:10 p. m. Arrive in Nagoya
        Tommy, Office Manager at Nagoya branch, will pick you up at the

	airport and take you to the Hotel.
	Stay at New Nagoya Hotel (Double room with bath booked)
3:00 p. m.	Conference scheduled at branch company
5:30 p. m.	Company dinner will be held at New Nagoya Hotel

Thursday, April 5 (Nagoya to Beijing)

9:30 a. m.	Tommy will pick you up at the hotel and take you to Nagoya International Airport
11:40 a. m.	Check in at air terminal.
12:40 p. m.	Departure.
	Japan Airline Flight No. 117 (First class, Lunch)

II. Suggested version

Agenda of a Director's Meeting
Company Conference Room 2
8th July 2017 (Thursday) at 1:30 p. m.

1:30 – 1:50	To discuss the minutes of the meeting held on 8th May, 2017
1:50 – 2:30	To discuss the possibilities of establishing some branches in New York and Singapore
2:30 – 3:00	To decide on the amount of investment in the branch company in Japan
3:00 – 4:00	Report on sales strategy in 2018 by Will Smith
4:00 – 4:30	To select a new manager among the candidates to replace Mr. Liu Yang who has handed in his resignation
4:30	Close the meeting

Unit 9 Business Reports

I. Comments and reference solution

Comments:

It seems a grim defect in the argument: If you have 4,000 teachers waiting to share a student pool of merely 10,000, it is hardly a big market for training. The readers of this conclusion will wonder where the "great potential" lies. Either the writer was not serious or had failed to give enough emphasis to his pre-writing research. The reference solution provided below is simply for demonstrating technical improvement possibilities, and the author of this book does not, by doing this, imply that one can change statistics for report-composing purpose.

Reference solution:

The present market of English-training in Wuci County is enormous with a great potential for growth. Our weeklong research shows that with more than 210 teachers working at county and vocational schools, and more than 20,000 young people aged between 15 and 25 wanting to learn English, the English Training Center in town will have training opportunities more than it can meet.

The center is rich in lecturer and trainer resources and has its own well-equipped facilities. With better public relations and greater promotion efforts, it should have a bright prospect in the English-training market in Wuci County at least for three years to come.

II. Reference solution

3. CONCLUSIONS

The Area Manager concludes:

—the major geographical differences between the north and south were not taken into account when planning the distribution in China.

—the problem of late payments will continue as long as the legal framework is loose, slow, and inefficient.

The District Manager concludes:

—the differences between the east and west were not taken into account when setting production targets.

—the problem of water supplies will continue as long as the regional water supplies infrastructure remains as it is.

—the problem of recruitment will continue as long as the company offers unattractive salaries in comparison with local rivals.

4. RECOMMENDATIONS

With the distribution difficulties, Mr. Zhang, the Area Manager, recommends the following measures:

—the feasibility of warehousing more goods in the north should be considered.

—the feasibility of transferring some staff and transport vehicles from the north to the south should be considered.

—a clause allowing for delays in deliveries due to bad weather conditions should be included in all delivery contracts.

On the production front, Mr. Li, the District Manager, recommends the following measures:

—Production targets should be reduced in the west and increased in the east of China.

Concerning employee compensation, Mr. Kang, the Human Resources Manager recommends that:

—working conditions in the west be improved;

—an increase in salaries for technical staff be considered; and

—employee benefits be improved.

III. Reference solution

A Recommendation Report
on
Reducing Prices of Passenger Cars
in Metropolitan China

CONTENTS
1. SUMMARY
2. INTRODUCTION
   2.1 Purpose
   2.2 Background
   2.3 Methodology
   2.4 Scope
3. FINDINGS
   3.1 Price—the Factor Directly Influences Purchasing Behavior
   3.2 Great Potential in China
      3.2.1 The Great Profit Margin of Car Industry
      3.2.2 Large Demand for Economical Family Cars in China
4. CONCLUSION
5. RECOMMENDATIONS
6. BIBLIOGRAPHY
7. APPENDIX: QUESTIONNAIRE

We Have to Reduce Prices of
Passenger Cars in Metropolitan China

1. SUMMARY

We found that there is a great potential demand in the family car market of China. Cars that sell for under RMB 100,000 enjoy the greatest popularity, and price is the main factor that directly influences consumer decision to buy.

It is, therefore, necessary to reduce the price of cars. For this, we recommend that the manufacturing costs be reduced and, step by step, the average price of a family car be lowered to around RMB 50,000 in five years.

2. INTRODUCTION

2.1 Purpose

This report has been drawn up to look into the necessity of reducing the prices of cars and to recommend suggestions about how to achieve the price reduction objective.

The purpose of this report is to look into the necessity and possibility of reducing prices in the family automobile industry in China and to recommend feasible solutions to this proposition.

2.2 Background

We conducted a questionnaire to generate data on public opinions (see appendices) of owning a family car. We looked into important parameters of Chinese consumers towards owning a car, such as income, housing, and affordability.

Meanwhile, we considered the profitability of the passenger car manufacturing industry.

Middling Company is one of the pioneer car companies in China, which was also one of the first joint venture players in the Chinese market. In 1983,... Ten years later, our first car manufactured in South China ... Moreover, our outputs and earnings in recent years are promising, too. See table 1.

Table 1. Annual sales and earnings of Middling Company in China

Year	Unit sales	Annual earnings*
1998	×××	×××,×××
1999	×××	×××,×××
2000	×××	×××,×××
2001	×××	×××,×××

* in millions RMB

However, with China's entry into the WTO, more international automobile makers are coming to China and the competition is becoming fiercer. Now, the most threatening competitors are Japanese Honda, which now focuses on economical family cars, and some Chinese manufacturers. Therefore, it is urgent for us to make some constructive strategies.

2.3 Methodology

The information for this report mainly gathered from 3,000 families in Beijing (see appendices) through the distribution and filling of the said questionnaire. Some supporting and background data are from the news media.

2.4 Scope

This report investigates Chinese consumer opinions on owning a family car, promotions by the automobile manufacturers, and their expected prices of five named car makes.

Also, the report looks into income, housing and other related factors to find out more about the market potential.

3. FINDINGS

3.1 Price—the Factor Directly Influencing Purchasing Behavior

According to our market research, price is the most direct factor influencing consumers' buying behavior. 68% of the investigated consumers say they will buy a car if the price is lowered. Considering their price expectation, we divide cars into three levels: high-grade cars, middle-grade cars and low-grade cars. See the following table.

Grade	Cars	Current Price*
High-grade	Buick (Shanghai GM)	360,000
High-grade	Red Flag	260,000
High-grade	Honda (Guangzhou)	250,000

续表

Grade	Cars	Current Price*
High-grade	Audi	250,000
Middle-grade	Fukang	140,000
Middle-grade	Jetta	130,000
Middle-grade	Santana	110,000
Low-grade	Xiali	90,000
Low-grade	Auto	60,000

* in RMB

3.2　Great Market Potential in China

3.2.1　The Great Profit Margin of Car Industry

According to some media, the profit of car industry has reached billions. In 1999, Jetta earned RMB 12 billion; Buick earned 6 billion RMB; and our Santana earned RMB 40 billion. No other market but Chinese car market can bring to a car company such a big profit. So it is reasonable for us to try to hold this market.

3.2.2　Large Demand for Economical Family Cars in China

A) Need for cars due to housing in suburbs

In many old cities, such as Beijing, Shanghai, Guangzhou and Tianjin, a lot of apartment buildings are being built in the suburbs. Thousands of people live in these areas, where the transportation is not very convenient. Therefore, for the sake of work, it is necessary for them to buy a car in the near future.

B) Need for economical cars because of low income

In our research, 2,000 of the 3,000 families express their desires to own a car. Low income, however, keeps them from doing so. The average income is RMB 2,000 – 3,000 per month and only a few people enjoy high salary. So they can only afford low-priced economical family cars.

4. CONCLUSION

The above findings show that there is great sales potential in Chinese car market and it is necessary for us to lower the prices of cars.

5. RECOMMENDATIONS

In view of the current situation regarding price reduction, the following suggestions are recommended.

5.1　The Price Reduction Should Be Conducted Gradually.

The price should be placed under RMB 100,000 per unit and, in the future 5 years, the price will be lowered gradually to RMB 50,000 per unit.

5.2　A New Production Should Be Built.

One billion dollars should be invested to build a new production line because mass production will reduce the cost and so lower the price. About the source of capital, our

suggestions are:
   a) USD 4 billion from the World Bank
   b) USD 6 billion being loans from Bank of China
6. BIBLIOGRAPHY
   Beijing Evening News
   Beijing Daily
   www.chinacar.online.com
7. APPENDICES: A QUESTIONNAIRE
   Omitted for short of space.

Unit 10　Business Letters

1. Establishing business relations

I.

(1) fall within　　(2) in the line of　　(3) be of interest
(4) enter into　　(5) enclosed　　(6) refer to

II.

(1) Having obtained your address from our agent in Holland, we are writing with a desire to establish business relations with you.

(2) We specialize in the importation of various kinds of household electrical appliances.

(3) We enclose a copy of the latest illustrated catalogue of our firm and we hope that you can contact us if any of the items interests you.

(4) Our banker is Bank of China Nanjing Branch, which can provide you with information about our character and finances.

III.

敬启者：

我们从渣打银行获悉贵公司想进口中国纺织品和棉布，而我们正好经营此商品的出口业务。

我公司能够根据客户提供的样品花样、规格和包装要求供货。

为使贵公司对我公司所供产品有个大概了解，我们随信附上一份最新商品目录供参考。如果贵公司对其中的商品感兴趣，请联系我们。我们将很乐意根据你们的具体询价单进行报价并寄送样品。

盼早复！

谨上

2. Making enquiries

I.

(1) enquiry   (2) price list   (3) supplier   (4) terms of payment
(5) quantity discount (6) freight   (7) place an order
(8) irrevocable L/C   (9) to quote CIF London   (10) commission

II.

We are interested to buy large quantities of Iron Nails of all sizes and should be obliged if you would give us a quotation per metric ton C. F. R. Lagos, Nigeria. It would also be appreciated if samples or brochure could be forwarded to us.

We used to purchase this article from other sources but we now prefer to buy from your corporation because we are given to understand you are able to supply large quantities at more attractive prices. Besides, we have confidence in the quality of Chinese Products.

We look forward to hearing from you by return.

III.

(1)
We are informed that you can supply large quantities of stationery.
Please give us your lowest quotation FOB Shanghai for 4500 gross "Good Friends" Brand pencils.
To acquaint us with the qualities and specifications of your goods, we will appreciate it very much if you will send us some samples and catalogues.
We hope to receive your early reply.

(2)
We are a leading importer of various textile products. Recently we have received a number of enquiries from customers for cotton bed sheets and should be glad if you would send us full particulars of your range, including colors, sizes and prices inclusive of packing and delivery charges. If illustrated brochures or pamphlets are available it would be helpful if you would send us copies.

3. Making offers and counter-offers

I.

(1) firm offer   (2) non-firm offer   (3) counter-offer   (4) retail price

(5) wholesale price　　(6) FOB　　　　　　(7) C&F　　　　　　(8) profit
(9) subject to　　　　 (10) confirmation

II.

（1）该报价是票面价值 2 000 美元以下的订货价，对于 2 000 美元以上的订单，我们给予 5％的额外折扣。
（2）如能给予 3％的折扣，我们可以考虑并接受你们的报盘。
（3）本报盘以货物未被售出为准。
（4）在收到有效订单后即可装货。
（5）我们准备分几批等量发运。
（6）你方价格似乎偏高，使我们无法向你们订购。
（7）考虑到你们的交易金额，我们同意折中处理。
（8）很遗憾我们不能再降价。

III.

Dear Sirs,

Thank you for your enquiry and we are pleased to offer as follows:
Hand-made Gloves in Genuine Leather

200 men's medium　　　　　US＄3.00 each
200 men's small　　　　　　US＄2.80 each
200 women's medium　　　　US＄2.60 each
200 women's small　　　　　US＄2.50 each
CIF London
Terms: By L/C at sight
Shipment: July

This offer is to subject to our final confirmation.

As you requested, we are airmailing you a copy of illustrated catalogue with a range of samples of the various leathers used in the manufacture of our gloves. We hope the colors will be just what you want, and the superb workmanship as well as the novel designs will appeal to your customers.

We look forward to your reply.

Yours faithfully,

4. Placing orders and confirmation

I.

(1) dispatch   (2) offer   (3) the package   (4) sample
(5) the first order (6) satisfactory (7) Purchase Confirmation (8) for our file

II.

(1) We are very interested in the different models of bicycles you offer and have decided to place a trial order.
(2) All these items are urgently required by our customers. We, therefore, hope you will make delivery at an early date.
(3) The relevant L/C has been issued by Bank of China, Shanghai Branch. Upon receipt of the said, please arrange the shipment and inform us by fax of the name of vessel and the date of sailing.
(4) Shipment will be made within 3 weeks from acceptance of your order. Our terms by payment are draft at sight under an irrevocable L/C. Marine insurance will be covered by us.
(5) We acknowledge with thanks the receipt of your Order No. WG721/BP dated 20th September.
(6) We regret to say that we are unable to accept your order of 1,000 computers owing to heavy commitments.

III.

Dear Sirs,

We have accepted your Order No. 16 for handkerchiefs, leather shoes and socks and are sending you herewith our Sales Confirmation No. Garm-263 in duplicate. Would you please sign and return one copy to us for file?

It is understood that a letter of credit in our favor covering the above-mentioned goods will be established at once. Please note that the stipulations in the relevant credit should strictly conform to the terms stated in our Sales Confirmation so as to avoid subsequent amendments.

You may rest assured that we shall effect shipment with the least possible delay upon receipt of the credit.

We appreciate your cooperation and look forward to receiving your further orders.

Faithfully yours,

5. Making payments

I.

(1) to establish an L/C in one's favor (2) to amend an L/C
(3) urge to open/issue/establish an L/C (4) shipping documents
(5) opening/issuing bank (6) negotiating bank
(7) time/usance L/C (8) sight L/C
(9) transferable L/C (10) deadline

II.

(1) 我方已于2004年6月21日通过中国银行南京分行开立以贵公司为受益人的、金额为32 000美元的、保兑的、不可撤销的信用证,编号为36745,有效期至2004年7月21日。特此奉告。请及时安排装运事宜。
(2) 凭贵方开具的以我行为付款人的按发票金额100%计算的即期汇票付款。
(3) 所有单证必须用快邮整套寄至香港汇丰银行。
(4) 基于上述情况,我们很抱歉希望你方能将3661号订单的信用证有效期延后两周。

III.

Dear Sirs,

We have received your L/C No. 4785 issued through the Standard Chartered Bank, Liverpool against our S/C No. 1249.

In accordance with the stipulations of the captioned L/C the total quantity should be shipped not later than May 21, and transshipment is not allowed. Although we have been making great efforts to book shipping spaces on time, much to our regret, we were told no direct steamer for your port before May 26. Therefore, we hereby request you to extend the date of shipment and the validity of the L/C to May 31 and June 16 respectively or to allow transshipment.

As we can do nothing until the above L/C is duly amended, we would advise you to attend to the matter with the least possible delay.

Yours sincerely,

6. Shipping

I.

(1) 装货港 (2) 卸货港 (3) 装运标志/唛头 (4) 货轮 (5) 集装箱船

(6) 提单　　　(7) 租船运输　(8) 原产地证　　(9) 装箱单　(10) 商业发票

II.

(1) complaining　　(2) shipment/shipping　(3) delay　　(4) due to
(5) contract　　　　(6) delivery date　　　 (7) within　 (8) inconvenience

III.

(1) We are pleased to inform you that the goods under your Order No. 1134 has now been shipped and taken on board S.S. Eastwind which, we are informed, will be sailing tomorrow.

(2) Please check and confirm the relevant shipping documents attached.

(3) We agreed on a delivery of June, 2004 under the terms of our Sales Contract No. 310. However, we would now like to bring delivery forward to April/May, 2004 for our buyers are in urgent need of these goods.

(4) We regret to inform that we have to postpone the delivery to the next month since we failed to fix the desired shipping space this month. Please write back to confirm it ASAP.

(5) The consignment will leave Xiamen on 8 Oct. on board SS Sailor and is due to arrive at London on 23 Oct.

(6) Please accept transshipment to ensure timely delivery.

7. Complaints & claims

I.

(1) claimant　　　　　　　　　　　　(2) to claim/to lodge a claim against …
(3) Damage Survey　　　　　　　　　(4) to meet/grant/justify a claim
(5) to refuse/reject/decline a claim　　(6) short delivery
(7) settlement　　　　　　　　　　　 (8) be responsible/liable for …
(9) Inspection Certificate　　　　　　　(10) compensation

II.

Dear Sirs,

We regret to inform you that the 20 cases of car parts we received this morning, consigned by you on 12th August, do not correspond with your invoice of the same date. We guess it was a mistake. We are holding the goods in our warehouse and are waiting for your instruction as to how to handle them.

Please fax us as soon as possible when we may expect to receive the goods we ordered.

Yours faithfully,

III.

Dear Sirs,

We acknowledge receipt of your letter of 15th May, with enclosures, claiming for shortage in weight and inferior quality on the consignment of the down quilt shipped by S. S. Patriot.

Having immediately looked into the matter, we find that our down quilt was properly weighed at the time of loading and the quality of the consignment was up to standard. We really cannot account for the reason for your complaint. Since the goods were examined by a public surveyor, we cannot but accept your claims as tendered.

We therefore enclose our check No. 22314 for US \$ 4,628.60 in full and final settlement of your claims PBC78 and PBC79. Kindly acknowledge receipt at your convenience.

We believe this is a fair adjustment of your claim, and trust that it will be completely acceptable to you.

Yours truly,

Unit 11　Contracts & Agreements

I. Key to blanks

(1) of, to, in, to, against, on　　(2) of, with
(3) of, for, with, on, for, for, by, of　　(4) by, of, under, with, by, of, of, from

II. Suggested translations

(1) This Contract is made on 15th of Oct., 2018 in Nanjing, China by and between ABC (Full Name) Company under the law of ~, having its registered address in ~, its legal address in ~ (hereafter referred to as the "Buyer") and the DEF (Full Name) Company under the law of ~, having its registered address in ~, its legal address in ~ (hereafter referred to as the "Seller"); whereby the Buyer agrees to buy and the Seller agrees to sell the following goods on the terms and conditions as below:

(2) ① Name of Commodity;
　　② Specifications, Quantity and Unit Price;
　　③ Total Value (USD);
　　④ Country of Origin and Manufacturers;

⑤ Packing:

Packing must be suitable for ocean shipment and sufficiently strong to withstand rough handling. Bales must be press-packed and hooped, with adequate inside waterproof protection and the outer wrapping must comprise good quality canvas. Cases or other outside containers must be externally of the smallest cubic dimension consistent with adequate protection of the goods.

Package must bear full marks and shipping numbers stenciled in good quality stencil ink in large plain characters on two sides and one end of each package. All bales must be marked "use no hooks".

(3) ① This Contract is made out in two origins, each copy written in Chinese and English languages, both texts being equally valid. In case of any divergence of interpretation, the Chinese text shall prevail.

② The annexes as listed in Articles 20 to this Contract shall form an integral part of this Contract.

③ Any amendment and/or supplement to this Contract shall be valid only after the authorized representatives of both parties have signed written document(s), forming integral part(s) of the Contract.

④ This Contract shall come into force after the signatures by the authorized representatives of both parties.

(4) If the other party fails to perform its obligation in the contract within the time limit agreed upon in this Contract, and fails to eliminate or remedy such breach within 15 days following the receipt of the notice thereof from the non-breaching party and still again fails to perform the Contract within the period of time allowed for delayed performance, in such case the non-breaching party shall be entitled to rescind the Contract by a written notice to the defaulting party and still have the right to claim damages from the defaulting party.

Unit 12 Advertisements

I.

1. 达成协议
2. 按照……条件;受……支配
3. 投标报价
4. 密封投标
5. 广告投标
6. joint venture
7. open bidding
8. bid bond
9. make an offer

10. win a tender

II.

1. 我们是美国一家具有领先地位的出口商,主要从事化学制品业。我们以 50 年来丰富的商业经验享有很高的声誉。我们保证你们将会对我们的服务和出色的产品质量满意的。
2. 附上我们的报价表,如果这些产品的质量和价格符合你们市场需求,请尽快向我们订货,好让我们为你们做必要的准备。
3. 作为答复,我们很高兴地通知你们,我们于国家银行开立了保兑不可撤销信用证,编号为 6783,以你方为受益人,总共 63 000 美元,需要即期汇票付款并附上全套运输单据。
4. 根据合同约定,上述货物将分三次运达;4 月,6 月和 8 月,但时至目前为止,第一批货物才到。我们的最终用户很惊讶你们竟然延迟那么长时间。
5. 如你所见,我们的调查报告里面讲 20 台空调严重损坏。所以,我们要求你们尽快运送替代空调,我们将准备文件向保险公司索赔。我们相信这件事情会引起你们足够的重视。
6. 它们在亚洲市场的贸易中所占的份额以达到 60%。
7. 根据国际惯例,投标人在投标时要缴纳投资保证金,或有银行出具保函。
8. 许多公司参加了这座大桥的投标,只有标价最低的才能中标。
9. 我们已经颁布了一系列有关设立合资企业的法律规定。
10. 贵国政府对提成费和初付费征收什么税?

III.

投标保函

……

ABC 银行保证按照下列文件支付本保函上述金额:

如保函申请人,由于纯属其本身的原因未同受益人订立合同,上述金额将通过你行支付给受益人。

本保函有效期截止到 20〔 〕年〔 〕月〔 〕日。期满后即失效并应立即退还我行。

如保函申请人未中标,本保函立即全部失效。

Unit 13　Advertisements

I. Rewrite

(1) A new car.

　　A new way to build it.

　　A new way to buy ESCORT.

　　It still has four tires and the steering wheel in on the left.

　　Other than that, everything else has changed for the 90's.

(2) Stronger, thicker hair guaranteed in just 7 DAYS!

　　Healthier, shinier hair doesn't happen overnight.

It could take as long as 14 DAYS.

II. Decide types of products

wine, drink, dress, cigarette, beauty, car, water, wine, vacuum, camera, medicine, TV, shoe, mobile phone, food, TV, car, beauty, shoe, food, mobile phone, jewelry, PC, beauty, PC

III. Advertisement Writing

(1) We need 2 new persons with secretarial & organizational skills. Reporting to the manager. Responsible for daily running of office.

We also need 3 marketing persons concerning foreign affairs. Male. Well up in English. With at least 5 years' marketing experience. Need to go on errands regularly.

(2)   ITS Intertek Testing Services ETL SEMKO
    has the following vacancies due to business growth:

① Certificated Project Engineer

- University graduates or above majoring in electricity, electronics, mechanics or refrigeration

Minimum 3 years' work experience in electrical or other related fields

- Previous experience in international testing body highly appreciated
- Good interpersonal skills and team work spirit
- Mature and independent

② Customer Services Officer

- Bachelor degree or above
- Major in English or foreign trade
- Good command of English listening, speaking, reading and writing
- Minimum 3 years of relevant work experience

③ Assistant Certification Engineer

- College graduates of electrical, electronic or mechanical major
- Good interpersonal skills and esprit de corps
- Honest, self-motivated, and willing to learn
- High sense of responsibility

Good command of English and PC skills are prerequisites for all above positions.

Applicants are requested to send their résumés (English and Chinese), school certification, relevant certificates, copies of ID cards, and a recent photo to:

    HRD of ETL SEMKO
   201 Shanxi Road, Pudong New Area
     Shanghai 200120

IV. Translation

(1)
The Pearl River Hotel
Finest Japanese Food
Cozy Atmosphere & Light Music

If you are looking for the most delicious Japanese cuisine in town, why not rendezvous at this delightful spot where appetizing dishes are always served?

888, South Zunyi Road
Tel: 7364621

(2) 招租

市中心南京东路768号房屋一幢,前为丽华床上用品公司。一幢五层楼砖结构大厦,占地面积约20英亩,其底层为一大服装商店铺面,另有宽大的二层楼仓库,其后为天井及一汽车库。

住房共10大间,备有浴室等设施。全租分租皆可。水、电、气俱全。宜辟为写字间。

有意者请至中山东一路上海服装进出口公司面洽。

邮编:200001

(3) 克莱斯勒汽车
创新标准,领新潮流

1925年以来,美国克莱斯勒汽车厂在美国汽车制造史上不断开创新的里程。今天,在全球一百多个国家里,我们同样肩负这项重任,蜚声国际!

在全球最先进的克莱斯勒汽车科研中心,诞生了无数的崭新型号和汽车新发明。克莱斯勒的汽车工程师和设计师经验丰富。他们的努力结果为克莱斯勒汽车写下了许多光辉篇章,大放异彩!

我们遵循一贯的宗旨,不但研制国际级的优质汽车;同时更是超越群伦,精益求精,领导新潮流,奠定了今天汽车世界的先导地位。我们邀请您亲自前往品鉴。

(4) 精工表荣获用户最高评价

无论款式或性能都远远超过一般钟表,达到了尽善尽美的境地,那就是精工牌手表。其石英元件走时无比精确,精细打磨,做工考究,造型轻薄。精工表使你赏心悦目,百看不厌。

Unit 14　Introduction of Company

I.

(1) 骨干企业　　　　(2) 外汇
(3) 创汇量　　　　　(4) 供应商
(5) 生产线　　　　　(6) 耐磨的
(7) 规格　　　　　　(8) 耐用
(9) 划算的　　　　　(10) 面向未来的

II.

(1) The products were awarded the "National Scientific Achievements" prize.

(2) The good quality and the high reliability of the machines produced in a big range of specifications have gained the company a world standing.

(3) The factory possesses a well-trained technical force as well as advanced production technology and equipment.

(4) For years, the company has been the first among all the companies of its kind in terms of annual output, export and foreign currency earned.

(5) We sincerely welcome friends from various parts of the world to establish trading relations and build up economic or technical cooperation with us.

(6) It is convenient for operation and maintenance.

(7) It has won high praises from the users.

(8) The carpet has an obviously-curved surface with solid water-wave patterns, bright luster, strong tensile strength, of latest design, and is soft, thick and good at keeping warm.

(9) General Electric Company is the leading manufacturer of industrial switchboards.

III.
(1) Hard work　(2) Pride　(3) Integrity　(4) Respect　(5) Recognition
(6) Diversity　(7) Passion　(8) Intensity　(9) Good Neighbor　(10) Growth

Unit 15　Brochures, Instructions & Manuals

I. Write table of contents

(1) Location
　　Rooms
　　The Continental Club
　　Business Center
　　Meeting & Conference Facilities
　　Recreation
　　Restaurant & Bar
　　Hotel Facilities

(2) Preparations
　　Sound
　　Radio Reception
　　CD Playing
　　Tape Playback
　　Recording
　　Clock And Timer
　　Other Connections
　　General

(3) About Us
　　Our Products
　　Training Service
　　Consultation Service
　　Management Service
　　Contact Us

II. Write a brochure of Xiamen

Located in the southern part of Fujian Province and on the west coast of the Taiwan Straits, separated from Quemoy island only by a narrow strip of water, Xiamen is a traditional trading port in southeast China and a famous tourist coastal city as well. It covers an area of 1,565 sq. kilometers and has a population of 1.26 million.

As one of the earliest Special Economic Zones (S.E.Z.) in China, Xiamen enjoys both provincial-level authority in economic administration and local legislative power. Thanks to the sustained, rapid and coordinated growth, Xiamen has been accredited as a National Hygienic City, National Garden City, National Model City for Environmental Protection and National Excellent Tourist City.

Xiamen Port is one of the top 10 ports of China. It boasts 80 berths of various sizes. There are navigation routes from Xiamen to over 60 ports in more than 40 countries and regions. With 62 international and domestic air routes, Xiamen Gaoqi International Airport is a main air hub in east China. The well-developed system of railway and highway transportation links the city with places all over the country. Xiamen enjoys various modern telecommunication services such as International Direct Dialing (IDD), Digital Data Special Telephone Line (DDN), Electronic Data Interchange (EDI) and Express Mail Service (EMS), giving quick and convenient connections to the outside world.

There are more than 600 financial institutions in operation in Xiamen. In addition to the state-owned banks and the joint venture banks in the city, overseas banks such as Citibank (USA), Standard Chartered Bank (UK), Credit Lyonnais Bank (France), ING Bank (Netherlands), the Daiichi Kangyo Bank Ltd. (Japan) and Hong Kong & Shanghai Banking Corporation Ltd. have all established their branches or representative offices in Xiamen.

Xiamen has established economic and trade relations with 162 countries and regions worldwide and the total value of imports and exports for the whole city in 1998 reached USD 7.7 billion. Xiamen is recognized as one of the most attractive locations for foreign investors. By the end of 1998, 4,523 projects with foreign direct investment have been approved currently in operation, the aggregate industrial output of which constitutes 80.4% of the city's total.

Xiamen is one of China's most famous cities for hosting conventions and exhibitions. The newly completed Xiamen International Conference & Exhibition Center is renowned as one of the nation's best convention and exhibition centers for its complete facilities and the most satisfying services.

III. Translation

The Asia Forest Partnership AFP

Collaborating for the sustainable management of Asia's forests

Introducing the AFP

The Asia Forest Partnership (AFP) is a voluntary, multi-stakeholder collaboration of governments, intergovernmental and civil society groups promoting sustainable forest management in Asia.

From Rio to the AFP

The AFP was launched at the 2002 World Summit on Sustainable Development in Johannesburg. It is one of over 200 partnerships registered with the United Nations Division for Sustainable Development. The common aim of these partnerships is the implementation of sustainable development based on the 1992 Rio Earth Summit Declaration and UN's Millennium Development Goals. Partnerships do not substitute for but complement intergovernmental commitments. The AFP's first phase extends until 2007.

AFP's Focus Areas

The AFP promotes sustainable forest management in Asia by focusing on three critical issues:
- Combating illegal logging
- Control of forest fires
- Rehabilitation and reforestation of degraded lands

The partnership also works on building capacity, good governance and better forest law enforcement for effective forest management. Work in these underlying and cross cutting issues will help achieve better results in the three focus areas.

AFP—A Unique Approach

The partnership acts as a catalyst for already existing initiatives by increasing synergies and reducing duplication between programs and activities. By providing a formal framework for sharing information and experience, the AFP is strengthening existing programs and, where appropriate, initiating new activities. The AFP collaborates with national, bilateral, multilateral and regional initiatives. The egalitarian, voluntary and open nature of the partnership encourages collaboration between a wide variety of partners with differing interests and perspectives.

Civil Society
- The Nature Conservancy (TNC) (leading partner)
- World Resources Institute (WRI)
- The Institute for Global Environmental Strategies (IGES)
- Global Environmental Forum (GEF)

Government
- Australia
- Cambodia
- China
- European Union
- Finland
- France
- Indonesia (leading partner)
- Japan (leading partner)
- Republic of Korea
- Malaysia
- Philippines
- Switzerland
- Thailand

- United Kingdom
- United States of America
- Vietnam

Intergovernmental Organization

- Asian Productivity Organization (APO)
- Asian Development Bank (ADB)
- Center for International Forestry Research (CIFOR) (leading partner)
- Food and Agriculture Organization of the United Nations (FAO)
- International Tropical Timber Organization (ITTO)
- Secretariat of the United Nations Forum on Forests (UNFF)
- United Nations Economic and Social Commission for Asia and the Pacific (ESCAP)
- United Nations University (UNU)

AFP welcomes additional partners

Contacts

The AFP information-sharing secretariat

Center for International Forestry Research (CIFOR)

Jl. Cifor, Situ Gede, Sindangbarang

Bogor Barat 16680

Indonesia

Phone: +62-251-622 622

Fax: +62-251-622 100

E-mail: afp@cgiar.org

Website: www.asiaforests.org

Unit 16 Invitations

I. Suggested rewritten version

> Dear Mr. and Mrs. Ellis Chambers,
>
>   I hope you haven't any plan for Saturday, November the fifth, at six o'clock p.m. as we'd like you to spend it with us at Scarlet Club. It is a wonderful place for get-together.
>
>   We hope nothing will prevent you from coming, as we're looking forward to your visit. Please contact us with the telephone: 37-7836.
>
> Sincerely Yours,
Rod Robert and Jane Robert

II. Suggested rewritten version

Dear Joanna Thomas,

Please accept our hearty thanks for your kind invitation to your party with several intimate friends on Sunday at the Country Musical Bar. However, we shall be unable to join you on account of a previous engagement for the same day.

Thank you again for including us among the limited number of your guests, and wish you a very successful party.

Sincerely yours,
Mr. and Mrs. Daniel Becker

III. Suggested version

(1)

Mr. and Mrs. David Bird
request the honor of
Dr. and Mrs. Dustin Harman's presence
at the marriage of their daughter
Christine
to
Mr. Charles M. Durham
on Saturday, the eighteenth of August
at three o'clock p. m.
Maple Church

R. S. V. P.   Telephone: 687-5452

(2)

Dear Betty,

We have four seats for a new film of the *Titanic* next Friday, the twelfth of April, at eight o'clock p. m. Will you and Dave join us here for dinner at half past six and then go on with us later to the film? We'll be waiting for you next Friday night, so don't disappoint us!

Affectionately Yours,
Joan

(3)

Dear Joan,
　　I'm very delighted to receive your kind invitation! We'll be there next Friday at half past six, and go with you afterward to the cinema. How wonderful of you and Joe to ask us!
　　　　　　　　　　　　　　　　　　　　　　　　　　　　Affectionately Yours,
　　　　　　　　　　　　　　　　　　　　　　　　　　　　　　　　　　Betty

(4)

Dear Joan,
　　Thank you for your kind invitation. However, Dave will go to Beijing for business and won't be back next week. Please accept our sincere regrets for not being able to join you. I think you'd better ask some other couple for next Friday. Thanks for asking us. I'm certainly sorry to disappoint you.
　　　　　　　　　　　　　　　　　　　　　　　　　　　　Affectionately Yours,
　　　　　　　　　　　　　　　　　　　　　　　　　　　　　　　　　　Betty

5.

Dear Fellow Students of the School of Foreign Languages,
　　Next Saturday, December the twenty-fourth, is Christmas Eve. We thought it would be pleasant to have some of our friends here to celebrate it. Will you come? We'll have been dancing from seven to eleven.
　　We are all very eager to see you here, so don't disappoint us!
　　　　　　　　　　　　　　　　　　　　　　　　　　　　Students of the School
　　　　　　　　　　　　　　　　　　　　　　　　　　　　of Math and Science

Unit 17　Social Letters

I.

Dear Ms Wang,
　　Further to our discussion today over the telephone regarding the problems of defective containers, you suggested that I simply mail you a statement monthly on the number of return by customers rather than send the defective containers to you.
　　I plan to put this into effect at once. But, I first want to make sure that I understand you correctly. If I don't hear from you within the coming week in written form, I'll assume that you approve.

II.

March 16, 2000

Dear Mr. Jack Smith,

Thank you very much for your letter of March 14. Could you come over to my company on May 25 so that we can discuss the details of our cooperation? If yes, please inform me of your flight. Miss Wu of our company will pick you up at the airport.

I'm looking forward to meeting you soon.

Yours sincerely,
Wang Gang

III.

A Letter Extending New Year Greetings

Dear Mr. Bool,

As the New Year is quickly approaching, I take this opportunity to send my greetings and best wishes to you for 2022.

I hope that the coming year will bring a further increase in exchange between our two countries and we look forward to continued friendly relations with you.

Yours faithfully,
Tom

Unit 18 Public Speeches

1.

Ladies and gentlemen,

We feel very much honored to have such a distinguished group of guests come all the way from Canada to visit our company.

Our staff and employees will do all we can to make your visit comfortable and worthwhile. Today, we will introduce you to our newly-established economic development zone and research center. Please do not hesitate to ask any questions you may have.

At last I want to extend my warmest welcome to all of you, and sincerely hope that your visit here will be really worthwhile and meaningful.

2.

Ladies and gentlemen,

Time flies! Over two months ago we happily gathered here in this hall to give Mr. and Mrs. Smith a warm welcome. It is with a special sense of cordiality and joy that we are now gathering here again with them after they have concluded a tour to many parts of our country. During their stay in China, they have carefully studied our educational system as well as politics, economy and culture. They are leaving for home tomorrow. Here we ask them to convey our profound friendship to the people of the United States. We wish them a pleasant journey home and good health. Let's now warmly welcome Mr. Smith to address us.

3.

Ladies and gentlemen,

 Your hospitality is extraordinary.

 For myself and for our entire delegation, I thank you for your warm welcome.

 I don't know how I can thank you sufficiently for holding this welcome party for us. It has been a long cherished hope of ours to visit China some day. We are fortunate to have had this rare chance today. We feel specially honored to be given this opportunity to meet such a nice group of distinguished people like you. We are sure our stay here will be a enjoyable and fruitful one. We do hope to see more of you while we are here.

4.

Dear friends,

 First of all, allow me to thank you for your kind invitation to attend the party. I am greatly honored once again to have an opportunity to visit your beautiful country and meet with so many of its people. This visit has been full of interesting things and everything here left me a deep impression. I have visited companies, schools, and cultural institutions. I have talked with and made friends with many people here and I have learnt a lot during my short stay here.

 I wish to take this opportunity to express my heartfelt gratitude to you again.

 May the friendship ties between our two peoples be further developed and consolidated.

5.

Ladies and gentlemen,

 It gives me great pleasure on behalf of this company to extend a warm welcome to the members of Chinese delegation who have been invited to this country by this company. I understand that arrangements are being made for a comprehensive program and I need not say more about this now.

 We are confident that this will surely help further the development of the two companies' cooperation. I should, therefore, like to propose a toast to the broad prospects of extensive cooperation and exchange between us, to our growing personal as well as commercial ties!

References(参考文献)

[1] 曹步峰,王晓英,丁建宁. 剑桥商务英语证书考试指南. 南京:河海大学出版社,1995.
[2] 常玉田. 英语商务报告写作. 北京:外文出版社,2001.
[3] 崔刚. 公关文秘英语. 北京:北京理工大学出版社,1993.
[4] 崔以泰. 对外交流书信和文件. 北京:学苑出版社,1990.
[5] 董晓波. 实用文体英语写作. 北京:对外经济贸易大学出版社,2012.
[6] 葛亚军. 合同英语. 天津:天津科技翻译出版公司,2002.
[7] 付美榕. 现代商务英语写作. 北京:北京理工大学出版社,2000.
[8] 傅似逸. 英汉应用手册. 北京:北京大学出版社,1999.
[9] 胡庚申,王春晖. 国际商务合同起草与翻译. 北京:外文出版社,2001.
[10] 希比. 国际合同:如何起草国际销售合同. 李力,译. 北京:经济科学出版社,1999.
[11] 梁婷,夏天. 英文广告实用手册. 成都:西南财经大学出版社,2003.
[12] 廖瑛. 实用英语应用文写作. 长沙:中南大学出版社,2003.
[13] 廖世楚. 英语应用文大全. 北京:机械工业出版社,1987.
[14] 刘书琴,李伯芳,张菊香. 求职英语应用文大全. 北京:机械工业出版社,2004.
[15] 刘鸿章,孔庆炎. 英汉商务应用文手册. 上海:汉语大词典出版社,2004.
[16] 刘惠玲,王俊. 国际商务函电. 北京:对外经济贸易大学出版社,2002.
[17] 陆乃胜. 最新英语应用文大全. 北京:世界图书出版公司,2002.
[18] 鲁瑛. 英语应用文写作教程. 北京:对外经济贸易大学出版社,2007.
[19] 福赛斯. 报告的写作. 常玉田,译. 北京:对外经济贸易大学出版社,1998.
[20] 单丽萍. 秘书实用英语. 北京:测绘出版社,1993.
[21] 王立非. 日常生活礼仪应用文大全. 南京:江苏科学技术出版社,2004.
[22] 王乃彦. 外贸英语函电. 北京:中国对外经济贸易出版社,2002.
[23] 王兴懿. 商贸英语应用文大全. 北京:机械工业出版社,2004.
[24] 王兴孙. 新编进出口英语函电. 上海:上海交通大学出版社,2003.
[25] 翁凤翔. 当代国际商务英语. 上海:上海交通大学出版社,2007.
[26] 徐小娟. 广告英语. 北京:首都经济贸易大学出版社,2004.
[27] 于干. 英文书信大全. 长沙:湖南科学技术出版社,1993.
[28] 张传德. 商务英语. 西安:西安交通大学出版社,2003.
[29] 张立民. 应用文大全. 南京:江苏科学技术出版社,1994.
[30] 张益明. 文本写作. 杭州:浙江大学出版社,2002.

[31] 赵静. 广告英语. 北京：外语教学与研究出版社，1997.

[32] 赵伟华，张艳敏. 实用商务英语写作. 大连：大连理工大学出版社，2003.

[33] 沃特森. 商务英语写作指南. 鲁刚译. 北京：世界图书出版公司，2004.

[34] SHIPPERY K C. International contracts. Shanghai：Shanghai Foreign Language Education Press, 2000.

[35] TREECE M. Effective reports for managerial communication. Boston：Allyn and Bacon, 1991.